May I have a word with you?

The Surprising Origins of Everyday Words of Religion and Spirituality

by David Tickner

 FriesenPress

Suite 300 - 990 Fort St
Victoria, BC, V8V 3K2
Canada

www.friesenpress.com

ISBN
978-1-5255-6361-4 (Hardcover)
978-1-5255-6362-1 (Paperback)
978-1-5255-6363-8 (eBook)

1. LANGUAGE ARTS & DISCIPLINES, LINGUISTICS, ETYMOLOGY

Distributed to the trade by The Ingram Book Company

Table of Contents

Introduction

"Words are not indifferent labels.
Products of human creativity, they are coined to render the speaker's attitude
toward the world… every word owes its existence to an individual act of
creativity" (Liberman, 2009, pp. 40, 127).

"Words designating such general concepts as love, hatred, and fear usually refer,
in the beginning, to concrete sensations" (Liberman, 2009, p. 193).

A childhood memory

One of my earliest memories as a small child was of playing in my bedroom and suddenly wondering how things got their names. My mind went to the corner store next door to where we lived at the edge of Prince Albert. Inside the store there was a back room that seemed dark and foreboding whenever I stopped and looked through the half-open doorway. As I wondered, I thought of this back room and saw in my imagination a group of adults sitting in a circle holding up in turn various objects. I saw an adult hold up an object and ask, "What about this one?" I heard various sounds expressed and murmurs of disapproval until someone said, "Fork," and everyone agreed. Then on to the next object.

I have no idea how or why such thoughts and images came into my pre-school mind, but this interest in the origin of words is still strongly with me.

Why have I written this book?

My interest in words and their origins and evolution has grown to include an interest in words related to the church, specifically to Christianity. I grew up in a family active in the life of the Anglican church.

As a child, I liked the Bible stories. They seemed just like the many other stories I heard or read. I liked or feared the characters as a story required. I watched to see how a story would unfold. I was sad when a story ended. I had no sense that these stories were meant to be 'real' or 'literal'; they were just stories. I had no conscious appreciation of the power of stories until I was older and realized the experiences, feelings, insights that stories can evoke.

I enjoyed the ritual liturgy of the church. It felt like a comfortable blanket. As a choir boy, I would look forward to certain parts of the sung liturgy—the *Te Deum Laudamus*, the *Jubilate Deo*, and the *Venite* were favourites. I remember asking my mother what the word 'heaven' meant or what it meant when the priest said that he was 'called to the ministry'. I don't remember my mother's answer to the first question but I do remember that her answer to the second question was, "You'll know."

I recall the bedtime prayers that as a child I would say each night with my parents. I vividly recall one night lying in bed and precociously thinking that I would make up my own prayer—so I did. I remember feeling very alert, very self-conscious, very aware that I was stepping somehow across a boundary into unknown territory. The prayer seemed very real as if I was actually talking with God. And then it hit me with a shock—what if God or Jesus actually appeared at that moment in my bedroom! A wave of fear swept over me. I shuddered. "Whoa... I won't do that again," I said to myself. And that was that.

Even though I found church interesting and somehow knew it to be important and I liked the people, I found less and less inspiration. I remember growing angrier as I grew into my teenage years as if I was becoming disconnected from something. The words of the hymns and the liturgy began to seem like wallpaper. I didn't notice them or even think about them anymore. The priest could have been speaking Latin. Intoning and hearing the words with the congregation seemed more important than having an understanding of what the words meant.[1]

Still, I continued to be curious and to ask questions. I wanted to know what these words and concepts meant and where they came from. However, I grew more irritated. No one had a satisfactory answer or even seemed too concerned about my questions. What was being said in church didn't make any sense to my enquiring high school mind. I couldn't make my own sense of it. I remember the adults in my life saying, "Just believe" or "Have faith."

I remember as a sixteen-year old trying to put my notes and thoughts together into some kind of coherent statement of what I believed, almost like trying to put together my own creed. In the pre-Post-It Notes and pre-digital world in which I lived I put my notes on numerous 3x5 cards, tried to put them in some kind of order, and then tried again and again to write something that made sense. I felt like I was wallowing in abstraction. One day in frustration I showed my notes to the priest of my church who looked through them and then said, "Boy, you've sure opened a can of worms here!"

At university, in spite of or perhaps because of my growing irritation, I became very involved in the life of the Anglican 'coffee house' chaplaincy, liturgical renewal and experimentation, social action, and endless late night discussions and arguments about religion.

However, eventually my church attendance dropped off. Was it me? Was it the church? Now, sometimes I wonder *Did I leave the church or did the church leave me?* I had left home and school and had entered the adult world of work and family. Yet, going to church seemed more and more

---

1   Many years later as I write, I am grateful for Borg's statement that "the primary purpose in worship is not propositional but sacramental: through these clunky words that stumble in the presence of mystery … the point is to let the drone of these words that we know by heart become a thin place" [a 'thin place', or 'open heart', being metaphors for where the visible physical world of ordinary experience and the 'other' divine or imaginal world intersect](Borg, 2004, 155 - 159). That is, worship is not a time to rehearse doctrine or to 'learn' something, but to be in the presence of the divine or the mystery and wonder in the midst of daily life. Borg describes the 'sacramental' or 'thin space' view of religion in several ways, one of which is that "religions are aesthetic traditions [which] have valued and created beauty"; e.g., beauty and artfulness in worship and ritual (Borg, 2004, 204).

to me like being stuck in childhood, in an innocent and unthinking way of being.

Paradoxically, over the years as I became less and less active in the church, I became more and more interested in the history of the church and in words related to this history. Curiosity overcame my estrangement. This book reflects my intentions to look again at the church words of my upbringing, to examine their origins and evolution, and to consider what these origins might now illuminate for me and others.

Words and the power of words, not just church-related words, have always been of interest to me. In my work life, I spent many years working with college instructors on curriculum and faculty development projects. A great part of my work involved helping instructors find the appropriate words to describe what their students needed to learn and what students would do that would indicate that such learning had occurred. During my work, I became interested in the origins of words related to education and training and often shared these with my own students—words such as teacher and learner, trainer and coach, evaluation and assessment, book, desk, chair, facilitate, education and training, lecture and de*mon*stration (you might be interested to know that this word shares its origins with words related to *mon*ster!), and many others. But that's another book![2]

---

[2]   During my work with college faculty and professional trainers I was not only helping these people develop their instructional and training skills but also helping them figure out ways to enable the learning of their own students. One thing I have learned from this work is the importance of focusing on the ways in which the brain uses affect, emotion, feeling, meaning, and relevance to affix learning in short and long term memory. My work involved helping faculty and trainers reflect on and learn from their own experiences so as to help them help their students integrate new learning into prior learning and experience.

Key pieces in the working of the brain's movement of information from short-term to long-term memory are affect and emotion. We learn or remember things that have some kind of emotional attachment. For example, falling in love with our Grade One teacher may set the stage for the rest of our educational experience or discovering the wonder of the Fibonacci spiral sequence may kindle a life-long love of mathematics. We will quite likely remember the high school teacher who killed our love of physics; we remember a short cut for installing a three-way switch because it saves us time and avoids frustration, and so on. We learn or remember things that provide context through meaning and relevance.

While doing course development work, we would spend considerable time discerning words which would best describe what students would be seen doing as a result of instruction; in particular, verb choices. For example, are students being asked to 'list the steps of a procedure' or to 'analyze the steps

After many years, as I turned my attention back to the words of the church, questions arose: What words describe what religious people do? What is the difference between belief and faith? Between contemplation and meditation? Between hallelujah and alleluia? When people have spiritual or religious experiences, what kind of words do they use to describe them? Where do these words come from?

It seems to me that the experiential dimension of many words related to religion and spirituality has been lost or buried. Most discourse about religion and spirituality seems rooted instead in concepts and logic, concepts that must be proven to be true before they can be believed. Faith seems to be something that you possess rather than something that you do or the way in which you live.

I write to find how we can use words as windows or mirrors to evoke some of the mystery and wonder of spiritual experiences. My hope is to recapture or renew the meaning and power of such words, to use them to name or point to experiences of awe, wonder—experiences which are by definition, of course, paradoxically beyond words. I hope to provoke reflection, to prompt the reader to think about the words of the church. I would like to think that one does not have to be religious to appreciate this experiential aspect of the origin of words related to religion.

I would like to delight the reader with the surprising origins of some words. I write this book for fellow readers who love words and who are interested in the origin of words, any words. I write for people who, like me, are curious about the experiences under the words. I write for people

---

of a procedure' or to 'perform the steps of the procedure'? The choice of such words informs both how the course will be a taught as well as how the students will learn and be evaluated.

Part of our work would be a discussion of when the course would be 'running' again or how often the course would 'run'? Knowing my interest in words, sometimes my colleagues would ask, why do we talk about 'running' a course? The words course and curriculum come from Latin currere which in turn, comes from the ancient Proto-Indo-European (PIE) word kers (to run). PIE kers is also the origin of the word horse. The words 'course' and 'horse' could be considered distant cousins. Could we consider doing curriculum work as a bit of horsing around!? (https://www.etymonline.com/search?q=horse) Similarly, another question which would often come up in our work was 'what is the purpose' or 'focus' of this course? I would ask, "Would it help to know that the word 'focus' is the Latin word for fireplace or hearth?!" In ancient times, the focus was the source of heat and light in a home. To ask, "What is the source of heat and light (i.e., energy and insight) in a course?" makes a difference to how you think about the course. A course is not just about information, it is also about inspiration.

who want to see through the wallpaper of words in their lives. In particular, I focus on the words of Christianity because that is my heritage. I hope to provide a resource for people who work at finding ways to write about their experiences and to understand the experiences of others.

Outline and Purpose

This book traces the evolution and development of over 200 words from origins to current use. Generally speaking, I use the terms 'church' or 'religious' when referring to words which can be linked to shared experiences of people. When referring to words naming inner or personal experiences of people, I use the terms 'spiritual' or 'mystical'. The dates used refer to when the word was first seen; in particular, when the word was first seen in modern English.

This book is not meant to be a replication of many other well-documented etymologies and word histories. Neither is the book intended as a theoretical or theological explanation of concepts related to such words. I write with great respect for these words and with an appreciation of the strong feelings many readers might have for such words: as Stark (1997) states, "No sacrilege is entailed in the search to understand human actions in human terms" (p. 4).

This book focuses on etymology and the origin of words, not the origin and development of language. Etymology is the study of the history of words, the explanations of where they came from, and how their meanings change through history. Etymology is like genealogy except with words instead of people. Every word, like every person, has a history. Each word has a life of its own. For an outline of the study and practice of etymology, refer to a later section of this Introduction. In brief, my approach in this book is to let the etymology of each word speak for itself and to add any reflections which have been prompted.[3]

This Introduction includes a summary of

---

3   Etymology, from the late 14th century word *ethimolegia* (facts of the origin and development of a word), comes from Old French *etimologie*, Latin *etymologia*, and Greek *etymologia* (analysis of a word to find its true origin; the study of the true sense of a word). Etymology comprises Greek etymon (true sense, original meaning; related to *eteos* = true) + Greek *-logia* (the study of).

- my methodology and findings
- personal insights and general implications
- and some background context underlying this book:
  - an outline of the study and practice of etymology
  - an overview of the evolution of religion in prehistoric people, especially in light of current brain research
  - a description of the Proto-Indo-European (PIE) ancestry of most modern Indo-European languages, including English

To introduce and illustrate such connections between etymology, history, and experience, I would recount an experience I had while writing this book. One day, as I wrote, I found myself reflecting on a recent hiking trip in the Vezere River valley in France, the site of a multitude of prehistoric sites, notably the Lascaux Caves at Montignac. As I walked through the valley visiting various sites, I was continually reminded of the intelligence of prehistoric people as they responded to the experiences presented by their environment. As a teacher, I wondered how they learned and how they passed such learning from one generation to another—to say that they would have 'learned from experience'[4] is an understatement! I spent a day at the Lascaux Caves interpretation centre in Montignac, another day at the National Museum of Prehistory in Les Eyzies, and, later, spent some time in the prehistory section of the Museum of Mankind in Paris. A recurring theme in these museums and in the literature of the period relates to burial practices and the treatment of the dead—one of the first signs of the symbolic life of prehistoric peoples.

As I worked on this book, I came across one of the ancient words for a burial mound—Greek *khute gaia* (poured earth), from Greek *khein* (to pour), PIE *ghu* (to pour), PIE *gheu* (that which is evoked), and PIE *gheu(e)* (to call, to evoke; to make a sacrificial or ceremonial offering of a liquid, e.g., blood). From these PIE and Greek sources comes Proto-Germanic *guthan* (the spirit emerging from a burial mound). And, to my delight,

---

4   The word experience comes from Latin *experientia* (a trial, proof, experiment; knowledge gained by repeated trials), from *experiri* (to try, test), from ex (out of) + *peritus* (experience, tested), from PIE *peryo* (to try, to risk). PIE *peryo* is also the root of the word peril. To 'learn from experience' means to take a calculated risk and to reflect on the consequences of the action.

I learned that the English word which comes to us from *guthan* is the word *god*.

In brief, in this anecdote, I see a pattern: an experience (the death of a member of a family or tribe) and the concurrent associated feelings, a response (symbolic burial practices), a word (the word *guthan* or god), and, much later, beyond the scope of this book, the explanations and interpretations (e.g., theologizing) related to the word.

In sum, the focus of this book is on etymology and the related history and personal reflections sparked by such etymology. I try to set each word and its origins in the context of historical and current usage—a context which helps me to see and understand the meaning of the word.

Method and results of writing

Methodology

Generally speaking, my approach to writing this book has been to research the origins of each word in various etymological dictionaries and texts to see what experiences were indicated by the root word. I examined how the word and its meaning had evolved over the centuries, paying attention to any metaphors indicating meaning. I looked at how closely the current meaning and use of the word reflected or did not reflect its root origins and meaning. I looked for indications of emotion or feeling in the early origins. In particular, I looked for indications of why such a word might have stuck in the language and what might have made the word memorable and useful. I watched for moments that indicated how the word might inform or re-inform meaningful actions for us today.

Unless otherwise indicated, all word definitions and the dates when words were first attested in English are from the Online Etymological Dictionary. In my writing, I have *not* tried to indicate how words sounded or were pronounced.

Looking at the etymology of a word, I tried to discern how the name given to something reflected something in the experience of the name giver. As Liberman (2009), a noted etymologist, suggests, experience comes first. Then words are created to name or explain the experience.

In particular, when considering the etymology of a given spiritual or religious word, I asked questions such as: is this word an action (e.g., to pray) or an object (e.g., a prayer)? If a verb, does an action or a response (e.g., gasps of awe, surprise, fear) appear to precede the name of that which is being responded to (e.g., birth or death, beauty or tragedy)? In the etymological record, which appears to come first—the action or the object, the verb or the noun?

When researching and writing I asked: How do these original words or sounds track down to us through the ages? How closely does the original word or sound relate to the present use of the word? How much change in usage do we see related to cultural factors? What patterns recur? What themes emerge?

Summary of findings

1. Two streams of words: Almost all of the words related to religion and spirituality which I reviewed have origins in Proto-Indo-European (PIE). For a description of PIE, refer to a later section in this Introduction. These words come to English through two main streams: the Proto-Germanic and Germanic languages, and the Greek / Latin languages. A few words come to English from ancient India, ancient Iran, and Hebrew; e.g., mystic (from Sanskrit *mukah*), paradise (from Avestan *pairidaeza*), and and hallelujah (from Hebrew *hillel*), respectively.

2. Verbs before nouns: Two-thirds or more of the words I examined have origins in actions (i.e., verbs) rather than things (i.e., nouns), suggesting perhaps that such words emerge from people's responses to significant or memorable experience. I was struck by the very ordinariness of these verbs; for example: to put, to stand, to leap, to dip, to observe, to speak, to gush, to grasp, to weave a web, and so on.

In most cases with PIE words, a verb or action precedes a related noun: e.g., PIE *weg* (to weave) precedes web and, later, revelation; PIE *da* (to divide) precedes Greek *daemon* (divider); PIE *dyeu* (to shine, to gleam) precedes Latin *deus* (god); PIE *spek* (to observe) precedes Greek *episkopos* (observer) and Old English *bisceop* (bishop); PIE *sed* (to sit) precedes Latin *cathedra* (an easy chair) and English cathedral; PIE *gheu* (to pour out) precedes font; PIE *sam* (to sing) precedes hymn; PIE *pa* (to tend, to care for) precedes pastor; and so on. Words for actions appear to precede words for things.

In fewer cases with PIE words, a noun precedes a related verb or action: e.g., PIE *oino* (one) precedes the Latin verb *adunare* (to unite, to be at one; later, to atone); PIE *duwo* (two) precedes Latin *dubitare* (to doubt, to question, to hesitate); PIE *tris* (three), PIE *tristi* (a disinterested third party), Latin *testis* (witness), and Latin *testamentum* (a will) all precede Latin *testari* (to be a witness to) and the later English word testify; PIE *leu* (song, hymn) precedes Latin *laud* (to praise); PIE *tem* (a place set apart) and Latin *templum* (temple) precede Latin *contemplare* (to reflect, ponder, study).

3. Strong feelings and emotions: Many words come to English from PIE roots which indicate or suggest experiences of strong emotion or feeling. Such experiences are memorable as are the words which still carry hints of these experiences. For example, the PIE word for the experience of love (*leubh*) is the origin of the word belief; the PIE word for the experience of putting your heart into something or doing something 'whole-heartedly (*kerd-dhe*) is the origin of the word creed; the PIE word for an experience of fear (*aghes*) is the origin of the word awe; the PIE word for beloved (*priya*) is the origin of the word freedom; the PIE word for the feeling of a vitality or liveliness in oneself and the world (*aiw*) is the origin of the words eternal and eternity; the PIE word for 'to favor' (*gwere*) is the origin of the word grace; the PIE word 'to give birth' (*gene*) is the origin of numerous English words.

Words with PIE origins related to singing include hallelujah, hymn, laud, psalm. Words with PIE origins related to 'the ties that bind' include religion, secular, and peace. Interestingly, words related to conciliate and reconcile have origins in PIE *kele* (to shout, to proclaim); that is, we reconcile by vigorous discussion rather than by fighting.

PIE *eis* (strong passion) leads to Greek *hieros* (sacred, filled with the divine) which is the origin of words like hieroglyphics and hierarchy. (PIE *eis* is also the root of the word iron, an Iron Age word that likely aroused strong passions when people discovered how to forge and use iron tools and weapons. I can hear people saying, "We really need to remember how to do this!")

PIE words related to gleaming or shining are the origins of words related to the divine and to Easter.

Other words with PIE origins suggesting strong emotion or feeling include to bide (or have faith), blessing, ghost, miracle, pastor, and prayer.

4. Word clusters: Some PIE terms are the origin of more than one English word. For example, PIE *gene* (to give birth) is the source of general, generate, generation, generous, genesis, genetic, and many more.

Other clusters include PIE *stel, steno, sta* (to stand) are the source of apostle and destiny. PIE *dhe* and *dhes* (to put) are the source of atheist, facilitate, and justify. PIE bhel and bhlo-to (to thrive, to bloom, to gush, to spurt) are the origin of the word blessing.

PIE terms meaning to cut include PIE *leu* (to cut apart, loosen, divide), *skei* (to cut, to split), *tem* (to cut, to create a space apart), and *sker* (to cut, scrape, hack) are the respective origins of absolution, conscience, contemplate, scripture, and incarnation. Looking at these five words, it is interesting to contemplate what experiences these words might name that involve cutting or splitting from something.

PIE terms meaning to shine include *dyeu* (divine) and *bha(1)* (phenomenon).

PIE *weik* (clan, social unit larger than a household) and *swe, swed–you* (social group) are the origins of ecumenical, parish, and ethics. Again, it is interesting to consider the relationship of ethics to decisions about how to live together in an 'ecumenical parish' or a community of diversity. Is it coincidental that these words seem related?

PIE terms related to speaking, saying, telling, calling, and evoking; that is PIE *bha(2)* and *ghue* are the source of words blaspheme, confess, fate, god, and prophet. Similarly, PIE *ghu, gheu,* and *spend* (to pour, to pour a libation to the gods) are the origin of the words god and responsibility. We often speak of a relationship of obedience to one's god. What would a relationship of *responsibility* to god entail? I am reminded that PIE *spend* is also the root of the word spouse.

PIE *kem, kemen, kel* (also the origin of cellar), and *skem*, meaning to cover, to conceal, to be covered are the origins of heaven, hell, and shame respectively.

PIE terms *mei* and *men* meaning small or isolated are the origins of minister, mono (one), and monk.

PIE *sak* (to sanctify) is the root of sacred, sacrament, saint, and sanctification.

5. Unchanged words: Some words come to us from hundreds, even thousands of years ago, almost unchanged from original sources; for example: amen (unchanged from ancient Hebrew and Greek *amen*; also Arabic *amiyn*), awe (from PIE *agh-es*), evil (from PIE *upelo*, Old High German *ubil*, Old English *yfel*), hallelujah (from ancient Hebrew *hallel-yah*, *hillel*—a song of praise to God), love (from PIE *leubh*, German *liebe*, Old English *lufu*), good (from PIE *gheudh*), and sacred (from PIE *sak*; also Hittite *saklai*).

6. Substantial changes: On the other hand, in some words we see substantial changes from origins to current use; e.g., from PIE *sed* (to sit) to the word cathedral; from PIE *gwele* (to throw) to the word devil; from PIE *duwo* (two) to the word doubt; from PIE *kaito* (uncultivated land) to halo; from PIE *wiz-ga*, *weis* (to turn, twist; young shoots of a new plant) to virgin; from PIE *mei* (small) to minister; and, perhaps more controversially, from the PIE words *per* (forward, in front of) + *bous* (cow); i.e., the lead-cow or one who leads cows—one unsubstantiated theory regarding the origin of the word priest!

7. Proto-Germanic origins in contrast to Latin origins: English words with Germanic origins could be considered to have more everyday and familiar, tribal or 'clannish', and 'bottom up' connotations in contrast to words with Greek and Latin origins which tend to have or have become more academic, 'top down', or 'colonial / imperial (Roman Empire) connotations. Examples include Germanic Easter rather than Latin *Pascha*, god from Germanic *guthan* rather than Latin *deus*, forgiveness from German *vergeban* and Old English *forgiefan* rather than from Latin words related to pardon.

Other English words with Proto-Germanic rather than Latin origins include heaven rather than *caelum*, holy rather than *sanctus*, hope rather than *spes*, church rather than Greek *ekklesia* or Latin *basilica*, evil rather than *malum*, Hell rather than *Hades*, and soul rather than *psyche*.

In contrast, following the Norman invasion of English in 1066, many Germanic and Old English words were replaced by French words with Latin origins; e.g., saviour replaced *haeland* (healer), peace replaced *frio* (peace), sacred replaced *godcund* (sacred), carpenter replaced *treow-wyrhta* (tree-wright).[5]

8. Terms from business and commerce: Many words related to religion and spirituality have origins in words which reflect transactions of business and commerce; for example, guilt, mercy, praise, redeem, repent, penance, sacrament, and sin. In some Germanic languages sin and debt are seen as the same. (For example, the translation of the Lord's prayer which asks "forgive us our debts as we forgive our debtors". Other translations use sins or trespasses rather than debts.) We owe the concept of sin as debt to Augustine in his writings on sin and almsgiving; i.e., giving alms to the poor is a way to 'pay back' something for shortcomings or a guilty conscience. The root of mercy is Latin *merx* (merchandise, mercantile). In the word appraise, as in 'to appraise the value or worth of something', we see the word praise. Repent and penance come from Latin *poine* (fine, penalty, blood money). The word sacrament comes from Latin *sacramentum* (a sum of money deposited as a bond during a legal procedure). Also, a *sacramentum* was an oath sworn by a new soldier as an offering of his life to the Empire. In essence, his word was his bond.

The origin of these religious or spiritual words in such business and commerce terms suggests to me how people looked for everyday words or concepts to use to describe their religious or spiritual experiences. Buying and selling affects everyone; e.g., the experience of owing someone money is one that any person can understand.

I suspect that many other religious or spiritual words are rooted in such everyday experiences, not just business and commerce. For example: If someone might say to a friend, "I just had the most amazing experience, I can't really describe it, it was sort of like when..." And then they would use

---

5   Claiborne (1989) suggests that "...the Germanic, Latin, and Greek connections together have contributed close to 90 percent of the English tongue's ... vocabulary. And some 90 percent of that 90 percent—altogether perhaps 300,000 words—can be traced back to ... only about two thousand known Indo-European roots [however] a single Indo-European root can engender twenty or more words" (p. 25 – 27). In particular, Claiborne states "...Germanic words, though a minority in our dictionaries, paradoxically make up a majority of the words we speak or write ... of the hundred English words we use most often, every one is Germanic, of the second hundred, eighty-three were Germanic" (p. 11).

a metaphor or some other poetic phrase to try and describe the experience to another. Ancient people didn't have theological language to describe such experiences. They looked for metaphors in everyday life. The theological language came much later as scholars sought to ascribe meaning to these descriptions of experience.

9. Surprising origins: The words ritual and arithmetic have the same origin. The word truth comes from an ancient word for tree (tree of knowledge!?). Catechism comes from PIE *swagh* (to echo; i.e., a catechism is a 'repeat after me' method of learning). The name Eve is related to ancient words meaning teacher. The name Jason comes from the Greek word *Iesous* (i.e., later spelled as Jesus) meaning healer. The word virgin originally meant the new shoots of a young plant. The *mini* in minister indicates its origins in the word small; i.e., originally a minister was an unnoticed servant working behind the scenes. Revelation comes from PIE *weg* (to weave a web). Other words with interesting or surprising origins include belief, creed, fundamental, god, lord, and miracle.

I am puzzled by the origins of the word carpenter. Early church scholars, when translating the New Testament from Greek to Latin, appear to have translated the Greek term *tekton* (craftsman) into Latin as *carpentarius* (wagon maker). Was Joseph of Nazareth actually a wagon maker? And, much later, how did the Latin word *carpentarius* become the English word carpenter when the Latin word for carpenter is *lignarius*? The Old English word for carpenter is *treowwyrhta* (tree-wright, woodworker). Do these translation and etymology questions make any difference to the Christian message? Does it really matter whether Joseph was a carpenter or wagon maker?

10. Chronology / historical context: Some words are unchanged since the days of the early church; e.g., Adam, Eve, Christian. Some words which first appeared before the 12th century include amen, bishop, disciple, epistle, glory, god, heaven, hell (as the abode of the dead; hell as a place of torment comes to English in the 17th century), hymn, mass, monk, priest, psalm, soul, and others. This period in Western Europe, from the end of the Roman Empire in the 4th century to the early 12th century, has been known from a Western European point of view as the so-called

'Dark Ages'. In contrast, this period was the height of a Muslim empire dominating the Mediterranean area from the Middle East to Spain—an empire marked by the development of universities, high culture, trade and commerce, science and technology. In particular, during this period Spain was a cosmopolitan and affluent society, embracing Muslims, Christians, and Jews in relative harmony and prosperity.

Words which appear in the 12th century include baptize, blessing, charity, choir, devil, justice, mercy, miracle, pastor, and virtue. The 12th century is sometimes called the 'century of learning' as it was during this period that many of the major European universities were established, often based on the Islamic universities existing at that time in Spain. It was also a century in which women played prominent roles, notably in the church (Heloise d'Argenteuil), politics (Eleanor of Aquitaine), and even, in some cases, the military (e.g., Matilda of Canossa). The 12th century is also noted for the emergent 'cult of Mary' seen, for example, in the many Notre Dame churches built during this time, notably Notre Dame Cathedral in Paris (some suggest that the 'cult of Mary' may have been a reaction to the revival and enforcement of clerical celibacy at this time). The 12th century is also noted for romance and chivalry as seen in literature and courtly practices (e.g., the stories of the 'knights of the round table'). And, of course, the 12th century crusades cannot be ignored.

Words which appear in the 13th century include absolution, blasphemy, doubt, faith, forgive, grace, hope, love, penance, purgatory, sacrament, and others. This was the time when Thomas Aquinas produced his massive work (*Summa Theologica*) documenting Roman Catholic church theology. This is also the time when the Western European societies which were emerging from the remnants of the Roman Empire were almost overrun and destroyed by Mongol invasions from Central Asia.

Most of the words described in this book came to English in the 14th century—words such as angel, awe, Christmas, confession, destiny, eternity, Lent, moral, parish, praise, prayer, prophecy, religion, sacred, saint, sanctuary, secular, truth, and others. The 14th century was notable for the Black Death plague (1347 – 1351) in which it is estimated that anywhere from one-third to more than half of Europe's population died. The plague resulted in dramatic changes in trade and commerce, in shortages of labour, and a societal crisis of faith. One result was the Peasant's Revolt in England in 1381 which marked the beginning of the end of the medieval feudal system. This was also the time during which first vernacular translations of the Bible are seen, most notably John Wycliffe's English translation. It can be said that the turmoil of the 14th century set the stage for the 15th century Renaissance and the 16th century Reformation.

The 15th century is marked by the recovery and revival of the culture of classical Greece and Rome and a growing interest in humanism marked by a shift in approaches to religion, notably translations of the Bible based on original Greek and Hebrew rather than Latin. The 15th century development of the printing press led to the easy dissemination of such work. Words which came to English in the 15th century include beatitude, belief, fate, intuition, justification, redeem, and sanctify.

The term Renaissance (rebirth) describes the 14th- 17th centuries period in Western Europe from the crisis of faith prompted by the 14th century Black Death and the discontent with and within the late 15th century Papacy leading to the 16th century Reformation and the 17th - 18th century Enlightenment or Age of Reason.

Words which came to English during the 16th century Reformation include afterlife, atheist, atonement, conciliate, creed, ecumenical, evangelical, holy, immortality, mission, righteous, sanctification, spirituality, temptation (as that which tempts), tutor, and others.

Words appearing more recently in English include apocalypse, hell, missionary, mystic, self-righteous (all from the 17th century), catechism, evil (as a thing in itself, not a descriptor), mysticism, responsibility (all from the 18th century), and agnostic, parochial, secularist (from the 19th century). The 20th century gave us the words fundamental (related to Protestant doctrine), non-secular, and Pentecostal (a Protestant denomination).

Tables found at the end of this Introduction categorize all the words of this book by the century in which they are first seen in their current English version.

Insights and Implications

Personal insights

As outlined earlier, a basic premise of etymology is that experience precedes naming. Words are created in order to name or describe an experience. When considering the words of religion and spirituality, and the experiences that lie beneath such words, people not only name or describe the experience but in addition they explain and interpret the experience,

I was recently asked if any given word implies that people would have had the same experience named by the word. For example, does the word 'awe' suggest that my experience is the same as anyone else's experience? Such explanation and interpretation are first of all done by individuals. Something happens to me, I think about it, I talk about it with others. When individuals talk with each other, compare notes, so to speak, and share insights, a common sense of the experience and the meaning of the experience emerge. For example, if I was to say, "I had a dog experience yesterday", others could also recall a 'dog experience' even though the dogs and the experiences will be different for each person. Over time a cultural consensus develops related to the use of the word.

I recall an incident from many years ago when I was a student hitchhiking across Canada, standing on the side of the highway on a sunny Sunday morning in northern Ontario, waiting and waiting for a ride. Hours passed. I grew discouraged, not just from waiting, but from the growing sense that my future at that point seemed empty, almost as bleak and as empty as the road. I was conscious that sooner or later I would have to make some career and relationship decisions that would shape my life. I took a break and sat in the shade of some trees by the roadside. I took out a book and started to read. A while later, without warning or intention, I felt a feeling washing over me like a wave, a feeling that I was

19

loved. My whole attitude was transformed. It didn't matter at that moment what I decided. I went back to the roadside feeling refreshed, confident, empowered. I felt nothing except gratitude for that passing feeling I had just experienced. When I look back at my journal from that day, I see few words of description or explanation, only the record that something amazing had happened.

Only much later, after years of reading, conversation, and reflection, I looked back at that incident and dared to name what I had experienced with the word grace—a word that someone in the distant past had created to describe a similar experience of their own.

Not only are words created in order to name or describe such experience, but stories and meaning are also created to explain and interpret such experience. Such explanations and interpretations are not fixed or given. People respond to and create the meaning of their own and other's shared experience. Such shared meaning is a foundation of any culture.

As seen in the evolution of words and their meanings over centuries, this process evolves. Not only do the words themselves evolve but the meanings of words evolve--some slightly, some substantially.

Looking at the etymology and history of the words we use implies re-examining the meaning and use of these words. Given the traditions of the past, what is the meaning of these words for today? And tomorrow? What is implied about the shape of future religious and spiritual life for individuals who work to interpret and re-interpret religious language and create meaning for themselves?

One of the main insights for me in writing this book has been the importance of intentionality regarding the religious and spiritual words I use. In particular, this means not only paying attention to my choice and use of such words but also paying attention to how such words describe and inform my experience regardless of whether it is mundane or extraordinary.[6]

Words related to religion and spirituality have been passed to us from generation to generation. Do we take them for granted? Do we assume that we

---

6   Such intention is as much about listening and feeling as it is about talking and thinking: "Sacredness is realized in the act of intention because reality is communicative and the mind is made, grace assisting exquisite effort, to experience its meaning" (Robinson, 2019, 294).

know what they mean? When we say 'fear of the Lord', do we mean that we are afraid of the Lord or that we respect the Lord? Does the word 'missionary' mean the same thing now as it did 150 years ago? Do we assume that words mean the same to us as to our ancestors, even as to our grandparents? Do we use the word 'awesome' in the same way that our grandparents would have used it?! What about the words heaven and hell—do we use these words as they would have been used a thousand years ago?

Writing this book has made me stop and look at the wallpaper of the religious and spiritual words around me. Not that I haven't seen and heard them almost every day of my life, but rather to stop and actually look at these words as objects or as miniature art forms. Sometimes now, I find myself looking at a word the same way I would look at a painting. When I hear or see words such as faith or belief or god or redemption or sin or forgiveness, I ask "What experiences do I see in my life to which such words would apply? What words would I use to describe the ineffable experiences of wonder and mystery in my life? Are these experiences similar to those of other people? What words would they use?"

This notion of experience as the foundation of religious expression seems in contrast with much of the adult religious education of my past in which the point seemed to be "What is the theological interpretation of this book or of the Bible chapter and verse?" I remember the frustration of feeling as though I was being guided to study the Bible as if it was a college textbook rather than using it to help illuminate something in my own life. It felt as though I was being given pre-digested answers to someone else's questions. It made me think of Sunday School lessons in which I was asked to memorize Bible verses week by week for no apparent reason. Such study felt like second-hand news, like hearing or reading about the experience of others but with no connection or relevance to my experience.[7]

---

7   Borg, citing William James, describes people who "experience firsthand the realities of which religion speaks and carefully distinguishes this primal experience from what he calls 'second hand' religion, the beliefs that people acquire through tradition" (Borg, 2018, 248).

Gauchet writes: "The successive totality of religious techniques may be legitimately understood as having shaped the question [of how difficult it is for humans to accept themselves] opened at our very centre ... which means taking responsibility for the self—and also responding to the question. Hence we see what separates us from the world of religions: **we ourselves are uncomfortably experiencing**

In particular, writing this book has made me think about how we talk about experiences that are seemingly ineffable, beyond words, regardless of whether or not we call such experiences 'religious' or 'spiritual'. How do we begin to find the words to describe and explain what such an experience means to us, an experience for which we say, "There are no words to describe it"?

If we are considering religion and spirituality in terms of significant and memorable experiences of meaning, as the etymology and history of these words seems to suggest, what are some implications for religious and spiritual life as individuals and community?

General implications

First, I will say again that my intention in this book is not to theologize. However, given the premise of this book that explanations follow from the words people create and use to name their experiences, I would like to think that when theologians arrive on the scene after such experiences that they are helping people understand and describe such experiences. As Tillich (1951) suggests, the work of the theologian is to connect such words and experiences with theology; in particular, to help people discern insight and meaning in such experience. And then, what are the implications of such experiences? How do such connections and insights prompt actions?[8]

---

as problematic what spiritual systems had presented to us as *resolved* [Emphasis added]. Hence the endless fascination that the tirelessly recapitulated memory of the worlds of faith holds for us." We are enticed but cannot follow. Simply believing is not enough—we need to act in some way (Gauchet, 1997, 205).

8   "Theology moves back and forth between two poles, the eternal truth of its foundations and the temporal situation in which the eternal truth must be received"; i.e., between the pole or meaning and the pole of experience (Tillich, 1951). https://www.etymonline.com/word/theology#etymonline_v_10731

Also: "The point is not to try and find a certain theological language that is somehow 'correct', but rather to encourage a form of dialectic movement in those who participate in the rituals and practices of the radical church" (Rollins, 2015, 173).

Second, when considering how to identify or describe a spiritual or religious experience, I found the set of guidelines provided by William James, cited by Borg (2017, pp. 31 – 32), very useful as I read and wrote:

- Does the experience describe or suggest 'illumination' (i.e., new clarity, enlightenment) or 'union' (a sense of connectedness, a softening or disappearance of distinction between self and world)?
- Is the experience ineffable (hard to describe in words) and transient (brief)?
- Was the experience simply received or passive (something happened to me, I didn't make something happen)?
- Could the experience be described as 'noetic' (a vivid sense of knowing without words or an intensity of feeling)?

Such guidelines could be used as a rubric or template when considering the naming, description, and theologizing related to spiritual experience.[9]

Third, the words we choose to explain and describe these experiences say as much about us as they do about the experience. We tell our story of what happened. The words we choose are often poetic or metaphoric. I believe that such reflection and storytelling are as much a part of understanding and appreciating such experiences as theologizing, if not more so. A good story catches our attention and sticks in our memory often much more than does a logical explanation (Kearney, 2002).

While reading countless novels over the years since my hitch-hiking experience, I have made a point of watching for and collecting examples of similar experiences in such writing which remind me of my own experience. These books are fiction. They are not autobiographies or theologies or moral lessons. They simply tell a story of what happened to a particular character in a particular situation without the use of any religious language. I read the story and am reminded both of the story of my own experience as well as the religious words which I could also use to describe this experience. The religious words used do not necessarily make the experience a 'religious' experience—it is simply an experience.

---

9   Also: "The question is no longer about the existence or inexistence of some being, but rather about whether or not one is responding to a call that throws him [or her] into a deep concern and care for the world" (Rollins, 2015, 172).

Rather, the words remind me that the words we use when telling our story describe our *relationship* to our experience. I might call the experience grace, others might call it a blessing or good karma or hormones or indigestion. However, when we use the same words as other people to describe our relationship to such experience, for example, the word grace, we can also enter into a community of such shared words and meanings.[10]

In sum, experience is the basis of words related to religion and spirituality. Words are chosen to describe such experiences. Such words deserve our respect. The words chosen often come from the words used by our ancestors who named and described their own similar experiences. And, yet, also, I would suggest, we have a responsibility to consider how we might create or re-create the words we need to describe our experiences within the particular culture and context in which we now live.

---

10   Some examples outlining this aesthetic response to experience include:
"It is crucial that the unmediated perception of the divine, that most glorious and more inward human privilege, is an aesthetic experience ... if concepts with religious history such as soul and conscience can be sufficiently redescribed in other language, this in no way diminishes their reality ..; if they cannot be redescribed in a nonreligious language, then we need to consider what is threatened or lost when religious language is lost" (Robinson, 2019; 198, 204).
Borg suggests that "Within modernity, a third view of religion and the religions is emerging [as an alternative to absolutist or reductionist views]. It sees religions as sacraments of the sacred. [Borg outlines several points describing this sacramental understanding of religion, one of which is] ... aesthetic traditions. All of the enduring religions have valued and created beauty: in their music, poetry, stories, art, architecture, worship, and rituals. They see beauty as a mediator of 'the real'" (Borg, 2004, 214).
"Our engagement with things is pervaded and articulated by the imagination ... the imminent possibility of an aesthetic experience—that is, an experience of difference making this involvement irresistibly meaningful for us by showing it to us in an unfamiliar light, by presenting it as other, as opening onto an unknown mystery ... it is an experience of the sacred, that is, of the divine presence in the world ... And art, in the specific sense that we moderns understand it, is the continuation of the sacred by other means" (Gauchet, 1997, 203).

Background Contexts

Etymology: Where do words come from?
How do things get their names?

Etymology is about explanations of how things got their names. It is the study of how sounds became words. It is not directly concerned with the origins and development of language. Etymology assumes that human consciousness, physiology, and language development are already well-established. Liberman suggests that "the speakers who chose those sounds had a reason to do so. The entire science of etymology is centered on finding that reason" (Liberman, 2009, p. 15).

In *Word Origins,* Liberman states: "...yet we still wonder at how the first words were coined. We turn again to the child (farmer, poet, scholar?) who examined a yellow flower and called it a *day's eye* ... [it seems as if] every word is the product of an individual act of creativity ... [words are] products of human creativity, they are coined to render the speaker's attitude toward the world" (Liberman, 2009, p. 10, 40). Someone looked at a such a flower with aroused emotion and awakened imagination.

Words are tools. They were created by early people's just as they created tools like axes or spears or ceramic bowls. A word, like a tool, must be functional and usable. A word, like a tool, is made in response to a particular task or a particular experience. "The news of an invention spreads, and acceptance or rejection follows ... words are hallowed by convention" (Liberman, 2009, p. 10 - 11).

It's easy to see the origin of words related to things. For example, the English word squirrel comes from ancient Greek *skiouros* (squirrel) which comes from a combination of other more ancient words, PIE *skia* (shadow) and *oura* (tail); i.e., shadow-tailed (*oura* is also the root of our word 'arse', but that's another story). Over thousands of years *skia* +

oura became squirrel. Ancient peoples didn't look in a tree and say, "Oh, there's a squirrel!" Rather, it's more likely they said, "Look, there's a small animal with a tail like a shadow... you know, a shadow tail." In contrast, the German word for squirrel comes from words meaning 'a little oakhorn'. The Russian word for squirrel comes from words meaning 'white fish'! (Liberman, 2009, 45)(https://www.etymonline.com/search?q=squirrel).

This naming process is relatively straightforward if we are speaking of daisies or squirrels or hammers. However, the process becomes more complex when speaking of internal experiences. Liberman suggests that words related to concepts such as love, hatred, fear "usually refer, in the beginning, to concrete sensations." Prehistoric people didn't start with an *idea* of fear but with a *feeling* or *sensation* of fear. Perhaps a person was startled by an unexpected encounter with a bear in the forest. Only later when trying to explain to others the feeling rather than the experience did this person begin to look for words that would describe or communicate or evoke 'fear'. And, suggests Liberman, as concepts become more abstract, the words used to describe them become narrower in meaning and more specialized. For example, people differentiated the sensations of 'god' (i.e., the 'other-ness' or the 'one-ness') experienced in the forest or trees in contrast to sensations of 'god' experienced in the water or the home (Liberman, 2009, 193 – 194).

Regardless of the words chosen to name or describe experience, Liberman (2009) states, "our knowledge is the result of our experience; it has nothing to do with language" (p. 196). Liberman also states, "If the origin of a word is to be sought in a people's way of life, the more we learn about 'things', the better … The knowledge of things cannot be derived from names: words lead us to things and thus get an explanation" (Liberman, 2009, 218).

So, in particular, how do words get invented? Liberman describes the many ways in which words are formed from sensations and experiences.

Some words come from sounds; for example, many words begin with 'gr', the ominous 'grrrr' sound; words such as grim, grimace, groan, grouch, growl, grudge, gruesome, grumble—or, re'gret'. Liberman suggests that such a 'gr' sound whose meaning can be construed as discontent or unease. Similarly, the 'gl' sound conveys the idea of sheen and smoothness; e.g.,

26

glow, gleam, glitter, glacier. Some words come from sound symbolism; i.e., onomatopoeia; e.g., pump (from the sound of a pump), splash (from the sound of something falling into water), gurgle, belch, rustle, slap, drizzle, murmur, jingle, and dozens of others.

Some words come from folk etymology; i.e., people make up their own words from other words; e.g., kitty-corner (does this word mean that there is a cat in the corner?), from cater-corner, from a misspelling of French *quatre* (four) corners, now meaning the diagonal line between two opposite corners of a four-sided figure.

Some words come from play; e.g., dilly-dally, shilly-shally, tick-tack-toe, heebie-jeebies, hugger-mugger, flip flop, hurly burly, and so on. Or razzamatazz from razzle-dazzle. Or cock-a-doodle, peek-a-boo, rub-a-dub-dub, hush-a-by, and ragamuffin. Some words shrink with age; e.g., holiday (a holy day), breakfast (break the fast), shepherd (Old English *sceaphierde*), gospel (goodspell), and so on.

Some words come from combining other words; e.g., smog (smoke + fog), chortle (chuckle + snort—one can hardly say the word snort without snorting!), dumbfound (dumb + confound), blurt (blow + spurt), and not to forget brunch (coined in 1895 as English university slang).

Many words (eponyms) are named after actual people; e.g., volt, sandwich, diesel, bayonet, guillotine, nicotine, and many others.

Many words were coined by people who are known. William Shakespeare is credited with inventing and adapting over 1,700 words now used in English; e.g., bloodstained, cold-blooded, luggage, eyesore, bedazzled, dauntless, madcap, puking, rant, swagger, scuffle, grovel, bump, zany, and many others that did not make the cut: tanling, slugabed, kicky-wicky, and congreeing. The Flemish chemist Jan Baptista van Helmont (1577 – 1644) coined the word 'gas' (something not a solid or liquid), from the Greek word *chaos* (the opposite of Greek *cosmos*, the ordered universe.[11] Boondoggle was coined by R.H. Link, an American scoutmaster, to describe a plaited leather cord worn around the neck. The word superman was coined by George Bernard Shaw, boredom by Charles

---

11   Dare I add that a cosmetic, from cosmos, could be considered a product for bringing order to the chaos of a face!

Dickens (1853), freelance by Sir Walter Scott (1820), hard-boiled, to describe someone hard-headed, by Mark Twain (1886), nerd by Dr Seuss (1950), robot by Karel Capek (1920), and, of course, many others. My own children innocently coined words when they were young. My son called an electric wall socket a 'shocket'. My daughter called the spear used for hunting whales a 'sharpoon'!

Hundreds of words come to English from other languages. No other modern European language has borrowed or absorbed or taken so many words from other languages as English.[12]

To summarize, Liberman provides many examples of where words come from. Also, let us remember Liberman's (2009) guiding principle in etymology is that "the knowledge of things cannot be derived from names" (p. 9). That is, we cannot learn anything about *dog* or *gadolinium* just by looking at or saying the word. A word points to an object or thing or experience. To understand the word we must look past or through the word to examine or reflect upon that to which it is pointing. As Liberman suggests, "only exact knowledge of things will allow us to reconstruct the process of name giving ... Words name and classify things for the speaking individual. They do not merge with things, but it would be strange if the original meaning of words could be disclosed without recourse to the properties of the objects to which they stick" (p. 14).

Finally, "etymology is not about the word's 'true meaning', because any meaning acceptable to a given community is 'true'" (Liberman, 2009, p. 167). The meaning of any word depends on its context. It also depends upon who is providing or constructing such meaning. However, regardless of whoever determines such meaning, whether the meaning is acceptable or not depends on the community in which the word is being used. Meaning is dependent on community.

---

12   For example: https://en.wikipedia.org/wiki/Lists_of_English_words_by_country_or_language_of_origin

Ancient peoples, the development of the brain, and the evolution of religion

As prehistoric peoples became more and more conscious of themselves and others, they created ways to communicate those things which they wanted or needed to tell others: let me tell you what happened to me, let me tell you what I learned, the deer are in the meadow, you can cross the stream over there, and so on. People communicated first by gestures and sounds, later by words, and later by symbols. People began to name things in their environment and in themselves. Words were as important tools as axes. Such naming, remembering, and communicating were essential survival skills.

Words are the result of experiences of high emotion or affect, experiences which get and hold our attention, experiences which become memorable for one reason or another. For example, we witness a birth or a death, we feast after a period of little food, we experience comaraderie, we experience fear when lost in the dark of night, we feel awe at the beauty of a sunset. We look for words to describe such experiences to ourselves and to others. We try out words and see what works, what resonates. We take a chance that we've chosen or invented the appropriate word.

As I have been researching and writing this book, I have looked for hints of the brain at work in descriptions of the lives of early peoples. Their memorable experiences would have had high levels of affect or emotion, meaning, and relevance, similar to what makes our own experiences memorable today.

While researching the brain and prehistory, I found Brandon Ambrosino's two-part series for the BBC on the evolution of religion— a clear, concise, and very helpful pull together of research on this topic. Reading this material provided a link between my own experiences described earlier, hiking in the Vezere River valley, my teaching related to brain-based learning, and to etymology. I acknowledge my debt to Ambrosio. The following paragraphs are a paraphrase of this work.[13]

---

13   Ambrosino, B. (2019, 30 May). How and why did religion evolve? Retrieved from http://www.bbc.com/future/story/20190418-how-and-why-did-religion-evolve
Ambrosino, B. (2019, 19 April). Do humans have a religion instinct? http://www.bbc.com/future/

First of all, for ancient people, experience was just experience. What in some experiences would have led to a sense that these were what we would call religious experiences? What, if any, is the difference between an experience and a religious experience?

Ambrosino suggests that religion emerged as early humans developed the capacity to form cohesive social bonds. Brain development and the subsequent development of enhanced emotions were instrumental in promoting such bonding. In particular, Ambrosino cites research which identifies four primary emotions observed in primate studies: aggression, fear, sadness, and happiness. We also see second-order emotions: happiness and anger lead to vengeance; anger and fear lead to jealousy; fear and happiness lead to awe; and sadness, fear, and anger lead to guilt and shame.

These emotions are balanced by other emotions such as love, happiness, satisfaction, caring, and loyalty which are generated and sustained by "rituals and other emotion-arousing behaviors to enhance solidarities" (Ambrosino, 2019). Such rituals appear to generate sensations of 'otherness' which are not necessarily 'religious'; for example, today we might use terms such as 'school spirit' or 'team spirit' or 'esprit de corps' to describe such sensations.

Such rituals involve a sense of play or drama; such ritual is "embodied requiring shared intention and shared attention" (Ambrosino, 2019). Such ritual implies an empathy which arises in the body; for example, yawning and smiling are often contagious. Just as when I yawn and then you yawn, almost involuntarily, so also can a simple ritual (e.g., shaking hands) generate or symbolize empathy or friendship.

"Empathy is absolutely central to what we call morality" (Ambrosino, 2019). Empathy indicates that each person has a stake in each other's well being and behaviour toward self and others. Such morality and resultant actions, suggests Ambrosino, *precede* religion. In this sense, such

---

story/20190529-do-humans-have-a-religion-instinct

Ambrosino draws upon the work of Justin Barrett (cognitive science), Robert Bellah (sociology), Pascal Boyer (neuroscience and religion), Antony Black (history), David Christian (history), Daniel Dennett (philosophy, cognitive science), Frans de Waal (primatology), Robin Dunbar (evolutionary psychology), Barbara Fruth (research on bonobos and food sharing), Karl Jaspers (philosophy), Andrew Newberg (neuroscience and religious experience), Jonathan H. Turner (evolution of religion).

pre-religion morality could be considered embodied in the same way that empathy and ritual are embodied—they all originate within the workings of the brain.

> "With a broader set of emotions, the hominin brain was then able to enhance some of its capabilities, some of which quite naturally lent themselves a religious way of being. As these capacities got more acutely enhanced with the growth of the *homo* brain and the development of the neo-cortex, behaviours such as play and ritual entered a new phase in hominin development, becoming the raw materials out of which cultural evolution would begin to institutionalize religion" (Ambrosino, 2019).

Another factor which Ambrosino outlines in the development of religion (proto-religion?) in early hominins is the notion of agency; that is, the awareness that something 'other' seems to cause us do something or that there is something 'out there' through which power or influence over us is exerted. For example, if early people heard a noise in nearby bushes, would they likely stop and think? No, they would likely run from a potential predator (flee) or at least be on the alert (freeze). If there was no predator, then fine, everything was okay. But it they didn't pay attention to this sense of an unknown other or agent, the consequences could be disastrous. Similarly, suggests Ambrosino, we may have similar feelings when we hear a creak in the floor or a banging on the window in the next room. Our attention is aroused. We "attribute agency to such events with no clear physical cause" (Ambrosino, 2019) especially when urgency is involved. Our actions at such times are automatic or non-reflective. Our brain alerts us. We are startled. We don't stop and think that we should be startled.

Other times, with experience, our actions can be more intentional such as readying a weapon rather than running; fight or hunt, rather than freeze or flee. Hominins learned to take the right actions considering the circumstances, especially when acting in relation to other members of the group.

In sum, early peoples learned to respond in certain ways to emotions related to empathy or fear that lead both to community and to survival. They used forms of ritual not only to remember such experiences but also as a way for one generation to pass such learning to the next. Rituals, as ways of intentionally passing memory of experience from generation to generation, are also ways to establishing an intentional relationship to experience. Experience is only 'religious' experience when we take such a relationship to experience. And so, suggests Ambrosino, "For brains that seem wired to find agency and intention everywhere, religion comes very naturally" (2019).

How did prehistoric people learn such things from one another? How did they learn the rules of the game, so to speak? One theory: they learned not only from their elders but from their ancestors. Even today,

> "we talk about our deceased loved ones as if they're still around, telling stories about them, reminding ourselves that they would approve of our decisions. In short, we keep them around.   But not physically because ... dead bodies are a problem. Something must be done with them. Indeed, religion may be much less about death than dead bodies. For this reason, some   suggest that the earliest forms of 'supernatural agency' were the departed, the ghosts of whom are minimally ... almost like us, except for the disappearing through the wall [between this world and the other world] ... our teachers were our dead ancestors" (Ambrosino, 2019).

And so we come again to the prehistoric sites, the burial mounds, and the etymology of the word god which I have earlier described. Prehistoric people experienced a sense of both empathy and agency in the presence of a burial mound containing their ancestors. The words they chose to name such experiences include PIE *gheu* (to evoke) and Proto-Germanic *guthan* (the spirit emanating from a burial mound).

Etymology: Proto-Indo-European (PIE) and the roots of the English language

"What is the oldest thing that you have in your home?" I used to ask this question to participants of my instructor training courses. After hearing the usual answers such as my grandmother's tea set or an antique chair or a family photo, I'd suggest that some of the words they use are perhaps the oldest things in their home.

Such words, those closest to hearth and home, come to us with seemingly little change from Proto-Indo-European (PIE), a linguistic reconstruction of the common ancestor of English and other Indo-European (IE) languages. Indo-European is the generic term (similar to the terms European or Asian) for the peoples who spoke the languages which are the sources of these common roots. In brief, the term Indo-European (IE) refers to people; Proto-Indo-European (PIE) refers to the words and culture of such people. PIE cultures first appeared 6,000 to 10,000 years ago in areas surrounding the Black Sea, including what is now eastern Europe, southern Russia, and the northern Middle East.

English words rooted in PIE include, for example, sister (PIE *swesor*) or brother (PIE *bhrater*), mother (*mater*) or father (*pater*), son (*sunus*) or daughter (*dhugheter*), love (*leubh*), or deity (*deiwo*). PIE is the common ancestor of many languages now used not only in Europe but also from Persia (Iran) to South Asia; e.g., the Hindi word for brother is *bhratar*. Such similarities between modern and ancient languages were first described in the late 18th century.

Such PIE words that have come to us relatively unchanged over the centuries are often words that carry high levels of emotion or affect. It's as if brain biology itself has rooted these words in our minds as these words are passed from generation to generation.

From these origins in central Asia, Indo-European peoples migrated in various directions. For example, the Hittites, a Indo-European people, migrated to Anatolia, now eastern Turkey, around 2,000 BCE. Other Indo-Europeans, notably the Aryans, migrated east into what is now Persia and India around 1500 BCE. Some Indo-Europeans moved into Italy at this time becoming ancestors of the Latin-speaking people who would later establish the Roman Empire. The Myceneans migrated south to Crete, establishing a flourishing civilization in the mid-2nd century BCE. Around 1,100 BCE the Dorians migrated to Greece and laid the foundations of what would become classical Greece. During this period, other Indo-European peoples migrated north and east, becoming ancestors of modern

Slavs; some migrated west becoming ancestors of Celtic and Germanic peoples who emerged in central Europe around 1200 BCE.

Many of these early proto-Celtic people migrated to what is now Britain between 2000 – 400 BCE, merging with earlier people already been living there. The early peoples were ancestors of the Cornish, Welsh, Scots, Irish, and Britons (people who lived in what is now Brittany in France).

In brief, English is the mongrel child and grandchild of many older European languages, notably French, German, Latin, and Greek which, in turn, come from Proto-Indo-European (PIE). As languages go, modern English is very young, about 400 years old. Prompted by the invention of the printing press in the 15th century, English began to take its current written form. This process was accelerated in the late 16th and early 17th centuries by the popularity of the works of William Shakespeare and of the new King James Version of the Bible. Earlier versions of English (Middle or medieval English, and Old English) are almost unintelligible to us today. And let us not forget the countless words from many other languages which have quietly slipped into use as part of the English language.

THE WORDS

Adam, Eve

Adam

The name Adam comes from Hebrew *adamah* meaning ground and Hebrew *adam* meaning man; i.e., one formed from the ground. Similarly, Latin *homo* meaning man and *humanus* meaning human are rooted in Latin *humus* (earth, ground, soil).

Consider the many different connotations of the word ground in addition to earth or soil: ground as a basis for belief or action; a fundamental condition or cause; a surrounding area (background); ground as the surface of the earth; an area used for a specific purpose (e.g., parade ground, fairground); an area to be won or defended in battle; an area of knowledge (e.g., she covered a lot of ground in her presentation); to make an electrical connection with the earth; a conducting body used as a common return for an electrical circuit (e.g., a ground wire); a 'ground game' in football or a 'grounder' in baseball; 'from the ground up'; getting a project 'off the ground'; being 'on the ground'; to hide or 'go to ground'; and so on.

Adam is from and of the earth. Adam is grounded in each here and now moment.

Adam's apple (first seen in English in 1731) comes from Latin *pomum Adami* and from Hebrew *tappuah haadam* meaning Adam's swelling; i.e., Hebrew *tappuah* meaning anything swollen. One ancient legend suggests that this swelling is a piece of the forbidden fruit given by Eve to Adam which became stuck in his throat.

The term adamite, from the 1620s, refers to people who practice nudism, in reference to the state of Adam before his expulsion from the garden.

Eve

Did you ever think that Eve may have been the original teacher? Consider the following: Eve comes from Latin *eva* and *heva*, which in turn come from Hebrew *hawwah* (source of life, living being); similar to *haya* (to live).

Let's follow this trail. First, *hawwah* and the Old Testament *Yahweh* both derive from the Hebrew verb 'to be'. Does this imply that *hawwah* and *yahweh* are the feminine and masculine forms of the verb 'to be'? Dare we wonder out loud whether or not *hawwah* and *yahweh* might even be equal in stature (i.e., simply the female and male names for being) as suggested by some of the rabbinic literature.[14] In the Old Testament, when Yahweh speaks of being "a jealous god", is he as jealous of his own grammatical sibling as he is of the other gods in the surrounding cultures of first millenium BCE!?

Second, the Hebrew word *hawwah* resembles two other Hebrew words: *hawa* (to teach) and *hewya* (serpent).[15] In some early creation stories from the ancient world, Eve (life) is sent by her mother Sophia (wisdom) to give life to Adam and to instruct him (i.e., to eat from the tree of the knowledge of good and evil). What are we to make of these stories that Eve preceded Adam?

Such stories, mythologies, and other cultural traditions are formed as people select and express those things in life which they feel are of significance, value, and meaning, and which are passed from generation to generation. As we know, as the Old Testament evolved in the centuries of the ancient world, this story of Eve and Sophia did not 'make the cut', so to speak, as the Genesis story came into being.

I find it fascinating how the origins of words can reveal to us, even in the vaguest way, hints of how our ancestors struggled to find the words and expressions to describe the experiences of their lives. Even now, as we

---

14   Midrash Rabbah Genesis VIII:1 interprets "male and female He created them" to mean that God originally created *Adam* as a hermaphrodite. In this way, adam was bodily and spiritually male and female. https://en.wikipedia.org/wiki/Eve

15   In ancient myths, serpents are almost always associated with the feminine. Some suggest that the written name Eve bears resemblance to an Aramaic word for snake which forms the basis for rabbinic puns related to the book of Genesis.

In ancient Greece, the caduceus, a staff entwined with two serpents was carried by Hermes, messenger of the gods. The caduceus was used as a symbol in various trades-related occupations (especially, printing trades) and in commerce and negotiation. The caduceus is also associated with eloquence, trickery, alchemy, and wisdom.

The Rod of Asclepius, the symbol of medicine and healthcare used from ancient to the present time, consists of *one* serpent entwined around a staff.

write and read, we struggle to find the words which express our deepest meanings and desire, words in which we find both our own ground and our common ground, and which we pass on to future generations.

Alleluia, Hallelujah

What's the difference between these two words? They both mean the same thing. The difference is found in their origins.

Alleluia, in the context of its use in the English language, is the older word. It comes to English in the 14th century from Latin *alleluja*, Greek *allelouia*, and Hebrew *hallelu-yah* (praise Jehovah).

In the 1530s, hallelujah comes to English more directly from Hebrew *hallalu-yah* (praise Jehovah). *Hallalu* comes from *hallel* (to praise, a song of praise) and from *hillel* (he praised). In its origins *hillel* has the sense of being 'to trill'. *Yah* is the short form of *Yahweh*, the Hebrew name of God.

When you think about it, you can almost hear the trill in *hillel*, *hillel*, *hillel*.

Listen to the ululations in the music and cultural traditions of countries of North Africa and of what is commonly known as the Middle East. Consider how much these sounds sound like hallelujah.

Altar

Altar is almost unchanged from its origins in Latin *altare* (high altar, altar for sacrifice to the great gods), a word influenced by Latin *altus* (high). The notion of an altar for burnt offerings comes, perhaps, from Latin *adolere* (to worship, to offer sacrifice, to honor by burning sacrifices to the gods).

From these Latin origins come Old English *alter* or *altar*. For a time, Middle English *auter*, from Old French *auter*, was used, but the use of altar from was restored in the 1500s.

Altar piece is from the 1640s. Altar-boy is from 1772. Altar, as a symbol of marriage, is from 1820.

Amen

Amen is a word or sound that appears to have remained unchanged for most of its history.

Amen has been part of English since before the 12th century. At that time, Old English *amen* was used only at the end of a reading of the Gospels. Amen has been used as an expression of concurrence after prayers only from the early 13th century.

Old English amen comes from Latin *amen*, from Ecclesiastical Greek *amen*, and from Hebrew *amen* (truth) all used adverbially as an expression of agreement. Amen in Arabic is *amiyn* (pronounced *ah-meen*). Amen has its roots in the Semitic *a-m-n* (to be trustworthy, confirm, support). Amen means 'so be it', verily, surely, to be firm, confirmed, reliable, faithful, to have faith, and to believe, depending on the context in which it is being used.

Do we say "ah-men" or "ay-men"? Both pronunciations are acceptable. 'Ah-men' is generally used in performances of classical music, in liberal and mainline Protestant churches with formal rituals and liturgy, and in Jewish congregations using modern Hebrew pronunciation. 'Ay-men' is generally used in Irish Protestantism, conservative evangelical churches, and in gospel music.

Amen is used in a similar manner in Christianity, Judaism, and Islam.

Angel

Do you ever have a hunch or intuition or gut feeling about something? I sometimes wonder what ancient people would have thought when they experienced such sensations, such knowing. Perhaps these experiences felt like voices from outside themselves, like messengers from another realm. Perhaps imagining angels were a way to give form to such voices.

Angels are part of most world religions, including Christianity, Hinduism, Islam, and Judaism. They are represented as men and women although female angels seem to become more prevalent in modern times.

Angels are not ghosts or spirits or apparitions. They are found in both religious and secular contexts. They are ubiquitous.

The word angel comes to English in the 14th century from the Old English *engel* and the Old French *angele*. Both words come from Latin *angelus* and Greek *angelos* (messenger, envoy, one that announces) and possibly from Greek *angaros* (mounted courier). Before this, the origins of the word angel are uncertain. Some suggest a possible relation to Sanskrit *aijira* (swift) or Hebrew *malakh* (messenger, to send). Another Old English word for angel was the delightful *aerendgast* (errand-spirit).

Much discussion exists regarding whether angels are male or female or both or neither. Some suggest that angels in early Christianity and Judaism were male (with few exceptions). In Christian art angels tend to be androgynous although in modern times they are most often seen as female. Artists seem to struggle with representing a being that is neither male nor female (or that is both). Some discussion suggests that even though angels are described as male, they are in fact both male and female in the same way that the term 'man' or 'mankind' was formerly used to describe all people.

Other discussions revolve around whether or not angels have wings. Some suggest that the image of wings for angels comes to Christianity from non-Christian cultures.

Angels have been categorized into various systems and hierarchies. For example, in the 13th century, St Thomas Aquinas determined that there were three hierarchies of angels with each hierarchy containing thee orders or choirs of angels.[16]

In any case, whether we are talking of the gender or the wings or the hierarchy of angels, or of whether or not they exist outside of our imaginations, the discussion continues.

---

16   In Aquinas' system, the three hierarchies and their related orders are as follows. The 'heavenly counsellors' hierarchy, closest to the divine, includes the three orders of seraphim, cherubim, and thrones. The second hierarchy, the 'heavenly governors', includes the three orders of dominions (or lordships), virtues (or strongholds), and powers (or authorities). At the lowest level, closest to humans, is the 'heavenly messengers' hierarchy which includes the orders of principalities (or rulers), archangels, and, finally, at the low end of this hierarchy, angels. That is, within this organization of three hierarchies and nine orders, angels are the closest of the nine orders to people (https://en.wikipedia.org/wiki/Christian_angelology).

In my own experience, I've seen angels carved into the wall behind a 1,500-year old sleeping Vishnu in a cave on India's Coromandel Coast. I've seen angels portrayed in Islamic art. My grandmother swore that during World War One she awoke one night to see an angel standing at the foot of her bed who told her that my grandfather, who had just been wounded in battle at Vimy Ridge, would be all right.

Annunciation

Have you been in a public space when an announcement comes over the PA system? Can you hear or even make sense of the message? Is it garbled? Do you wonder if this might have something to do with you—like, maybe your flight has been delayed or the departure gate has been changed? Perhaps you get a memo at the office announcing that the Friday meeting has been cancelled. Or the chair of a meeting makes an announcement calling for volunteers to help set up an event. Responding to such announcements may not make much difference to your life; or, you may not realize until much later how much your response actually did change your life. If you had not missed that flight, who knows where you might have ended up.

Our lives are full of such announcements. Most of them are mundane. An announcement can be a command, a request, an invitation, a piece of information: "Do not back into this parking spot", "Will you take out the garbage?", "You are invited to our anniversary celebration?", "The elevator will be out of service until noon." We respond accordingly.

Some announcements can call forth more significant responses: you hear or see an announcement for a job posting that seems to have your name on it. If you got the job it might mean moving to the other side of town or maybe to the other side of the country. Or you meet someone. You know at such moments that whatever you decide, the consequences will be life changing.

An annunciation is an announcement regardless of what it is that is being announced. The word annunciation comes from PIE *neu* (to shout)[17] and Latin *annuntiare* and *adnuntiare* (to announce, make known; i.e., to bring news to, from *ad* (to) + *nuntiare* (to relate, to report). Latin *nuntius* (messenger) also comes from PIE *neu*. From these Latin words come Old French *anoncier* (to announce, proclaim) and later French *annoncer* (to announce). A Papal nuncio is a messenger sent by the Pope or the Vatican.

Latin *annuntiatum* (announcement), from *annuntiare*, leads to Old French *anonciacion*, Anglo-French *anunciacioun* (announcement, news), and later to English annunciation in the 14th century. Annunciation as the general sense of an announcing is from the 1560s.

In the Biblical story of the annunciation (Luke 1: 26 – 38), a young woman, Mary, who is engaged to be married, receives a messenger in her home who announces that Mary will give birth to a son called Jesus.[18]

In early medieval times, the annunciation was celebrated as Lady Day or Our Lady's Day and often coincided with a New Year celebration. Lady Day also marked the change from a harvesting season to a planting season. The Old English word for Lady Day was *bodungdaeg*. In the early 14th century, Lady Day became more commonly known as the Feast of the Annunciation and came to be celebrated each year on 25 March, perhaps not surprisingly, nine months before Christmas.[19]

---

17   PIE neu is also the root of words such as announce, denounce, enunciate, nuncio, pronounce, renounce. There are also suggestions that PIE new is related to Greek *neuo* (to nod, beckon), Latin *nuntius* (messenger), and Old Irish *noid* (make known). https://www.etymonline.com/word/*neu-?ref=etymonline_crossreference
See also NUMEN.

18   For me, the most striking part of this story is Mary's response to this announcement or annunciation. First of all, she is troubled but not intimidated by the messenger's words. She ponders. She asks questions. You can almost hear her inner voice, "Are you sure you've got the right person?" After consideration and deliberation with the messenger, she replies, "Yes, may it be as you have said." Richard Kearney comments, "If Mary had said no, there would be no incarnation, no Christ, no Christianity. If Mary does not accept the freedom, integral to choice … if we see in her only 'meek obedience' to a Word that's going to happen anyway, if we read Mary as submitting to a Logos of imperial divinity which imposes itself on her—then, I think we have misunderstood a fundamental message of Judeo-Christianity; namely, that God is a call, a solicitation, a desire" (Kearney, 2016, 254). See also Denise Levertov's poem, "The Annunciation" for another interpretation of this story.

19   The Annunciation is not to be confused with the feast day of Immaculate Conception first celebrated as early as the 5th century. Immaculate Conception, the doctrine that Mary was made sinless

See also ANGEL, HOLY SPIRIT, VIRGIN MARY, VOCATION, WILL.

Apocalypse, Revelation

Apocalypse

An apocalypse is a revelation. Apocalypse means to bring something from concealment or to uncover something or to reveal something. The word apocalypse does not refer specifically to what it is that is being revealed.

Apocalypse comes from the combining of Greek *kalyptein*[20] (to cover, to conceal) with the prefix *apo-* (from); Greek *apokalyptein* means to uncover, reveal, disclose. In the late 14th century the Latin term *apocalypsis* (revelation) used in a religious context became the English word apocalypse (revelation, disclosure).

When the book of Revelation in the Bible was written in the late 1st century (i.e., ~80s - 90s CE) the writer[21] used the term *Apokalypsis* which was translated into English around 1320 as Apocalypse. During the Middle Ages, the term apocalypse was used in reference to insight, vision, or hallucination. In his translation of the Bible into English around 1380, John Wycliffe used the word Revelation when translating the Latin *Apocalysis*. The English word apocalyptic, when referring to the book of Revelation, dates from the 1660s.

---

by an act of God, was officially announced in 1854 by Pope Pius IX. The Feast Day of the Immaculate Conception is 8 December. Almost one hundred years later, on 1 November 1950, Pope Pius XII officially declared the assumption of Mary into heaven as part of Roman Catholic doctrine.

20   *Kalyptein* comes from PIE kel (to cover, conceal, save) which is the origin of the English words cell, cellar, and hell. *Kalyptein* is also the root of Calypso, a sea nymph in Greek mythology. Calypso music, from the Caribbean, is named as such from 1934—the origin of the name for this music is unknown.

21   Since the days of the early church, several writers named John have been suggested as the writer of *Apokalypsis*—i.e., John of Patmos, John the Apostle (Evangelist), John the Presbyter, and John the Divine.
https://en.wikipedia.org/wiki/Book_of_Revelation

The use of apocalypse to describe a cataclysmic event is relatively modern (e.g., modern apocalyptic 'end of the world' fiction has its origins in the early 19th century). The use of apocalyptic to refer to the imminent end of the world first appears in the 1880s.[22]

Revelation

Revelation comes from reveal which comes from veil. Veil is rooted in PIE *weg* (to weave a web) and Latin *velum* (a veil) and *velare* (to cover, to veil). Reveal, from Latin *revelare* (reveal, uncover, disclose), is comprised of *re-* (opposite of) + *velare*. Latin *revelare* leads to Old French *reveler* (to unveil, to uncover).

Revelation, the noun related to the verb reveal, comes from Latin *revelationem* and Old French *revelacion*. The word revelation comes to English around 1300 meaning to disclose information to people by divine or supernatural agency. Revelation meaning disclosure of facts comes from

---

22   [3] I confess that when I sat down to write I realized that I had always thought that the word apocalypse meant the end of the world. I was surprised to learn that the word simply means revelation. In particular, the word revelation has the connotation that what is revealed changes your attitude or your life in some large or small way. I think of times when my attitude or outlook toward a student changed when something surprising was revealed. For example, I recall my irritation with a student who had been coming late to class in the morning. I thought she was late simply because she was lazy or not interested or disorganized. When I checked with her, she apologized and told me that she had to take her children to daycare before she comes to school. Or, I recall a student from a course I'd taught several years before who came up to me at a conference and told me that that course had changed her life. Then she burst into tears. I almost burst into tears.

The irony in this for me is that the etymology of the word apocalypse changed my negative 'end of the world' perception of the nature of the apocalypse to something more positive and part of everyday experience: that is, seeing something revealed from a different point of view can be both life affirming and life changing.

So how did apocalypse change from being something revealed to something being the end of the world? Why is that? For example: https://theconversation.com/philosophy-and-fallout-4-whats-the-appeal-of-the-post-apocalypse-50759 or https://blogs.scientificamerican.com/observations/psychology-reveals-the-comforts-of-the-apocalypse/. What has lead to the current wide range of apocalyptic books and movies? For example: https://en.wikipedia.org/wiki/Apocalyptic_and_post-apocalyptic_fiction.

Such questions are beyond the scope of this book. For now, I am content to simply let the words and the etymology speak for themselves.

the late 14th century. Revelation meaning a 'striking disclosure' comes from 1862.

Apologetics

Why would you want to apologize for what you believe?

We usually apologize or say "I'm sorry" when expressing regret for doing something wrong. This is a relatively recent use of the word. The English word apology used in this sense is first seen in the 1590s and became common in the 18th century. By the mid-19th century we see the use of apologize to regretfully acknowledge failure.

However, the word apology has its origins in words meaning to defend or to justify a point of view or to state or prove innocence.

The word apology comes from Latin *apologia*, Greek *apologia* (a speech in defense), Greek *apologeisthai* (to speak in one's defense), and *apologos* (an account, story). Greek *apologos* comprises *apo* (away from, off) + *logos* (speech). *Logos* comes from PIE *leg* (to gather, to collect; in particular, to speak, to pick out words. PIE *leg* is also the root of words such as lecture and legend). In classical Greek, an apology was a well-reasoned reply or response to accusations.

Latin *apologia* was used in early Christian writings in defense of the faith. The word apologetics, first seen in 1733 as the branch of theology which defends Christian belief, comes from apologetic, first seen in the 15th century to mean a formal defense.

In sum, an apology is a heartfelt expression of regret for a wrongdoing. On the other hand, apologetics is a term used to defend and justify Christian belief using concepts and practices of logic and rationality.

Apostle, Epistle

Both apostle and epistle have the same origin in PIE *stel* (to put, to stand), the origin of many words related to standing objects or places.[23]

Apostle

PIE *stel* leads to Greek *stellein* (to set in order, arrange, array, equip, make ready, to put—perhaps in the sense of moving from one place to another or putting something in another place). The Greek prefix *apo-* (from, away from, separate, free from) added to *stellein* creates the Greek word *apostellein* (to send away, send forth) and *apostolos* (messenger, person sent forth). From these Greek words comes Latin *apostolus* and eventually Old English *apostol* (messenger).

The English word apostle is from the 16th century. The use of apostle to mean the chief advocate of a new principle or system is from 1810.

Epistle

Adding the Greek prefix *epi-* (upon, at, close upon [in space or time], on the occasion of, in addition) to Greek *stellein* creates *epistellein* (to dispatch, send). From *epistellein* comes Greek *epistole* (message, letter, command, commission) and Latin Latin *epistola* (a letter). From these sources come Old French *epistre* and Old English *epistol*.

The use of epistle to refer to a letter from an apostle forming part of canonical scripture is from around 1200.

In brief...

Perhaps an apostle is one who says, "This is where I stand." An epistle is a document that describes what the apostle stands for.

---

23   For example: install, stable, stall, stallion, stele, stolid. Also, apostle and epistle are related to Latin *ponere* (to place, to put) which is one source of 'to post'; i.e., to post a letter, postage, postal, post office, and so on.

Ascension, Exaltation

Ascension

The word ascension has its earliest roots in PIE *skand* (to spring, leap, climb) which leads to Latin *scandere*, a term used in poetry meaning 'to scan verse'; that is, to note the rising and falling of poetic rhythms. When the Latin prefix *ad-* (to; toward in space or time; with regard to; in relation to) is combined with Latin *scandere*, the word *ascendere*[24] (to climb up, to mount, to ascend, to rise, to reach) is formed.

Around 1300, the word ascension came to English from Latin *ascensionem* and *ascensio* (a rising), words related to *ascendere*. At that time, the word ascension was used to mean the ascent of Christ into heaven on the 40th day after the resurrection.

By the late 14th century, *ascendere* had come to English as the verb 'to ascend'.[25]

Exaltation

The words 'to exalt' and 'exaltation' come to English in the late 14th century from the Old French *exalter* and *exaltacion*. Both words come from Latin *exaltere* (to raise, to elevate) and *exaltationem*, *exaltatio* (elevation, pride). Latin *exaltere* comes from the combining of *ex-* (out, up, upwards) and *altus* (high). Latin *altus* has its origins in PIE *al-* (to grow, to nourish).

PIE *al-* is also the root of Proto-Germanic *althaz* (grown up, adult), West Saxon *eald* (aged, antique, primeval; elder, experienced), and Old English *ald* (old).[26]

---

24   In Latin, when *ad-* precedes a word beginning with 'sc', the 'd' in *ad-* is dropped.

25   You may (or may not) be interested to know that in 15th century the verb ascend was also used with the sense of 'to mount (a female) for copulation'.

26   We see remnants of these old words in current words such as alderman, alumnus, and elder (and not to forget the Scots auld, as in auld lang syne). The Olympic motto 'Citius, Altius, Fortius' is Latin for 'faster, higher, stronger'.

In brief...

Ascension carries the connotation that something is arising of its own volition whereas exaltation carries the connotation that something is exalted by others; for example, an elder may be held in respect or 'exalted' by younger people.

Atheist, Agnostic

Atheist

The word atheist comes from PIE *dhes* and *dhe* (to set or to put), root words which are the origins of Greek *theos* (a god). Adding the Greek prefix *a-* (without) to *theos* creates *atheos* (without a god, denying the gods, abandoned of the gods, godless, ungodly).

In this context, in ancient times *atheos* did not necessarily mean that a person did not believe that a god or gods existed—rather, the word and its various meanings indicate a person's relationship to the god or gods. That is, to say "I deny God" is a statement more about the person than about the god. The concept of 'no gods' was not something that anyone at that time would even consider (sort of like a modern person denying or not believing in gravity).[27]

The English word atheist, from the 1570s (a godless person, one who denies the existence of a supreme, intelligent being to whom moral obligation is due) comes from 16th century French *atheiste* which, in turn, is from Greek *atheos*. Interestingly, the word atheist emerges at the time of the vicious wars of religion in Europe at this time.

---

27   "Only rarely did [the word atheist] refer to someone who denied the existence of any divine being at all. Rather, it was used to refer to those who thought the gods were radically disinterested and uninvolved with human affairs—the view of the Epicurean philosophers—or to those who did not ascribe any true divinity to the traditional gods" (Ehrman, 2018, p. 188).

PIE *dhes* is also forms the basis of many other words with religious connotations; e.g., enthusiasm, fanatic, feast, festival, pantheon, profane, theology, tiffany, and names such as Dorothy, Theodore, and Timothy).

Agnostic

In contrast to an atheist who says that they do not believe, an agnostic says that they do not or cannot know. In particular, the agnostic takes the view that knowledge of god and the essential nature of things are not or cannot be known. The word agnostic comes from a combination of Greek *a-* (not) + *gnostos* (to be known), from PIE root *gno* (to know; also the root of English words know, knowledge).

The word agnostic was reputedly coined by T.H. Huxley, a noted English biologist and anthropologist, in 1869.

Atone, Atonement

The noun atonement has its origins first of all in words relating to oneness and later in words relating to the condition of being in a state of oneness with others or God. Later, the verb 'to atone' emerges meaning the actions relating to achieving a state of atonement.

The word atone comes from Latin *adunare*; that is, *ad-* (to, at, toward) plus *unum* (one); i.e., 'at one' or 'toward oneness'. Latin *unum* is related to PIE *oino* (one, unique), Greek *oinos* (ace; as on cards or dice), and Latin *unus* (one).

Atonement, as the condition of being at one with others, comes from the 1510. Atonement, meaning the theological state of reconciliation of sinners with God, is from the 1520s (the beginning of the Reformation).

The use of atone as an action (to atone) originates around 1300 in Middle English *atonen* (to be in accord, literally to be 'at one' or to be in harmony) and comes to English as 'to atone' in the 1590s; that is, 'to atone' suggests the actions necessary to restore a peaceful and harmonious state between people.

Atonement meaning the state which follows the addressing of damage or disharmony caused by one's behaviour is from the 1610s.

The more secular use of the verb 'to atone' is first seen in the 1660s (to make up for deficiencies or errors) and the 1680s (to make reparations).

In sum, to atone or to be atoned is to be at one with yourself and/or with others and/or with God.[28]

Awe

Before it was a word, awe was a sound—a gasp, a cry, a sigh—a first response to some experience of heightened emotion. We can almost hear the word awe in responses such as "Aaaaaah!" or "Arghhhh!" or "Ahhhhh!"[29]

---

28   Several theories of atonement and how it occurs are found in Christianity. The two most common conceptions are related to the 'moral influence' theory and the 'penal substitution' theory.

Moral influence theory, originating in the writings of the early Church, outlines how Christianity is about doing good (e.g., almsgiving) and ensuring positive moral change in one's life. Through repentance and forgiveness one's prior wrongdoings are erased and one is 're-born', so to speak, to a new life. In contrast, penal substitution theory, highlighted in the writings of the Reformation, outlines how one's prior wrongdoings are never forgotten or erased. Only through Jesus' sacrifice can one be saved—his punishment is a substitute for our punishment.

Other theories of atonement which have developed over the centuries include *Christus victor* theory, governmental theory, non-penal substitution theory, recapitulation theory, ransom theory, satisfaction theory, scapegoat theory, shared atonement theory, substitutionary theory, and vicarious atonement theory. Needless to say, confusion can and does exist in the usage of such terms. Clarity depends on the context in which they are being used.

29   John McWhorter, describing the similarities in the words for 'mama' in many languages, and citing the linguist Roman Jakobson, states, "If you're a baby making a random sound, the easiest vowel is ah because you can make it without doing anything with your tongue or lips. Then, if you are going to vary things at all, the first impulse is to break up the stream of ahhh by closing your lips for a spell, especially since you've been doing that to nurse."

McWhorter, J. (12 Oct 2015). Why 'Mom' and 'Dad' sound so similar in so many languages. The Atlantic.

https://www.theatlantic.com/international/archive/2015/10/words-mom-dad-similar-languages/409810/

Also:

[Some etymologists] "found pantomimic words everywhere. For example, in awe, the mouth is open, suggestive of fear or surprise" (Liberman, 209, p. 223). Note: pantomimic from pantomime; i.e., expressing information or telling a story without words, using body movements and facial expressions.

The word awe began as PIE *agh-es* (to be afraid, to be depressed) and came to Greek as *akhos*[30] pain, grief) and to Gothic as *agis* (fear, anquish), Proto-Germanic *agiz* (fright; also the source of Old English *ege*; meaning fear), Old High German *agiso* (fright, terror) and to various Scandinavian words meaning fright; e.g., Old Norse *agi*. Around 1200, the word *aghe* (fright) came to English from Scandinavia.

In the 14th century *aghe* had become the word *aue* (fear, terror, reverence), later seen as the word awe (dread mixed with admiration and a healthy sense of respect, especially when used in relation to experiences that felt other worldly, to experiences of power and mystery, to experiences which seemed related to activities of god or the gods).

I try to imagine such experiences that would cause early peoples to gasp or cry out. I would imagine that they would be experiences which we would also find quite familiar—experiences of wonder and beauty and unexplained happiness, experiences of chaos and destruction ("shock and awe"), experiences of birth and death, experiences for which, at the time, there were no words or explanations—only the visceral inhalation or exhalation of breath.

Awe is rooted in such experiences of feeling alive, of being possessed by life. To me, awe is clearly not a word to be trifled with.

We see the expression 'to stand in awe' from the 15th century. The word awesome appears in the 1590s, meaning 'profoundly reverential'. Awe as a verb (to awe, as in the act of inspiring awe or dread) is from the 1670s. 'Awe-inspiring' is attested from 1814.

However, somewhere along the line, the word awe seems to have lost its edge. Since the early 1960s, and especially since the 1980s, the word awesome has become a slang term used to describe something impressive or very good: "Hey dude, awesome tunes" or "Awesome cheesecake"!

Also:

"For this soft 'ah!', immortals entered the world of bodies."
Hirshfield, J. (2007). Ah!: An assay. *After: poems.* New York: HarperPerennial, 67.

30   Not to be confused with PIE ag-es (fault, guilt) and Greek *ake* (a groaning, an ache) from which comes the English word ache.

Baptize, Baptism, Baptist, Anabaptist

Baptize comes to us from PIE *gwabh* (to dip, to sink). From these origins we have the Greek *baptizein* (immerse, dip in water, to be soaked in wine; also, to be 'over one's head'—e.g., to be deep in debt) and *baptein* (to dip, steep, dye, colour).

In early Christian usage, Greek *baptein* is the origin of baptize and baptism—the sacrament in which a person is marked by the ritual use of water, a symbol of life, as a sign of being admitted into Christian community.

From Greek comes Latin *baptizare*, Old French *batisier* (11th century), and by the 14th century baptize had come to English. In the 12th century, the term baptist was being used to name a person who baptized others.

The term baptism comes to English around 1300 as *bapteme* (the 's' in the word was restored in the late 14th century) from Old French *batesme* and *bapteme* from Latin *baptismus* and Greek *baptismos*.

The phrase 'baptism by fire' comes from Greek *baptisma pyros* meaning the grace of the Holy Spirit imparted through baptism. This phrase was later used to describe martyrdom by burning; i.e., burning at the stake. This phrase, baptism by fire, describing a soldier's first experience of battle, was first used in 1857.

The term anabaptist (one who baptizes over again) comes from Latin *anabaptismus* (*ana* meaning 'up' in place or time, back again, anew; i.e. *anabaptismus* means second baptism). Anabaptism, as the early Protestant practice of adult baptism, emerged in Germany in the 1520s. By the 1570s, Anabaptism had become a more formal religious denomination. And, as a Christian doctrine, anabaptism comes from the 1640s.[31]

The use of Mennonite to name the Anabaptist sect founded by Menno Simons in Friesland, a part of Germany, comes from the 1560s.

The use of Hutterite to name the Moravian Anabaptist sect founded by Jacob Hutter comes from the 1640s.

---

31   As often seen in the origin of such church-related terms, the practice comes first, the doctrine comes later.

The first use of Baptist to describe a member of the Protestant denomination that believes in adult baptism by immersion is attested from 1654.

Opponents of such adult baptism practices have used the term anabaptist as a derogatory term, perhaps derisively asking, "How many times does someone need to be baptized?! Weren't they baptized when a child?"

Belief

What is the difference between faith and belief? Have you noticed that these words are often used in everyday conversation as if they have the same meaning? Given these similarities in their usage, what do the origins of belief tell us about how belief and faith are different?

The word belief has its origins in ancient words for love; in particular, in PIE *leubh* (to care, to desire, to love). From *leubh* come many other words related to love; for example, Proto-Germanic *lubo* (love), Old High German *liubi* (joy), German *liebe* (love), Old Norse, Old Frisian, and Dutch *lof* (love), German *lob* (praise), Old Saxon *liof*, Old Frisian *liaf*, Dutch *lief*, Old High German *liob*, German *leib*, and Gothic *liufs*—all of which mean dear or beloved. From these Germanic words comes Old English *lufu* (love, affection, friendliness) and later the word love. The verb 'to believe' comes from PIE *leubh* and Old English *belyfan* (to believe, hold dear, love).

In PIE, the prefix 'ga' was added to indicate the intensity of a word; for example, *ga* added to *leubh* became *galaub* which led to words meaning dearly beloved or esteemed, words such as Old Saxon *gilobo*, Middle Dutch *gelove*, Old High German *giloubo*, and German *glaube*.

And from West Germanic *ga-laubon* (to hold dear, esteem, trust) comes Old English *geleafa* (belief and faith). In Old English, belief and faith were perceived as similar. Both were related to that which was held in affection, esteem, and trust. By the 12th century *geleafa* had become *bileave* and, by the 15th century, the noun belief.

During the 13th century, the meanings and usages for the words belief and faith began to diverge. The word faith began to be used in terms of a person's trust and duty and loyalty. The word belief and its meanings began a slow shift from the heart to the head, from affect to intellect. A belief was a statement or dogma, something that could be written down.

By the 16th century, the word belief had come to mean the mental acceptance of something as true; in particular, the sense of things held to be true as a matter of religious doctrine. If love was still present it was probably related to having strong feelings about the truth or doctrine which you believed.

In brief, in its origins, belief was first related to what we love and only later to what we think. See also FAITH.

Bible

During the period when Old English (or Anglo-Saxon) was spoken in what is now England (5th to 12th centuries), the ordinary word for Christian scripture was *bibliodece*, a word from Latin *bibliotheca* (library, room for books, collection of books) and Greek *bibliotheke* (book repository). The word bible meant a collection of books—just as the Bible is a collection of 'books' (i.e., not chapters).

In the 14th century, the word bible, from the Old French *bible*, replaced *bibliodece*. Old French *bible* is from Anglo-Latin *biblia* which referred to any large book, as in the Latin phrase *biblia sacra* (holy books), a translation of Greek *ta biblia to hagia* (the holy books). In turn, *biblia* comes from Greek *biblion* (paper, scroll) and from Greek *byblos*.

The ancient Greeks imported 'paper' (i.e., Egyptian papyrus) from the Phoenician port city, Byblos, now the modern city of Jubayl in Lebanon. There is some debate among etymologists regarding whether Greek *byblos* refers to the city or to the papyrus.[32]

---

32   https://en.wikipedia.org/wiki/Byblos

I can imagine ancient Greek merchants first saying, "We need to get more of that Egyptian papyrus from Byblos"; then, "We need get more of that Byblos papyrus"; then, "We need more *byblos*." Just as the word bible may come from the port city of Byblos, so also can we see other products named for the cities from which they come; e.g., port wine (from Porto, Portugal) or blue jeans (from medieval French *jean fustian,* a type of twilled cotton cloth from Genoa, Italy) or denim (de Nimes, i.e., from Nimes, France).

Other words related to bible and biblio include bibliography (a list of books on a particular topic or subject), biblioklept (someone who steals books), bibliolatry (worship or idolatry or excessive reverence of books), bibliomancy (divination by randomly opening a holy book and using the first verse presented as a form of prognostication of future events), bibliomania (crazy about books), bibliopegy (the art of book binding), bibliophile (lover of books), and bibliopole (a dealer in rare or curious books).

Bishop

In its origins, a bishop is someone who 'watches over' or who 'over sees'. Bishop comes from Greek *episkopos*[33] (a watcher, spiritual overseer; a title for various government officials which was later taken over by Church officials). *Episkopos* is from Greek *epi* (over) and *skopos* (one that watches, one that looks after; a guardian, protector. *Skopos* comes from PIE *spek* (to observe).[34] Old English *bisceop* (bishop, high priest—Jewish or pagan) comes from Greek via Latin *episcopus*.

The word bishop was used in the New Testament as a descriptive title for elders and continues as such in some non-hierarchical Christian sects.[35]

A bishopric, from Old English *bisceoprice*, is the diocese or province of a bishop. *Bisceoprice* comes from *bisceop* + *rice* (realm, dominion, province) from Proto-Germanic *rikja* (rule) from PIE *reg* (move in a straight line, to direct, to lead, to rule).

Archbishop, from the 9th century, is from Old English *aercebhisceop* and Latin *archiepiscopus*; arch from Greek *arkhi* (chief, ruler). The archbishop is the chief or ruler of bishops.

The chess piece called a bishop is from the 1560s. Before that, the piece had been known as the archer and before that the alfin.

---

33   *Episkopos* is also the root of episcopal (having to do with bishops) and Episcopalian (the US version of Anglicanism).

34   Greek *skopos* is also the origin of words such as telescope, microscrope, and so on. PIE *spek* is also the origin of words such as spectacles and respect (i.e., re + *spek* = 'to see again').

35   https://www.etymonline.com/search?q=bishop

Blaspheme, Blasphemy

Blaspheme

Blaspheme is a verb with its origins in Greek *blasphemein* (to speak lightly or amiss of sacred things, to slander) and *blasphemos* (evil speaking), both rooted in PIE *bha* (to speak, to tell). Blaspheme combines *blas* (origin uncertain; perhaps related to Greek *blaptikos* (hurtful) or *blax* (slack in mind, stupid]) and *-pheme* (from PIE *bha*).

The usage of words in the Old Testament, translated as blasphemy, meant irreverence for God with implications comparable to treason.

From these PIE and Greek sources, come Latin *blasphemare* (revile, reproach, blame) and Old French *blasfemer* (to blaspheme). The verb 'to blaspheme' (to speak impiously or irreverently of God and sacred things) comes to English in the mid-14th century. Before this time, versions of blaspheme had been used in Old English simply meaning 'to blame'.

Blasphemy

Blasphemy, a noun meaning impious or profane speaking of God or sacred things, is from the early 13th century, and comes from Old French *blasfemie*, Latin *blasphemia*, and Greek *blasphemia* (a speaking ill, impious speech, slander) and Greek *blasphemein* (to speak evil of).

Blessings, Beatitudes

What comes first—being happy or being blessed? Are we happy because we are blessed or are we blessed because we are happy? Does it matter!?

Bless, blessings

Blessing. Blood. Life blood.

Bless has its origins in the Proto-Germanic word *blodison* meaning to hallow with blood or to mark with blood. The Proto-Germanic word *blotham* meant the blood sprinkled on altars after a sacrificial offering to the gods. The word *blotham* is related to the Proto-Germanic word *blodam*[36] (blood) which in turn has its origins in PIE *bhlo-to* (to swell, to gush, to spurt, that which bursts out) and in PIE *bhel* meaning to thrive, to bloom.

From such origins, we see synonyms in the dictionary for such 'life blood' which include life force, life, driving force, vital spark, inspiration, essence, heart, soul, and core. These terms suggest, perhaps, that to bless something is to sprinkle it with life.

Bless comes from Proto-Germanic *blodison* to Old English as *bletsian* or *bledsian* and to Northumbrian as *bloedsian*, words meaning to consecrate by religious rite, to make holy, or to give thanks. In late Old English, *bletsian* meant 'to pronounce or to make happy'. *Bletsian* was the word used in Old English Bibles to translate Latin *beneficere* and Greek *eulogein*[37], words meaning 'to speak well of, to praise' as well as words used to translate Hebrew *barak* (to bend the knee, worship, praise, invoke blessings).[38]

In the late use of Old English, the meaning of blessing also included the sense of to pronounce or to make happy, prosperous, fortunate (i.e., to bless with good fortune).

By the late 12th century, the word blessed was used to mean both 'supremely happy' and 'consecrated'.

The 14th century noun blessing, meaning 'a gift from God' comes from the Old English *bletsunga* or *bledsunge*. The verb to bless, meaning 'to invoke or promise God's blessing upon', is also seen in English in the 14th century. By the mid-14th century the world blessing is also used to mean a benefit. The use of blessing, as in 'to say a blessing' (as prayer before a meal), is first seen in 1738.

---

36   Proto-Germanic *blodam* (blood) is the origin of Dutch *bloed*, Old Norse *bloo*, Old Saxon *blod*, and Old English *blod*.

37   *Eulogein* is also the origin of eulogy: *eu* (good) + *logis* (word); i.e., a eulogy is 'good words'.

38   The origins of the word bless are not to be confused with the word bliss. Bliss comes from Old English *blis* (meaning bliss, merriment, favor, grace, happiness) and from Proto-Germanic *blithsjo*, *blithiz* (meaning gentle, kind). The latter is also the origin of Old English *blibe* (joyful, kind, cheerful, pleasant) from which comes our word blithe.

Beatitude

The English word beatitude, from the early 15th century, means supreme happiness. Beatitude comes to English through Middle French *béatitude* from Latin *beatitudo* (a state of blessedness) and Latin *beare* (to make happy, to make blessed). Latin *beare* has its roots in PIE *dwene* and *deu* (to do, perform, show favor, revere).

The Vulgate Bible, translated from Greek to Latin the late 4th century, uses the Latin term *beatitudines* in reference to the Sermon on the Mount (Matthew 5: 1 – 12). The use of the English word beatitudes is from the 1520s.

The English verb 'to beatify', from the 1530s, means 'to make very happy' and comes from Middle French *beatifer*, Latin *beatificare* (to make happy, to make blessed; from *beare* meaning to make happy, to bless plus *ficare*, *facere* meaning to make, to do), and from Latin *beatus* (supremely happy, blessed).

The use of beatify meaning 'to pronounce as being in heavenly bliss', the first step in the canonization of a saint, comes from the 1620s. Beatification, also from Latin *beatificare*, as a papal declaration about the state of a deceased person dates from about the same time.

Summary

Blessings, whether given or received, evoke happiness. A blessing is an act, an expression of gratitude.

A beatitude is a state of being, an experience of extreme happiness. Formally, beatification is the acknowledgement of such a state, an official recognition or praise for work well done, for a life well-lived.

Happiness, whether experienced as a blessing or as a beatitude, is a gift. Happiness is something that happens in its own time whether or not it is actively pursued. When we are happy, we feel blessed.

Carpenter

Do you ever wonder about the 'car' in carpenter?

Carpenter has origins in PIE *krsos* and *kers* meaning to run.[39] From PIE *kers* emerge several ancient words related to wheeled vehicles: Breton *karr* (chariot); Old Irish and Welsh *carr* (cart or wagon); and Gaulish *karros*, the source of Latin *carrus* (a two-wheeled Celtic war chariot). From Latin *carrus* we get Anglo-French *carre* which in the early 14th century became the English word car. (What do cars carry? Among other things they carry cargo, from Spanish *cargar* meaning a load or burden which in turn also comes from the Latin *carrus*.)

Okay, so that's car—what about carpenter?

PIE *kers* leads to Old Celtic *carpentom* (carriage) and to Latin *carpentum* (wagon or two-wheeled carriage). In Latin, a person who made wagons or carts was called a *carpentarius*.[40]

And, so, what is the Latin word for carpenter? In Latin, a carpenter is a *lignarius* (carpenter, housewright, woodworker, joiner) from Latin *lignum* (wood).

In comparison, the ancient Greek word for carpenter was *tekton* (craftsman; in particular, a carpenter or woodworker), the origin of English words such as technical, technician, and technology. When the Bible was translated from Greek to Latin during the years of the early church, Greek *tekton* was translated as Latin *carpentarius*[41]; that is, Greek 'craftsman' or 'carpenter' was translated as Latin 'wagon maker'. Why was craftsman or carpenter not translated as *lignarius*? Why was Joseph of Nazareth referred to as a *carpentarius* rather than as a *lignarius*? In any case, for whatever reasons, over the following centuries Latin *carpentarius* replaced *lignarius* eventually becoming the French and then English words for carpenter.

---

39   *Kers* is also the origin of the English words course and curriculum; as in, "Is your course running again next semester?" *Kers* is also the origin of the words career, concurrent, currency, and horse.

40   Online   Etymological   Dictionary: carpenter.   https://www.etymonline.com/search?q=carpenter

41   https://en.wikipedia.org/wiki/Tekt%C5%8Dn

The original word for carpenter in Old English was *treowwyrtha* (a tree wright or tree worker, like shipwright or millwright or wainwright). After the Norman invasion of England in 1066, the Anglo-French word *carpenter* (from Old North French *carpentier*), from Latin *carpentarius*, eventually replaced *treowwyrtha*. The English word carpenter is first seen in the 12th century as a surname and is first seen meaning woodworker in the early 13th century.

In addition, Latin *carpentarius* leads to Spanish *carpentero* and Italian *carpentiero*, also words for carpenter or woodworker. However, the German word for carpenter, *zimmermann*, comes from Old High German *zimbarman* and *zimbar* (wood for building, timber).

Finally, how is carpenter a religious word in the context of this book? Maybe Joseph of Nazareth actually was a *carpentarius*—that is, a wagon maker or a cartwright. Would it make any difference to the Bible story if this was the case? Interestingly, some sources suggest that a related Hebrew word *kharash-etsim* (craftsman of wood, carpenter) or the related Aramaic word *naggara* (craftsman) may refer to someone who was also wise and learned in a religious sense.[42]

Catechism

Catechism is oral instruction or word of mouth instruction. Catechism has its origins in PIE *swagh* (to resound, to echo) and Greek *katekhein* (to instruct orally), from *kata* (down) + *ekhein* (to sound, to ring, to echo). From these Greek roots comes Latin *catechism* (oral instruction) and *catechismus* (book of instruction).

By 1500, Latin *catechism* was used to mean basic instruction in Christian principles using a question and answer or call / response methodology in

---

42   For example, such sources include well-known and respected scholars Geza Vermes and A.N. Wilson. Geza Vermes (1983) suggests that the use of the term 'carpenter' in the Talmud can signify a very learned man and so the New Testament description of Joseph as a carpenter could indicate that he was considered wise and literate with regard to the Torah. This theory was later popularized by A. N. Wilson to suggest that, as a carpenter, Joseph had some sort of elevated social status. https://en.wikipedia.org/wiki/Tekt%C5%8Dn

which the student echoes the teacher. In brief, "Here are the questions, memorize the answers, the test will be tomorrow!"

The word catechism comes to English in 1753.

Cathedral

Cathedral is related to words meaning a chair, sitting down, and falling down.

Cathedral, first seen in English in the 1580s meaning the church of a bishop, comes from Latin *cathedra* (meaning a comfortable easy chair, usually one used by women) and Greek *kathedra* meaning a seat or bench.[43]

Kathedra is formed from *kata* (down) + *hedra* (a seat) which is from PIE *sed* (to sit). *Kata* is the root of several falling down words such as cataclysm, catacomb, catalog, catalyst, catalytic, catapult, cataract, catastrophe, and catatonic. Perhaps this is why when someone calls with bad news they ask first if we are sitting down!

Speaking of falling or sitting down, a related term, PIE *dher*, means to support or to hold; i.e., to keep from falling down. PIE *dher* is the root of the Greek words *thronos* (a throne) and *theraps* (a servant), both of which support us. Related to *dher* and *theraps* is Greek *therapeia* (to care for, to cure) from which we get our words therapy and therapist. Perhaps this is why the chair or couch has become a symbol (or cliché?) for psychotherapy?!

Dher went to India and became the Sanskrit *dharma* meaning right conduct and cosmic order (i.e., harmony, things falling in their right place).

And, in Christianity, even though cathedral now means a church from which a bishop presides, originally, wherever the bishop sat was the cathedral!

---

43   Speaking of chairs, the word chair also comes to English from Latin *cathedra* through the Old French *chaire* (the chair or the office of a professor). Today we use the word 'chair' (chair of the meeting, chair of the board, and so on) in the same way that a bishop of the early church could be have been considered the 'chair' or *'cathedra'* of the church.

Celibacy

Celibacy is a word of unknown origin. It is first seen in Latin *caelibatus* (the state of being unmarried). The English word celibacy (again, the state of being unmarried, voluntary abstention from marriage) is from the 1660s.

The Online Etymological Dictionary suggests that the word may come from PIE *kaiwelo* (alone) + *libhs* (living); i.e., living alone. An alternative suggestion is PIE *kehi-lo* (whole), a word which is related to the word health.

The practice of celibacy is seen in varying forms and at different times in many world religions. In Christianity, celibacy laws are seen as early as the 4th century Council of Elvira. During these early centuries of the church, celibacy was both resisted and seen as a matter of personal choice. However, these laws were renewed in the 11th century reforms of Pope Gregory VII and began to be enforced (e.g., Second Lateran Council of 1139) during the period when Western Europe was emerging from the so-called Dark Ages.[44]

The noun celibate (the state of celibacy, especially as mandated to clergy in the Roman Catholic church) is from the 1610s. This was the only meaning of the word until the early 19th century. Celibate meaning someone who is sworn to celibacy is from 1838. Celibate as an adjective is from 1825.

In the 19th century, the word celibacy was used as the opposite of marriage. At that time, celibacy, except as a religious vow, was seen as leading to, or being an excuse for, sexual indulgence and debauchery among bachelors. By the 1950s, celibacy was used to mean voluntary abstinence from sexuality, without reference to marriage.[45]

---

44   https://en.wikipedia.org/wiki/Celibacy

45   https://www.etymonline.com/search?q=celibacy

Character

English contains many phrases related to character; for example, "She's quite a character," character reference, strength of character, character sketch, character-assassination, out of character, character arc (the journey of a character in a story), and so on.

So what is character or a character? How is character related to personality?

The word character has uncertain origins. One suggestion for the origin is the pre-Greek word *kharax* (a pointed stake). Perhaps from this word comes another ancient Greek word *kharessein* (to engrave) and *kharakter* (an engraved mark; a mark engraved on a coin; a symbol or imprint on the soul; an instrument for marking). In later Greek culture, *kharakter* was used metaphorically to mean a defining quality or individual feature of a person.

Character first comes to English in the mid-14th century as *carecter* (a symbol marked or branded or the body) from Greek *kharakter*, Latin *character*, and later, Old French *caratere* (feature, character). By the mid-15th century *carecter* meant a symbol or drawing used in sorcery. By the late 15th century it meant an alphabetic letter or graphic symbol standing for a sound or syllable. By the 16th century, the original '*ch*' of Latin *character* had re-emerged to form the current English word character.

By the 1640s, character referred to the sum of qualities that define a person or thing or which differentiate one person or thing from another. In particular, the word character describes the aggregate of moral qualities by which a person is judged *apart from* intelligence, competence, or special talents – perhaps an indication during this period of the emergence of the idea of an individual as a unique or differentiated person in relation to society in general.[46]

---

46   "When we speak of a moral virtue or an excellence of character, the emphasis is not on mere distinctiveness or individuality, but on the combination of qualities that make an individual the sort of ethically admirable person he or she is. ... This entry will discuss 'moral character' in the Greek sense of having or lacking moral virtue. ...Aristotle states ... that it is not easy to define in rules which actions deserve moral praise and blame, and that these matters require the judgment of the virtuous person." https://plato.stanford.edu/entries/moral-character/

Over the years, the word character took on other meanings: by the 1660s, character also meant a person in a play or novel; by 1712, a moral quality assigned by others to a person by repute; by 1749, an individual 'person' in the abstract, especially an eccentric person (1773); by 1886, character-building; by 1888, character-assassination; and, by 1931, character as a chap or fellow.

So, returning to the origins of the word character, how do we 'make our mark' in life; i.e., our *kharakter*? How is character be related to personality?

Character and personality are similar but not necessarily the same thing.[47] Personality is the expression of various traits (e.g., sociability, assertiveness, kindness, energetic, and so on—lists of traits seem endless) whereas character is more about the sum and expression of these traits as expressed in a context of a life of moral virtue (see ETHICS, MORALS, VIRTUE).

James Hillman (1999)[48] suggests that 'force of character' is what drives a person. He differentiates character and personality in several ways; for example, "the discourse of personality is human psychology; of character, imaginative description" (p. 197), e.g., story-telling. Hillman suggests that personality is individual whereas character is social (p. 198); that is, as individuals, we express our personality whereas others see and are influenced by our character. Finally, Hillman suggests that "character is to late years as the individual calling is to early years; [character] gives sense and purpose to the changes of aging" (p. 198).

In summary, could we say that personality is like the daily weather and character is like the climate? Or, that personality is the bricks and character is the wall? Some might say that personality is about 'spirit' (i.e., akin to 'team spirit' or 'school spirit') whereas character is about 'soul' (i.e., akin to 'soul food'

---

47   The dictionary (Merriam-Webster) tells us that personality is "the complex of characteristics that distinguishes an individual; especially, the totality of an individual's behavioural and emotional characteristics." On the other hand, the Stanford Encyclopedia of Philosophy states, "... the philosophical use of the word "character" has a different linguistic history [from the word personality]. ... for excellences of character —*ēthikai aretai*— we usually translate as 'moral virtue(s)' or 'moral excellence(s).' The Greek *ēthikos* (ethical) is the adjective [related to the noun] *ēthos* (character).

48   Hillman, J. (1999). *The force of character and the lasting life*. New York: Ballantine.

or 'soul mates'). Perhaps personality is 'who' we are whereas 'character' is more related to 'how' we are; i.e., how we live a virtuous and moral life.

Charisma, Charismatic

Charisma

Think of people you know who are charming, full of good cheer, creative, and love a good party. Such people are attractive. You want to be near them; in fact, when you are near such people you too may also become charming, cheerful, creative, and festive—perhaps in spite of yourself! You are drawn into that energy in the same way that you might be drawn into a good book or a moving piece of music or an inspiring teacher or an exciting football game. Such characteristics are seen in the origins of the word charisma.

The word charisma comes from Greek *kharis* (grace, beauty, kindness) and *khairein* (to rejoice at). In Greek mythology, a *charis* was one of the three goddesses of charm, beauty, nature, human creativity, and fertility. Some sources suggest that these three goddesses were attendants of the goddess of love, Aphrodite (or Venus, as she was known in Roman mythology). The three goddesses, also known as 'the three graces', from oldest to youngest, were Aglaea (elegance, brightness, splendor), Euphrosyne (mirth, joyfulness), and Thalia (youth, beauty, good cheer, festivity).

From Greek *kharis* come the words *kharizesthai* (to show favor to) and *kharisma* (favor, divine gift). The Latin version is *charisma*. The Middle English word *karisme* (spiritual gift, divine grace) is first seen around 1500. The English word charism (plural charismata) is attested from the 1640s. There were two kinds of gifts related to charism—the gift of healing and the gift of teaching (in particular, the gift of prophecy and the gift of tongues).

The current English form of the word charisma seems relatively new, first seen in 1875. At that time it named a special spiritual gift, a power divinely conferred, or a talent from God.

The secular use of the term charisma, meaning the gift of leadership or the power of authority, came to English around 1930, from the work of Max Weber (1864 – 1920), the noted German sociologist and philosopher. Charisma meaning personal charm is first seen in 1959.

To return for a moment to the Greek word *kharis*: its origins are in PIE *gher* (to like, to want) which is also the source of words such as eucharist, exhortation, greedy, and yearn. Some suggest that PIE *gher* is also the source of words such as Sanskrit *haryati* (finds pleasure, likes) and *harsate* (is aroused), Avestan *zara* (effort, aim), Latin *hortari* (exhort, encourage, urge, incite, instigate), Russian *zhariti* (awake desire, charm), Gothic *gairnei* (desire), and Old English *giernan* (to strive, desire, yearn). The number and variety of such words would seem to indicate that many people in many cultures have experienced something for which they would need to create and use such a word.

Charismatic

This adjective comes from noun charisma. Charismatic (of or pertaining to charisma) is first seen in 1851 in Bible commentary and theology in reference to the operation of the Holy Spirit and the prophetic ecstasy seen in the life of the early church. The English term 'charismatic movement' in modern Christianity, emphasizing the divine gifts of healing, tongues, and so on, is first seen in 1936.

Charity

The word charity has its roots in PIE *karo*, *ka* (to like, to desire). PIE *ka*, it seems, is not too far removed from the word care. PIE *ka* is the root of words such as caress, cherish, and, perhaps surprisingly, the word whore. PIE *ka* has also been noted as a possible source of Sanskrit *Kama* (a name for the Hindu god of love; also, the *Kama Sutra*), Sanskrit *kamah* (love, desire), Old Persian *kama* (desire), Latin *carus* (dear, valued), Old Irish *cara* (friend), and Old English *hore* (prostitute, whore).

From Latin *carus* come *caritatem* and *caritas* (costliness, esteem, affection) and from these, in the 12th century, we see Old French *charite* (Christian charity, mercy, compassion, alms, charitable foundation). From these origins we have the Old English *charity* (benevolence for the poor, Christian love in its highest manifestation).

Charity as "the sense of affections people ought to feel for one another" is from around 1300. Also from this time, charity is used to mean both an act of kindness or philanthropy and the alms bestowed on a person or persons in need. The use of charity to mean "liberality in judging others or their actions" is from the late 15th century. Charity, used in terms of a charitable foundation, is from the 1690s.[49]

The Vulgate Bible uses the Latin *carus* as a translation of Greek *agape* (love, love of humanity), likely to avoid the sexual suggestiveness of Latin *amor* (love). Early English translations of the Bible used either love or charity as translations of Greek *agape*; however, generally speaking, love was used more often and is now uniformly used in such translations.

The word charitable, first seen around 1200, was used to refer to the Christian virtues of benevolence, kindness, and the manifestation of Christian love in its highest and broadest form. Charitable, meaning the liberal (i.e., in the sense of generous) treatment of the poor is from around 1400. The use of charitable to impute favourable motives to others in from the 1620s.[50]

Choir, Chorus

The word chorus comes from PIE *gher* (to grasp, enclose), perhaps suggesting an enclosed dance floor. From PIE *gher* comes Greek *khoros* (band of dancers or singers, dance, dancing ground[51]) and then Latin *chorus* (a

---

49   https://www.etymonline.com/search?q=charity

50   Marilynne Robinson, discussing problems of translation of Latin and Greek words to English, describes the "persistence of words whose meanings have changed since they became classic or at least conventional" and suggests that "in English, charity, [is] a word which, sadly, has acquired a meaning having no inevitable connection at all with love" (Robinson, 2019, 242).

51   The term choreography (the movements done by dancers during a performance or the job of deciding how dancers will move) is from 1789. Choreography is from Greek *khoreia* (dance).

dance in a circle, the persons singing and dancing, the chorus of a play; e.g., a Greek tragedy). A rich patron of the arts in ancient Greece was a *khoregos*.

In ancient Greek culture, a chorus was a circle of people dancing and singing. The stories or plays presented during this dancing and singing gradually became the basis of the later tragedies and comedies of classical Greek drama. During the intervals in these dramatic presentations, a group of people known as a chorus spoke in a single collective voice on the moral and religious sentiments evoked by the actions of the play. This chorus was like a narrator or, perhaps, a representation of the inner reflective voices of the playwright and the audience.

The word chorus came to English in the 1560s. Chorus, meaning the refrain of a song (which the audience joins in singing) is from the 1590s. The use of the term chorus to mean a choir is first attested in the 1650s.

When we think of the word choir, we think of a group of people singing, usually in a church or concert hall; however, the word choir originally meant the place in a church from which the choir sang. The word choir came to English around 1300 as *queor* from Old French *cuer* (an architectural term; i.e., the choir part of a church). The use of the word choir to describe the people singing in a church came from 13th century Old French *choeur* and from Latin *chorus* (choir). The more generic use of choir simply to mean a band of singers is from the early 15th century.

The word chorister, a member of a choir, is from the mid-14th century. The adjective choral, from the 1580s, is from Latin *choralis* (belonging to a chorus or choir).

Choirboy is first seen in 1769. Chorus girl is from 1894. By 1885, the term choirboy was being used to suggest a sense of innocence; the term chorus girl, on the other hand, suggests a sense of, shall we say, something not so innocent.

Christian, Christianity

Christian

The origins of the word Christian reflect the cosmopolitan milieu of the early years in which the early church took shape. The word Christian comes from Greek *christianos*, from *christos* or *khristos* (the anointed one; a translation of Hebrew *mashiah* and Aramaic *meshiah* from which comes the word messiah). From Greek *christianos* comes Latin *christianus*, a word also borrowed for use in West Germanic languages from which comes Old English *cristen* and later *Christen*. By the 16th century, the word Christian had replaced these earlier words.[52]

In Latin, the suffix *-iani* (follower, servant) was added to Greek *khristos* to form the Latin word *christiani* (servants of the anointed one). At that time, the word described a role rather than a religion.[53]

The first reference to the word Christian, found in the New Testament book, Acts of the Apostles (i.e., Acts 11: 25 – 26), written toward the middle or end of the 1st century CE, describes the followers of Christ in the city of Antioch.

Christianity

The term Christianity, used to describe all Christians or the state of being a Christian, comes to English around 1300 from Old French *crestienté* (Christendom, spiritual authority, baptism) and Latin *christianitatem*. Christianity gradually replaced Christendom as the name of the religion.

---

52   The verb christen comes to English around 1200 from Old English *cristnian* (to baptize; to make Christian). According to the origins of word christen, a person is not born as a Christian but is made a Christian through baptism. A person of another religion can choose to convert to Christianity. In contrast, in some other religions (e.g., Islam) in which people are considered to be born as members of the religion, newcomers do not 'convert' to the religion but rather 'revert' to it; i.e., they revert to what is perceived as the original 'default' religion.

53   Ostler, 2016, 62 – 63.

Christmas

The word Christmas[54], as one would expect, is comprised of Christ + mass (See also JESUS CHRIST, MASS).

In Old English, Christmas was known as *Cristes maesse* and began to be written as one word in the mid-14th century. In the early 14th century, Old English *Cristenmesse Even*, or Christmas Eve, first appears.

The term 'Father Christmas' is first seen in a Devon carol from the late 14th century. The term 'Christmas present'; i.e., a gift, is from 1769. Christmas tree, in the modern sense, comes to English in 1835 from German *weihnachtsbaum*. Christmas cards appear in the 1840s and were popular by the 1860s.

Church

I recall when I was a child my mother insisting that the church isn't the building, it's the people. At the same time, I heard other people describe the church as the house of the Lord or the house of God. Other people said that God is everywhere. For some reason I didn't find these distinctions puzzling, I just accepted them. I grew to appreciate what my mother meant but, as a child, it seemed that church was just a building (perhaps, a somewhat special building) where I went on Sunday mornings with my family.

The sense of church as being the people comes from words meaning congregation or assembly, words which were used by early Christians before words related to church. In the early days, people didn't go to

---

54   "The clearest case of a specific Roman festival equated with a subsequent Christian feast is Saturnalia, the midwinter feast, which began on December 17 and culminated on December 25 with the birth of *Sol Invictus*, the 'invincible sun'. This day had in fact only been instituted as part of a cult for soldiers by the emperor Aurelian in 274 CE. Still, this could be reinterpreted as a celebration of Christ's birth, and the gold, incense, and myrrh that the magi brought from the east to honor the newborn Christ (according to Matthew 2: 1, 11) could now be taken as a sanction for the ancient Roman custom of gift-giving in this season" (Ostler, 2016, 84 – 85).

church, they were the church wherever they happened to meet. A particular building called a church came later.

So, where does the word church come from? Its roots are found in PIE *keue* which means swollen or to swell into something strong and powerful.[55] The Greek word *kyrios* (ruler, lord) is rooted in *keue*; i.e., *kyrios* is a person who has become a strong and powerful ruler.

Where does this *kyrios* live? The house of the ruler or lord was called *kryiake*. This term migrated from Greek to Proto-Germanic *kirika* (house of the lord or ruler) which evolved into the German word *kirche* (church). From these Germanic origins we get the Old English words *cirice* and *circe*, the Middle English word *chirche*, and to the current English word church. Given that modern English is a relatively new language, the word church, from before the 12th century, is one of its older words. We also still see other words meaning church, such as *kirk* and *kerk*, which also have Germanic origins.

The word ancient Greek word *kyriake* is also related to the Greek word *oikia*, meaning house or habitation. *Oikia* is the root of the Greek *oikoumenikos* (the inhabited world), the Latin *oecumenicus* (general, universal), and the English word *ecumenical* (all churches) first seen in 1587 during the turmoil of the Protestant Reformation in Europe. See ECUMENISM.

After Emperor Constantine's conversion to Christianity and the official recognition and promotion of Christianity after 313 CE, the Greek term *kyriakon* (an adjective meaning 'of the lord') was used to describe houses of Christian worship. However, over time, the use of this word declined in favor of the Latin terms *basilike* (basilica) and *ecclesia* (from Greek *ekklesia*), words used to describe houses of Christian worship, especially during the growing divergence over the centuries between Roman Catholic and Eastern Orthodox forms of Christianity.[56]

---

55   Keue is also the root of PIE kumolo and Latin cumulus = a heap, pile, mass, surplus. The word cumulus, naming a rounded mass of clouds, is first seen in 1803. The word accumulate comes from PIE keue.

56   The word church, from Greek kyriake and kyriakon, is an example of the migration of many words from Greek to Germanic via the Goths and West Germanic people. In contrast many words used in more western areas of Europe have their roots in Latin. For example, the French word for church (eglise) has its roots in the Latin ecclesia.

In brief, the Greek, Latin, and Germanic origins of the word church indicate its roots in terms related to the house or place of a ruler or lord.

So, today, should we consider the church as the people or the building? Sounds like it's both. A house without people is just a house. A building without people is just a building. A church is both people and place—it is a community, a group of people who happen to share common beliefs, and it is a place where such a community meets to celebrate through ritual and symbol these common beliefs. Church is a place for people who are or who 'live' the church to feel and to be at home.

As I think about the word church, I am intrigued by the sense of the original PIE *keue* as a 'swelling' or an 'enlargement'. This sense of the word has a dynamic rather than a static quality and suggests the notion of church as something continually growing, developing, and evolving. Like a garden or a forest, the word church contains an organic sense of aliveness.

And so, just as a growing or developing ruler creates a home so also does a growing or developing community of believers create a home. Communities create sacred or symbolic spaces which represent their understanding of and their relationship to their god.

Clergy, Laity

Clergy

The word clergy comes from PIE *kla* or *kel* (to strike). From PIE *kla* comes Greek *klastos* (broken in pieces).[57] From *klastos* comes *kleros* (first meaning a shard or wood chip used in casting lots; then meaning a lot, allotment; piece of land; heritage, inheritance).

What does all this have to do with the word clergy? Perhaps the clergy were people who were 'cut out' or 'set apart' to perform ritual duty in early Christian community. Perhaps they drew lots to see who would give the sermon each week?!

---

57   *Klastos* also the root of iconoclast (an image breaker) and pyroclastic (formed or involving fragmentation by fire).

By the second century CE, we see the ecclesiastical Greek word *klerikos* (pertaining to an inheritance) which was also being used to mean of the clergy or belonging to the clergy as opposed to the laity. Greek *kleros* was also used to describe matters relating to ministry; e.g., as seen in Deuteronomy 18.2 ("Therefore they shall have no inheritance among their brethren: The Lord is their inheritance").

From Greek *klerikos* come Latin *clericus* (clergyman, priest; priestly, belonging to the *clerus*) and Old French *clergie*, a word with two meanings: *clergie* meaning clerics, learned men, and *clergie* meaning learning, knowledge, erudition.

By around 1200 the word clergy appears in English meaning both the office or dignity of a clergyman. By around 1300 the word clergy also meant persons ordained for religious work. In 1274 English law exempted clergy from certain criminal processes before secular judges; however, this exemption was abolished in 1827.

Also, from Latin *clericus* comes Old French *clerc* and Old English *cleric* (both words meaning clergyman, priest, scholar, student). By around 1200, the word clerk appears (a man ordained in the ministry, a priest, an ecclesiastic). Also, by around 1200, the word clerk had also come to describe someone who could read and write.

At this time, the words clergy and clerk both mean clergyman or priest. However, during this early medieval period when the clergy were usually more literate than others in society, many clergy or 'clerks' were employed as scribes and account keepers by secular authorities. Over time, the word clerk took on a broader meaning than the word clergy. By around 1500 the word clerk meant someone who was an assistant in public or private business. In 1790 we see the use of the word clerk in American English to mean a retail salesman (i.e., a salesclerk). By 1879 we see the word clerk meaning someone who registers guests in a hotel.

The word clergyman (someone in holy orders) appears in the 1570s. The word clergywoman appears in the 1670s and usually meant someone who was a nun. The meaning of clergywoman as pastor or a woman of the clerical profession is from 1871.

Laity

The word laity, from the early 15th century, means a body of people not in religious orders. In church settings, the words laity and the lay people refer to those who are not the clergy. The word layman is from the 15th century. The word laywoman is from 1529. Laypeople is from 1972.

Originally the adjective lay (e.g., lay man) meant uneducated, non-professional, or non-clerical (i.e., not clergy). The word lay comes from Old French *lai* (secular, not of the clergy), 12th century *laique*, Latin *laicus*, and Greek *laikos* (of the people). *Laikos* comes from Greek *laos* (the common folk, people, the tribe).

Before these Greek words, the origins of the word laity are unknown.

Since the 19th century, the adjective laic (from the 1560s), also from Greek *laikos*, has been considered a more modern alternative to lay and laity.

Communion, Eucharist

The words communion and eucharist, often used interchangeably, in their origins generally mean expressing gratitude and thanks for being together. In brief, communion is about a group of people who have something in common, eucharist names a ritual in which these people participate.

Communion

Communion comes from common which in turn is rooted in PIE *ko-moin-i* (held in common, shared by all), from PIE *ko* (together) and *moin*, *mei* (change, exchange). From these roots come Latin *communis* (from *com* meaning together and *unus* meaning one) meaning in common, public, shared by all or many, general (not specific), familiar (not pretentious) and Old French *comun* meaning common, general, free, open, public. By the 14th century the word common was part of English—the commons were the common grazing lands for livestock; later, the House of Commons evolved as the 'house of the people'.

The Latin term *communionem*, meaning fellowship, mutual participation, and sharing, is based on *communis* and was used by St Augustine (354 – 430 CE) to mean participation in the sacrament known as the eucharist.

Eucharist

Regular Sunday worship in the second century early Church became known as *eukharistia* (thanksgiving), "a term which gradually replaced the more primitive term *breaking of bread*" (Chadwick, 1993, 261). Greek *eukharistia* comes from *eukaristos* (grateful), from *eu-* (well, good)[58] and *kharizethai* (to show favor), which in turn is from Greek *kharis* (grace, favor) and in its earliest form from PIE *gher* (to like, want).

In the Septuagint and the Greek New Testament *eukharisteo* is used to mean to thank and to be thankful.

Eucharist, meaning the sacrament of the Lord's Supper or Communion, comes to English in the mid-14th century from Old French *eurcariste*, Latin *eucharistia*, and Greek *eukharistia* (thanksgiving, gratitude; later, *eukharistia* came to mean the Lord's Supper).

Confession, Absolution

Confession

The word confession is rooted in PIE *bha* (to speak, to tell, to say) which is the root of two related Latin words *fari* (to speak) and *fama* (talk, rumour, reputation, public opinion, renown; also, ill-fame, scandal, reproach).[59]

First, Latin *confessare* comes from Latin *confiteri* (to acknowledge), from *com-* (together) and *fateri* (to admit) which is related to *fari* (to speak).

---

58   Greek *eu-* is a common prefix in English and comes from PIE *esu* (good, well). In addition to meaning good and well, *eu-* also means luckily and happily. The opposite of *eu-* is *dys-* (e.g., dysfunctional, dystrophy, and so on). Some words beginning with *eu-* include eulogy, euphemism, euphony, euphoria, euthanasia, and many others (but not Europe!).

59   Fama was the goddess of rumour in Roman mythology. *Fama* is also related to Latin *fabula* (fable) and Greek *pheme* (talk) and phone (voice, sound).

From *confessare* we see Old French *confesser* and by the late 14th century the English verb to confess. In these origins, to confess could be said to mean people coming together to say the words, to acknowledge commonly held beliefs, to say what they believe to be true.

In the early days of Christianity, a confession was the words uttered by someone avowing his or her religion in spite of persecution or danger but who did not necessarily suffer martyrdom. To be martyred was to 'witness' rather than to 'confess'. This sense of the word confession is seen in Old French *confesser* which had the connotation that to confess meant saying something that could likely bring you harm or suffering.

In brief, a confession was not a statement of sins committed but rather a statement, often in the face of danger or harm, of what you believed to be true.

Second, Latin *fama* appears to be a word related to the character or repute of the person saying the words. Confession, as related to *fama*, is not just about saying the words but also about the person saying the words— that is, practicing what you preach, embodying your beliefs. Confession was not just about what you said but was also about who you were and how you were perceived by others. By the 13th century, *fama* had come to English as the word fame (the character attributed to someone) and by the late 14th century we see the word infamous (of ill repute).

Perhaps it is this sense of *fama* that is the focus of a common understanding of confession (i.e., the confession in the confessional). In such a state of confession I state who I am and who I have been in relation to myself, to others, and to life in general.

The noun confession, seen in English from the 14th century, comes from Latin *confessionem* and *confessio* (a confession, an acknowledgement). Confession meaning 'that which is confessed' is seen from the mid-15th century. A confession in the context of the law is seen from the 1570s. The word confessional, the place where a priest hears a confession, is from 1727.

In brief, in common use, the word confession has evolved from a statement, often in the face of persecution, of what is believed to be true to a statement of what has been done wrong or where one has fallen short and for which one asks to be absolved.[60]

Absolution

The origins of the word absolution are found in PIE *leu* (to loosen, divide, cut apart) and Latin *solvere* (to loosen, dissolve, untie, release, detach).

From Latin *solvere* comes Latin *solutionem* and *solutio* (a loosening or unfastening), Old French *solucion* (division, dissolving, explanation), and in the 14th century, the English word solution.[61] Latin *solvere* also came to English in the 14th century as 'to solve' at which time it meant to disperse, dissipate, and loosen.

And, so to absolve, from the Latin *absolvere* (to set free, to acquit). The *ab-* prefix before *solvere* meaning 'off' or 'away from' has its origins in PIE *apo-* (off, away).[62] To absolve is not just to loosen or unfasten something but it is also to put that something away from you. To absolve is to cut something away and let it go.

From Latin *absolvere* we see the Old French *absolucion* and by around 1200 we see the English word absolution meaning remission or forgiveness. Originally, absolution was used to mean remission or forgiveness of sins (the words sin, debts, trespass were used interchangeably at various times in different translations of older Greek and Latin words). By the 1400s absolution was also being used more generally to mean the remission or forgiveness of a monetary debt.

---

60   Also, consider the difference between profession and confession; i.e., the 'pro' and the 'con'. To profess something is to state what you know or believe to be true, or to 'do' what you know (e.g., a professor or a professional). In the context of the church, a novice to a religious order will profess what they believe as part of their initiation to their order. On the other hand, to confess something is perhaps to 'profess' in the face of danger or to 'confess' the shortcomings seen or felt in one's beliefs or actions.

61   Solution meaning a liquid containing a dissolved substance is first seen in the 1590s.

62   See also APOCALYPSE (to take away the concealment, to reveal something).

Confession and Absolution

In brief, in the context of these word origins, a confession can be both a statement of what I believe and of how I have acted in relation to what I believe. An absolution, on the other side of such a confession, is the acknowledgement of the truth of what has been said as well as the permission for the release and letting go of the past. The past is past and I carry forward with hope into the future.

Conscience

Sometimes when I hear the word conscience I am reminded of cartoons I've seen of a little figure whispering into a person's ear. Sometimes a cartoon will show two figures, one with a halo, one with a pitchfork, competing for the person's attention.

Conscience, or inner voice, often shows up when least expected (or wanted!). The ancient Greeks had two words for this inner voice—*daemon*—from which we can trace our words demon (the voice that gets us into trouble) and *genius* (originally meaning the voice that keeps us on track toward our destiny). See DAEMON, DEMON.

The word conscience is rooted in PIE *skei* (to cut, to split) which seems appropriate given this sense of an 'other' voice that feels like it is part of me but not quite part of me.

PIE *skei* is related to Greek *skhizein* (to split, rend, cleave)[63], Old English *sceadan* (to divide, separate), and our verb 'to shed'—that is, to cast off, to leave behind.

PIE *skei* is also related to Latin *scire* (to know, to distinguish; that is, to be able to separate one thing from another) and Latin *scindere* (to cut, to divide).[64] Latin *scire* is related to *sciens* (intelligent, skilled) and *scientia* (knowledge, a knowing, expertness) which led to the 12th century Old French word *science* (knowledge, learning, application, a body of

63   Other words related to *skhizein* include schedule, schism, schist, and schizophrenia.

64   Other words related to *scindere* include scissors, scythe, shingle, and rescind.

knowledge). By the 14ᵗʰ century the word science had come to English meaning what is known, knowledge of something acquired by study, information; assurance of knowledge, certitude, certainty.[65]

During the 14th century, the word science took on several connotations: book-learning; a particular branch of knowledge or learning; skillfulness, cleverness; and, craftiness. By the late 14ᵗʰ century the word science referred to collective human knowledge; particularly, the knowledge gained by systematic observation, experiment, and reasoning. By the early 15ᵗʰ century the word science also meant experiential knowledge as well as a skill, handicraft, and a trade. The modern use of the word science to mean a body of regular or methodical observations or propositions concerning a particular subject or speculation is attested from 1725. The sense of science as related to non-arts studies is from the 1670s.

And so to the word conscience, from Latin *conscire* (to be mutually aware, perhaps in the sense of I and my inner voice being mutually aware) which is comprised of Latin *com* (with, thoroughly) and Latin *scire* (to know). Latin *conscire* seems to imply a sense of knowing what I know, of being self-conscious of what I know.

It is as if when confronted by choices ("Which voices to listen to?") I am beside myself listening to these voices discussing my knowing and considering various actions. The word conscience retains this experience of being of two minds about something or of having to stand outside myself in order to consider my options and values, and then to act accordingly. It feels as though through such a dialogue within myself, I not only construct and develop my knowledge but also my conscience. My conscience grows as I grow.

Latin *conscire* leads to Latin *conscientum* and *conscientia* (knowledge within oneself, sense of right, a moral sense). These Latin roots lead to the 12ᵗʰ century Old French *conscience* (conscience, innermost thoughts,

---

65   The modern concept and practice of the 'scientific method' comes from this period, particularly in the work of Roger Bacon (1214 – 1294) who drew upon methods which had been developed in the ancient world and in the medieval Muslim universities. Bacon also advocated the use of mathematics in scientific research. In this, some say, he was four centuries ahead of his time. For example, Isaac Newton (1642 – 1727) did not do his pioneering work in science and math until the 17ᵗʰ century.

desires, intentions, feelings) and in the early 13th century the English word conscience.

Perhaps conscience is the process of developing and considering what we know and do through mindfulness and self-consciousness.

Contemplation

A hint to understanding the origins and use of the word contemplate is the syllable 'temp', which is also the origin of the word temple, and which has its origins in PIE *tem* (to cut, to create a space that is set apart).

The sense of PIE *tem* meaning 'a place set apart' is also seen in PIE *temp* (a cleared space in front of an altar) and in Greek *temenos* (the sacred area around a temple). From these origins comes Latin *templum* (a piece of ground consecrated for the taking of auspices, a building for the worship of a god). The Old English word *tempel*, meaning a building for worship or an edifice dedicated to the service of a deity or any place regarded as occupied by divine presence, leads to the current English word temple.

And so, on to the word contemplation which is derived from Latin *templum*. When Latin *com-* (with, together) is added as a prefix to *templum*, the words *contemplari* (to set a place apart for observation, to gaze attentively, to observe), *contemplationem*, and *contemplatio* (the act of looking at) are formed. Perhaps in this sense, contemplation could be considered as the act of putting oneself in or near a sacred spot in order to gaze upon the divine.[66]

Contemplation, meaning a religious musing, comes to English around 1200 from Old French *contemplation* and Latin *contemplationem*. Contemplative is from the mid-14th century and the verb 'to contemplate' comes from the 1590s.

Could it be said that the act of contemplation is an act of not only putting yourself in a space that is set apart but also putting yourself in a time that is set apart? In addition, could it be said that in a way contemplation

---

66   Perhaps similar to the concept in Hinduism of 'doing darshan'; i.e., going to a temple to gaze upon the image of the god with the expectation that the god will look back favourably upon the viewer. Interestingly, the national public television broadcaster in India is called Doordarshan.

is putting yourself in a space and a time in which you experience being set apart from yourself? In a ritual fashion you put yourself in the presence of something other than yourself.[67]

Convert, Conversion

The verb 'to convert' comes from Latin *convertire*, *convertere* (to turn around, transform) from Latin *com-*, *con-* (with, together) + *vertere* (to turn); from PIE *wer* (to turn, bend). From these origins comes Old French *convertir* (to turn around, turn towards; change, transform; convert, win over) which came to English around 1300 as convert (a change or turn from one religion to another; especially to Christianity). The related Old English word before the arrival of Old French was *gecyrren*, *cierran* (to turn, return).

Conversion in the religious sense can be experienced as a sudden 'road to Damascus' experience or as a more gradual and subtle 'tap on the shoulder' experience.[68]

The more general sense of convert meaning to transmute or to change into another form or substance is from the late 14th century. The sense of turning from one use or destination to another is from the late 15th century.

---

67   So how are meditation, contemplation, and prayer different? What might the origins of these three words tell us?
Meditation, in its origins, seems to be about thoughtfulness, mindfulness, study, and reflection. Prayer, in its origins, seems to be about speaking with intention, perhaps on the other side of meditation, in the anticipation of some expected action or outcome. Contemplation, in its origins, seems to be about being present in a (sacred) space and time that is intentionally set apart from daily activity. Contemplation may include ritual action without necessarily any focus on particular thought or action.

68   Ehrman describes most conversions as a gradual step by step process in contrast to a more general belief that conversions are dramatic and instant changes of mind and heart. Conversion, says Ehrman, is "an exchange of one set of religious beliefs and practices for another. Some people –possibly very large numbers of people—will not make the change instantaneously, completely, or with full commitment ... But in the version of Christianity that was more or less authorized from its early centuries, conversion was *not 'both/and'* [i.e., both the old and the new beliefs co-existing as had been common in pre-Christian times when people tended to add new beliefs and practices to the old ones, reflecting a more polytheistic worldview] *but 'either/or'*. Christians ... understood their religion to be restrictive, not additive, exclusive not inclusive" (Ehrman, 2019, 109).

The noun convert (a person who converts; a person whose faith has been changed from one religion to another[69]) is from the 1560s (the time of the Reformation). The more general sense of a person converted from one opinion or practice to another is from the 1640s.

Covenant

The word covenant comes from PIE *gwa* (to go, to come). From PIE gwa come Latin *convenir* (to come together, to unite, to agree); i.e., Latin *com- + venire* (to come) and Latin *covenir* (to agree, to meet). These sources lead to 12th century Old French *covenant* (agreement, pact, promise) and by around 1300 to English as *covenaunt*, later covenant, (a mutual compact to do or not do something). In the law of the late 14th century, a covenant was a promise 'made by deed'.

The Hebrew word for covenant was *berith* which was translated in Greek as *diatheke* (covenant; also, a will [i.e., the legal document] and testament) and in Latin as *testamentum*. In the Latin Vulgate Bible *testamentum* put the emphasis on 'testament' rather than 'covenant'.

By the time that the Bible was translated into English in the 14th century both *testamentum* and *diatheke* were used as the basis for the translation of covenant. Also, by this time, *testamentum* had also come to refer to the legal terms 'will' (as in 'last will and testament') and 'testimony'. Confusion can be seen in English translations of the Bible at this time; e.g., Wycliffe's translation uses both 'covenant' (from Greek *diatheke*) and 'testament' (Latin *testamentum*). Such confusion might be reflected, for example, when talking about the 'New Testament' or the 'New Covenant'. Over time, 'New Testament' became the predominant term.

---

69   The opposite of conversion is reversion. For example, generally speaking, a Muslim belief is that children, regardless of the religion of their parents, are born with a natural faith in god, a concept related to *fitrah* (obedience to god). Given this view, non-Muslims do not 'convert' to Islam, rather it is believed that they 'revert' to what they originally were when they were born (https://www.learnreligions.com/convert-or-revert-to-islam-2004197).

Covenant meaning a solemn agreement between members of a church is from 1630s; specifically, those of the Scottish Presbyterians in 1638 and 1643 who were often called 'covenanters'.

See TESTAMENT.

Creed

A creed is where you put your heart.

Creed is rooted in PIE *kerd-dhe*; i.e., *dhe* (to put) your heart (*kerd*[70]). Creed comes to English from Old English *creda* (an article or statement of Christian belief) and Latin *credo* (I believe) and *credere* (to believe). The word credo came to English in the 12th century eventually becoming the word creed.

Credo meaning a formula or statement of belief is from the 1580s. By the 17th century, creed meant any statement of belief.

In sum, a creed is first of all about your heart not about your head. And let us not forget that the words belief and believe also come from another heart-related word; i.e., love.

Cross, Crucifixion, Crucifix

Cross

The word cross comes from Latin *crux* (a stake or cross; a word which may have Phoenician origins). Originally a *crux* was a tall pole on which criminals were impaled or hanged. The word cross comes to English in a roundabout way likely via Scandinavia to Irish *cros*, then to 10th century Old English *cros* (the instrument of Jesus' crucifixion; a symbol of Christianity),

---

70   PIE *kerd* is the root of medical words related to heart; e.g., medical words containing cardio, from Greek *kardia*. As well, *kerd* is the root of *cor*, the Latin word for heart, from which we see French *coeur* and later the English word courage. The English word heart comes from Old English *heorte* which has its origins in Proto-German *herton* and PIE *kerd*.

and later seen as cross. Latin *crux*[71] and Old English *cros* replaced the earlier Old English *rood*[72] (a pole or cross, especially that on which Jesus was crucified) from PIE *ret* (post).

The word cross has taken on various meanings. By around 1200, the word referred to an ornament (e.g., a necklace with a cross pendant) and to the sign of the cross made with or by the fingers. The word was also used in the figurative sense referring to the burden of Christian suffering or to a trial or affliction or to penance in Jesus' name (e.g., "This is a cross I have to bear.") At this time, the word Cross was also seen as a surname.

In the late 14th century a large cross-shaped outdoor structure or monument was referred to as a cross. Also at this time the word cross was used in a theological sense to refer to the crucifixion and death of Jesus as a necessary part of his mission. By the end of the 14th century the word cross was being used without any religious significance; e.g., a cross was simply two lines intersecting at right angles on a surface.

Crucifixion

The verb 'to crucify' came to English around 1300 from Old French *crucifer* and Latin *crucificare* (to fasten to a cross), words which come from Latin *crux* (cross) and Latin *figare* (to fasten). The word crucifixion comes to English in the early 15th century from Latin *crucifixionem* (to kill by crucifixion).

Crucifix

The word crucifix, meaning the symbol or ornament of Jesus affixed to a cross, comes to English in the early 13th century from Latin *crucifixus* (one fixed to a cross) and Old French *crucefix*.

---

71   Latin crux is also the origin of English crux, a word first seen in 1814 and used to mean 'the central difficulty' of something or a point in a text that is impossible to interpret; as in, "That seems to be the crux of the matter."

72   In medieval Church architecture a 'rood screen' was a divider between the congregation and the altar. Many churches still have a rood screen.

Daemon or Demon?

Daemon

In today's English, the word daemon has at least two different meanings. First, a daemon is a computer program that runs as a background process without being under the active control of the computer user. Second, daemon is a term used to describe several concepts from ancient Greek mythology; for example, deity, divine power; lesser god; guiding spirit, tutelary deity (sometimes including souls of the dead); one's genius; dispenser; one's lot or fortune. As you might expect, this second use of the word daemon will now be discussed.

Daemon (the original Greek word is also *daemon*) comes from PIE *daimon* (divider, provider of fortunes or destinies); from PIE *da* (to divide).[73]

In Greek mythology, daemons were similar to ghosts, spirit guides, or unseen forces of nature. Daemons were spirits that existed somewhere between the divine world of the gods and the metaphysical or philosophical world of people. For example, some in ancient Greece did not consider love to be a deity (e.g., love as personified by Eros or Aphrodite) but rather love was perceived as a 'great daemon'.

We also see other terms related to daemon. For example, *daimone* names the spirit of a venerated hero or other great figure which, after death, served a mortal human as a guardian spirit. Socrates (470 – 399 BCE) used the term *daimonion* to describe the divine principle, inner oracle, or inner voice which guided his actions. Aristotle (384 – 322) used the term *eudaimonia* in reference to human well-being, happiness, prosperity, and blessedness.

Several descriptions and interpretations of daemons can be found; however, generally speaking, they fall into two types: good daemons and bad daemons.

Good daemons were considered knowing and wise and were considered in a similar fashion as guardian angels are considered today. Such daemons were known in Latin as *genius*[74] and in Arabic as *jinn* (the origin

---

73   Da is also the root of the Greek word demos (people, land) and the English word democracy.
74   The word genius, meaning a tutelary god from classical mythology, came to English in the

of the word genie).[75] For example, in the Greek myth of Ur, as described by Plato (428 – 348 BCE), a daemon was the spirit of a dead person who returned to life as the daemon or guardian spirit of a person about to be born. According to the myth, every person was born with such a daemon or inner voice which drew the person toward their destiny.

Bad daemons were known as 'adversarial daemons'; i.e., those inner voices that get you into trouble. They were often seen as dangerous, if not evil, spirits.

I am reminded of the cartoons in which we see a person who has a haloed angel on one shoulder and a devil with a pitchfork on the other— each vying for the person's attention in making a decision. I'm also reminded of Paul's comment in Romans 7: 18 (NIV): "...for I have the desire to do what is good, but I cannot carry it out."

The Greek terms *daemon, daimone*, and *daimonion*, and the subsequent Latin term *daimon*, were used in early translations of the Bible. For example, in the Old Testament, Jewish authors used Greek *daemon* to render *shedim* (lords, idols) in the Septuagint. Other early translations of the Old Testament used Latin *daimon* (spirit; in particular, a natural spirit that is less than divine) to translate Hebrew words for idols, the gods of others, unclean spirits, and natural evils.

In the original text of the 2nd century Greek New Testament *daemon* was applied to the Judeo-Christian concept of an evil spirit. Jerome used the Latin *daimon* in his Vulgate as a translation for 'god of the heathen' and 'unclean spirit'. The use of *daimones* in Matthew 8: 31 was later translated as *deofol* in Old English, and as *feend* (fiend) or *deuil* (devil) in Middle English. A related Old English word was *hellcniht* (hell-knight).

---

late 14th century from Latin *genius*, a word with several meanings: a guardian deity or spirit which watches over each person from birth, spirit, incarnation, wit, talent, and prophetic skill. Originally the word genius meant generative power, from the Latin *gignere* (beget, produce), and from PIE *gen* (produce). Other related words include gene, genesis, genetic, generate, generation, genus, ingenuity, and so on, including the word engineer from *ingenius!*

Genius as a characteristic disposition of someone is from 1580s. Genius meaning a person of natural intelligence or talent and genius as natural ability are first recorded in the 1640s.

75   Genie came to English in the 1650s, again meaning a tutelary spirit, from French *génie* and Latin *genius*. In an (18th century?) French translation of the Arabian Nights stories, Arabic *jinn* (guardian spirit) was accidentally translated using the term genie. This use of genie in its now contemporary 'genie in a bottle' sense is first seen in English in 1748.

By the 5th century, *daemon* and *daimon* had come increasingly to refer to evil spirits in the early Christian world.

Demon

The word demon, first seen in English by the 12th century, comes from Greek *daemon* and Latin *daimon*. During the Middle Ages, the word *deuil* (devil), from the Old English translation of *daimone*, came to be used synonymously with demon—the words demon and devil were used interchangeably.

Demons (and devils) have been organized and classified in several ways; for example, in 1409 or 1410 an anonymous tract, *Lantern of Lights*, identified a different demon for each of the seven deadly sins. In 1467, Alphonso de Spina classified demons according to various criteria found in ancient legends and stories. In 1589 Peter Binsfeld, a German bishop and theologian as well as a noted witch-hunter, produced a document which classified demons according to each of the seven deadly sins and assigned each demon a separate room in hell. By the end of the 16th century each month of the year had been assigned its own demon. Sounds like pandemonium to me.[76]

In brief, since the word demon came to English, its common use to name an evil spirit or something that causes a person to have a lot of trouble or unhappiness has increasingly come to predominate. The positive connotations of *daemon* and *daimon* as outlined above have gradually fallen from common use.

Daemon and Demon?

So, what happened to the positive connotations of daemon? How did the word demon and its evil connotations come to be so predominant? In contrast, the sense of a daemon as an individual's positive 'inner voice' or 'inner guardian' was well-known in ancient classical societies.

---

76   Pandemominum; i.e., 'all demons', a term coined by John Milton in Paradise Lost, 1667, from Greek pan (all) + Latin *daemonium* (lesser god, evil spirit).

Perhaps the people of the early church considered the *daemon* as a foreign or non-Christian concept and not to be trusted. Perhaps the idea or experience of an inner voice itself was not to be trusted. Hence, perhaps, the use of demon to name such a not-to-be trusted or evil voice, overtook the more positive use of the term daemon.

Perhaps the modern equivalents of the positive form of daemon can be found in notions of the inner voice, conscience, intuition, conscious and unconscious impulses and actions, and meta-cognition (e.g., consciousness of consciousness). As such, daemon would seem to indicate an inner self-consciousness and sense of direction as the basis for a person's responsibility for the actions of their life.

See also DEVIL.

Deacon

Deacon comes from Middle English *deken* (one who reads the Gospel in divine worship, one of a body of assistants to a priest or clergyman), from Old English *deacon* or *diacon*, Latin *diaconus*, and Greek *diakonus* (servant of the church, a religious official). *Diakonus*, meaning servant, is from Greek *dia-* (here, thoroughly, from all sides) + PIE *kono, ken* (to hasten, to set oneself in motion); that is, a *diakonus* is a person scurrying this way and that to provide quick and efficient service.

And, of course, the *arch* (rule by) + deacon is the head or chief deacon.

Death, Resurrection

Death

The word death has not changed much since its ancient origins in PIE *dheu* (to die, to pass away, to become senseless).

The verb 'to die' came to English in the mid-12th century possibly from Old Danish *doja* or Old Norse *deyja* (to die, pass away), both from

Proto-Germanic *dawjan* and the related words in Old Frisian *deja (*to kill), Old Saxon *doian*, Old High German *touwen*, and Gothic *diwans* (mortal). Proto-Germanic *dawjan* is from PIE *dheu*.

The noun 'death' is seen in Old English as *dead* (death, dying, cause of death) from Proto-Germanic *dauthaz* (related to Old Saxon *doth*, Old Frisian *dath*, Dutch *dood*, Old High German *tod*, German *Tod*, Old Norse *daudi*, Danish *dod*, Swedish *dod*, Gothic *daubas*—all meaning death) and from the PIE verbal stem *dheu* (to die). PIE *dheu* is also related to Old Irish *dith* (end, death), Old Slavonic *daviti*, and Russian *davit (*to choke, suffer).

It's almost spooky how little the word has changed over the millennia as it has moved from culture to culture, language to language, and dialect to dialect. Perhaps this says something about the enduring power and significance of the word.

Resurrection

On the other hand, since its origins, the word resurrection has taken a path with many twists and turns.

The word resurrection is first seen in English around 1300 as the name of the Church festival commemorating Christ's rising from death and in reference to the rising of the dead on the last day. The use of resurrection to mean revival is from the 1640s.

The English word comes from 12th century Anglo-French *resurrectiun* (used in relation to the resurrection of Christ) and from Latin *resurrectionem* and *resurrectio* (a rising again from the dead).

These Latin words appear to have been created in response to the language needs of the early days of the Christian church (for example, what do we call this experience?) and of Christian theology (for example, how do we explain this experience?). These Latin words, *resurrectionem* and *resurrectio*, come from Latin *resurgere* (to rise again, to lift oneself, to be restored, to appear again).[77]

---

77   Latin *resurgere* is also the root of English words resurgent (1808) and resurgence (1834).

Latin *resurgere* is comprised of Latin *re-* (again) and *surgere* (to rise, to arise, to get up, to mount up, to ascend, to attack). In turn *surgere* is a contraction of Latin *surrigere*, originally *sub* (up from below) and *regere* (to keep straight, to guide).[78]

Latin *regere* is also related to the word regal (royal, kingly, belonging to a king, worthy of a king) which is first seen in English in the late 14th century. Both have their roots in PIE *reg* (to move in a straight line).[79]

So, in brief, the word resurrection has its roots in words related to moving in a straight line, rising again, restoring, appearing again, ascending, resurgence, guiding, and kings.

Despair

The word *despeir* (despair) comes to English around 1300 from French *despeir*, *desperer* (the total loss of hope, hopelessness) and Latin *desperare* (to despair, to lose hope), a word comprised of Latin *de* (without) + Latin *sperare* (to hope), from Latin *spes* (hope) and PIE *spes* (prosperity). The word *desperacioun* (desperation, hopelessness) comes to English in the 14th century. By the mid-14th century, the English verb *despeiren* appears (to lose hope, to be without hope, to despair). By the early 15th century the word also referred to a desperate state of mind.[80]

---

78   By the 1510s, Latin *surrigere* was used to mean the sense of an excited rising up of feelings. By the 1520s, Latin *surrigere* (also meaning a high, rolling swell of water) had become the English word 'surge'.

79   PIE *reg* is also the root of other related words such as Sanskrit *raj* (a king, a leader); Latin *rex* (a king, a leader); Latin *rectus* (right, correct); Old Irish *ri*, Gaelic *righ* and Gaulish *-rix* (all meaning 'a king'); Gothic *reiks* (a leader); Old English *rice* (kingdom), *-ric* (king), *rice* (rich, powerful), and *riht* (correct); and Old High German (correct).

80   The Oxford English Dictionary (OED) notes the noun and the verb 'respair' (the return of hope after a period of despair). It seems as though there might be a hint of a choice here; e.g., "After feeling down in the dumps for a while, I respaired." Unfortunately, the OED notes that most recent use of the word respair appears to be in 1425. It seems, perhaps, that we have no desire or use for such a word.

Johnson. (4 March 2017). Lexical treasures: Why words die (and how to stop a few of them from keeling over). *The Economist*, p. 69.

In brief, as can be seen in the origins of the word, despair is a state of being (something we have, not something we do). Unhelpful or unhealthy actions often arise from feelings or emotions of despair.

Early in the history of the Christian church despair (also called sadness or despondency at that time) was classified as one of the so-called seven deadly sins.[81] Even though despair was the least aggressive or intrusive sin on this list, it was the only one for which there was no forgiveness. For example, people in despair who committed suicide were denied burial in sacred ground. Why was this? Perhaps because the despairing person not only gave up the notion of hope or forgiveness but perhaps even gave up the notion being a sinner.[82]

Another early church interpretation of Latin *disperare* (despair) from 6th century Gregory of Tours) described people

"who were not panic-stricken persons, living in a world of gathering gloom, far from it. They had put the Last Judgment out of their minds. [For such people, the term despair] lacked the subjective overtones of fear and desperation that accompany the modern notion of 'despair'. Instead

---

81   An early Christian writer, Evagrius Ponticus (345 – 399) listed eight of humanity's evil thoughts or faults: gluttony, fornication, avarice, pride, sadness (despair), wrath, boasting (vainglory), and acedia (dejection, spiritual lethargy). His pupil, John Cassian (360 – 435), a theologian and pioneer of western Christian monasticism, revised this list and arranged them from least problematic to most problematic: gluttony, lust, avarice, sadness (despair), anger, spiritual lethargy, vanity, and pride.

Pope Gregory I the Great (540 – 604) revised and condensed Cassian's list, identifying seven 'deadly sins' (again, from bad to worst): lust, gluttony, sadness (despair), avarice (greed), wrath, envy (new to the list), and pride (pride combined with vainglory).

Later, the sin of sloth replaced that of sadness or despair. It was no longer a sin to be sad! Each of the seven deadly sins is matched with one of the seven cardinal virtues; i.e., self-control, temperance, generosity, zeal, kindness, love, and humility.

During the 16th century, various writers documented the different punishments in hell that were reserved for each of these sins. For example, the lusty ended up in fire and brimstone, the gluttons were force fed toads, rats, and snakes, the greedy were boiled in oil, sad (or slothful) folks ended up in a room full of snakes, angry people were dismembered alive, the envious ended up in freezing water, and the prideful were tortured and broken on the wheel. https://en.wikipedia.org/wiki/Seven_deadly_sins

82   A contemporary writer also suggests that despair is "a state of intense inwardness, thus independence. The despairing soul is a rebel." To despair was a political act—an act against external authority; i.e., against the church, in the context of early Christianity. Oates, J.C. (1993). *The deadly sins/despair; The one unforgivable sin.* The New York Times. https://www.nytimes.com/1993/07/25/books/the-deadly-sins-despair-the-one-unforgivable-sin.html

disperare meant, literally, *de + sperare*—to 'un-hope' oneself. It meant to give up hope, to cease to expect, even, quite bluntly, to give no thought to. [To despair was to act] as if God did not exist. [Such people] did not expect Him to intervene in their affairs."[83]

To 'un-hope' was not to give up hope but simply not to hope in the first place. Life is what it is, live now, get on with your life, live wisely and with good intentions. With 'un-hope', there seems no moral imperative to be hopeful.

Perhaps, this reflects the still powerful influence of ancient Greek and Roman religious world views (e.g., Stoicism) during the early years of the development of the Christian church, views in which God and the gods were more perceived as impersonal and 'out there' rather than as something more personal and 'in here'. Perhaps such views also reflect the unsettled state of church doctrine and interpretation given the multiple versions of Christianity emergent during the its early years.

Finally, from a contemporary point of view, despair is not to be confused with depression. Current definitions in psychology and counselling suggest that despair can be seen as a psycho-spiritual crisis (e.g., "dark night of the soul") whereas depression can be described in terms of a disease related to the body and is treated accordingly.[84]

When all is said and done, it is a mystery to me as to what it is that draws someone who is in the grip of the despair of no hope, the despair, even, of no forgiveness, back from the abyss of addictive or literal oblivion. Some, even with love and support, fall. But yet, many more step back or are pulled back from the edge: What is it that happens to someone that allows or even compels them to say 'Yes' rather than 'No'?

83   Brown, P. (2015). *The ransom of the soul: Afterlife and wealth in early Western Christianity*. Cambridge, MA: Harvard University Press, 156.

84   Diamond, S. (2011). Clinical despair: science, psychotherapy, and spirituality in the treatment of depression. P*sychology Today*. Download: https://www.psychologytoday.com/ca/blog/evil-deeds/201103/clinical-despair-science-psychotherapy-and-spirituality-in-the-treatment. 26 September 2018.

Devil

The word devil has its roots in ancient words related to throwing and dancing.

The word devil comes from Old English *deofol* meaning an evil spirit, a devil or *the* devil, a false god, a diabolical person. *Deofol* came from Latin diabolus,[85] Greek *diabolos*, and Greek *disballein*, words meaning to slander or attack—literally, to throw across. Greek *diaballein* comprises *dia* (across, through) and *ballein* (to throw). *Ballein* comes from PIE *gwele* (to throw, to reach, to pierce).[86]

The Greek term *diabolos* was used in early Christian and Jewish writings to refer to *the* Devil or Satan. Jerome used the term Satan when preparing his translation of the Vulgate Bible. In more general use, the term *diabolos* meant an accuser or slanderer.

The word devil, meaning a false or heathen god, is from around 1200. At this time, the term diabolical was also used to refer to a person who seemed devilish or demonic in character. The use of devil to mean 'a clever rogue' is from around 1600.

Devils (and demons)[87] have been organized and classified in various Christian demonologies; for example, in 1589 Peter Binsfeld, a German bishop and theologian as well as a noted witch-hunter, produced a document which classified devils according to each of the seven deadly sins. Each sin has its own room in hell and each sin has its own unique torment. A different devil presides over each room; for example, Beezelbub governs the room reserved for gluttony in which the tormented are force-fed toads, snakes, and rats; Lucifer governs the room reserved for pride in which the tormented are tortured (in particular, broken on the wheel); and so on.

---

85   Latin *diabolus* is also the root of Italian *diavolo*, French *diable*, and Spanish *diablo*. German teufel and Old High German *tiufal* also come from Latin but via Gothic *diabaulus*. And, of course, *diabolus* is also the root of English diabolic and diabolical.

86   *Ballein* is from Greek *ballistes* (to throw, to throw so as to hit). *Ballein* is the root of the English word ballistics and also the Greek word *ballizein* (to dance; i.e., to throw your body; e.g., ballet).

87   Generally speaking, the word devil usually refers to the figure of Satan whereas the word demon usually refers to evil spirits or agents of Satan.

Other classifications of devils have been produced at different times by different people.

See also DAEMON OR DEMON.

Disciple, Discipline

Disciple

Disciple comes to us along two paths: one related to learning and teaching, and a second related to comprehension and capability.

First, disciple is said to come from Old English *disipul* (feminine *discipula*), Latin *discipulus* (pupil, student, follower), Latin *discere* (to learn), and PIE *dek* (to take, to accept, to receive, to greet, to be suitable). PIE *dek* is also the root of Latin *decere* (to be fitting or suitable) and Latin *decentum* (becoming, seemly, fitting, proper—the origins of the English word decent, first seen in the 1530s). Latin *decere* is related to Latin *docere* (to teach) and the English word docent (a college or university teacher, or a museum guide) from 1880. So, it could be said that a disciple is not only one who learns but also one who teaches.

Second, disciple is also said to come from Latin *discipere* (to grasp intellectually, analyze thoroughly) from Latin *dis* (apart) plus Latin *capere* (to take hold of, to grasp, undertake, take in, comprehend), from PIE *kap* (to grasp). Latin *capere* is related to Latin *capabilis* (receptive, able to grasp) which came to English in the 1560s as the word capable.

The word discipleship is first seen in the 1540s.

Discipline

The word discipline comes from Latin *discipulus* (pupil, student, follower) and *disciplina* (instruction given, teaching, learning, knowledge, science; also, object of instruction, military discipline). Latin *disciplina* when used in the 14th century meant a field of study or a branch of instruction or education.

Over the years the word discipline took on a harsher tone than seen in its original meaning as a field of study. By the 11th century, the Old French word *descepline* (from Latin *disciplina*) was used to mean discipline, physical punishment, teaching, suffering, martyrdom.[88] By the early 13th century, the English word discipline was used to mean penitential chastisement and punishment.

This medieval sense of discipline as a something that corrects or punishes is from the sense that discipline provides the order or structure necessary for instruction; seemingly, from the idea that you have to correct, even punish, students so that they will learn. I sense a desperation here in this medieval usage. Learning was so important that you had to force students to learn. Learning was a life and death matter, not a form of pleasure. Learning was work, the work needed to build a society emerging from the so-called Dark Ages.

The verb 'to discipline' someone comes from the early 14th century. The use of 'undisciplined' to mean untrained comes from the late 14th century.

Discipline meaning military training is from the late 15th century. Discipline meaning orderly conduct as a result of training is from the early 16th century.

In the 1580s, the word disciplinarian was used by Puritans who wanted to establish the Presbyterian 'discipline' in England. The use of disciplinarian as someone who enforces order comes from the 1630s and as someone who is an advocate of greater discipline comes from 1746.

The use of self-discipline is first seen in 1796.

Divine

The word divine can be used as a noun, an adjective, or a verb. Each use means something different—a soothsayer, being god-like or wonderful, or to conjure or to guess.

---

88   I have to say that, as a teacher, I find it somewhat disturbing to see the words teaching, suffering, and martyrdom in the same sentence! Having said that, perhaps teaching can be seen as sacrificial act!

As a noun, the oldest use of divine in the English language is found in the early 14th century. A divine was a soothsayer, from the Old French *devin* and the Latin *divinus* (of a god) and the Latin *divus* (a god, the divine one). *Divus* is related to the Latin *deus* (god, deity) from PIE *dewos* (god) and PIE *dyeu* (to gleam, to shine). PIE *dewos* is also the root of Sanskrit *deva* (god). The use of divine to refer to an ecclesiastic or a theologian also comes from the late 14th century.

The noun divinity also comes from the late 14th century; i.e., divinity as the quality of being divine or god-like.

And, in 1883 we see the first use of the noun diva meaning a distinguished woman singer or prima donna. Diva comes from Italian *diva* (goddess, fine lady) from Latin *diva* (goddess); i.e., the feminine version of *divus*.

As an adjective, the use of divine also comes from the early 14th century and has the same origins as divine the noun. This use of divine as an adjective is the one that we are likely most familiar with in terms of religion and the church; that is, to say that something is divine is to say that it is in some way related to god; e.g., 'divine intervention' or 'divine right of kings' or Dante's 'Divine Comedy'. By the late 15th century, divine had also come to include a more secular meaning; that is, divine in the sense of wonderful or very good or excellent; e.g., "That dress is simply divine."

As a verb, the use of 'to divine' comes from the mid-14th century and means to conjure, to guess, or to make something out by supernatural insight. The verb 'to divine' comes from Old French *deviner*, Latin *devinare*, and Latin *divinare* and *divinus* (soothsayer). By the 1650s, we see words such as diviner and divining rod; e.g., to search for water using a divining rod.

Doctrine, Dogma

Doctrine and dogma originate in PIE *dek* (to take, accept); also the origin of the word doctor. From PIE *dek* come the Latin words *decere* (be seemly, fitting), *docere* (to show, to teach, to cause to show, to make to appear right), and *doctor* (religious teacher, advisor, scholar).

The words doctrine and dogma come from words related to doctor (a person knowledgeable and qualified in a given subject). Doctrine is "whatever is taught or laid down as true by a master or instructor," hence "any set of principles held as true." The truth of a doctrine or dogma would appear to depend on the authority and creditability of the person who created or proposed the doctrine (https://www.etymonline.com/search?q=doctrine).[89]

Other words coming from PIE *dek* include decent, decorate, dignity, disciple, docile, document, doxology, indignant, orthodox, and paradox.

Doctrine

The word doctrine meaning a body or principles or dogmas in a religion or a field of knowledge comes to English in the late 14th century. The word doctrine was also used in a general sense for learning, instruction, and education. Doctrine comes from 12th century Old French *doctrine* (teaching, doctrine), Latin *doctrina* (a teaching, body of teachings, learning), and Latin *doctor* (teacher).

Dogma

Dogma comes from PIE *dek* and Greek *dokein* (to seem good, think) and later from Greek *dogma* (opinion; literally that which one thinks is true). From these origins come Latin dogma (philosophical tenet) and by around 1600 the word dogma is seen in English meaning a settled opinion, a principle held as being firmly established.

By the 1680s we see the term dogmatic meaning, for example, someone disposed to make positive assertions without presenting arguments or evidence. "The *dogmatic* person insists strenuously upon the correctness of his

---

89   Doctor, meaning "holder of the highest degree in a university, one who has passed all the degrees of a faculty and is thereby empowered to teach the subjects included in it", is from late 14c. Hence "teacher, instructor, learned man; one skilled in a learned profession" (late 14c.).
The sense of doctor as a "medical professional, person duly licensed to practice medicine" grew gradually out of this although this use of the word was not common until late 16c.
https://www.etymonline.com/search?q=doctor

or her own opinions, and, being unable to see how others can fail to believe with her or him, dictatorially presses upon them his or her opinions as true without argument, while she or he tends also to blame and overbear those who venture to express dissent. [Century Dictionary]"; cited by the Online Etymological Dictionary (https://www.etymonline.com/word/dogmatic).

In sum, given the similarities in the origins of doctrine and dogma, how are these words different in meaning? It would seem that a doctrine is more an 'objective' statement related to argument and evidence whereas a dogma seems a more 'subjective' statement related to belief and opinion. Today, "a doctrine is a set of ideas or beliefs that are taught or believed to be true. Dogma is a belief or set of beliefs accepted by members of a group without being questioned or doubted" (Merriam-Webster Dictionary).

Doubt

Have you ever been 'of two minds' about something? Have you ever been in a situation in which you were presented with various options and from these you had to make a decision?

Even when both options are pleasant (e.g., chocolate or strawberry ice cream?) there's still a sensation of anxiety in that you have to choose one and leave the other behind. Or, in more ambiguous situations in which two or more options could have both positive and negative consequences, we could add fear to the sensations of anxiety when making a decision. Making the wrong choice could have serious unwanted consequences.

Such situations reflect the origins of the word doubt.

Doubt often has a negative connotation; i.e., to say "I doubt it" often implies "I don't believe it". In contrast, consider 'doubting Thomas': "I'd like to believe but I'd like my belief to be based on personal experience or on some evidence." Doubt is not about not believing; doubt is about the ambiguities and uncertainties involved in believing.

Doubt (and its cousin 'double') are rooted in ancient words meaning two or twin. The word doubt has its origins in the PIE *duwo* (two) which is the basis of the Greek and Latin word *duo* (two). PIE *duwo* is also the root of the Proto-Germanic *twa* leading to Old English *twa*, *twegen* (two), and *twain*[90]—all of which mean two.

Latin *duo* is the root of the Latin *dubitaire* (to doubt, question, hesitate, waver in opinion) and Latin *dubius* (to be uncertain; to have to choose between two things). From these Latin beginnings, *doute* (doubt, to be uncertain) came to English in the early 13th century via the Old French *dote* (fear, dread, doubt) and Old French *doter* (to doubt, to be doubtful, to be afraid). The association of fear with doubt, developed in Old French, passed on to English.

Doubt (from *doute*) is attested in English from around 1300. At some point someone added the 'b' into *doute*, a recognition of its Latin roots in *dubius* and *dubitaire*.

From these origins we also have the words indubitable (that which cannot be doubted) and dubious (vacillating, fluctuating, can go one way or the other).

So, what might be considered as doubt's double or twin?

At times life confronts and confounds us with ambiguities and uncertainties. There are times when what we feel strongly about is called into question. From time to time we face doubt. Doubt is the maybe between yes or no, between right or wrong. Doubt saves us from rigidity or collapse when our strongly held feelings or views are challenged.

If we say that doubt is about uncertainties and ambiguities, could we also say that doubt's double or twin is faith—that doubt is the foundation of faith?

Could we say that faith can not exist without doubt, without an awareness of our limitations? Faith without doubt would be blind faith, mindless stoicism, or passive acquiescence. In fact, it is doubt that calls forth faith.

See also BELIEF, FAITH.

---

90   In US nautical terminology, twain was first used in 1799 to mean 'a depth of two fathoms'. When the US writer Samuel Clemens was looking for a pen name, he chose 'Mark Twain', a term used by Mississippi river boat pilots.

Easter

As might be expected, the word Easter comes from words related to the word east, from PIE *aus* (to shine, of the dawn) and *aust* (east, toward the sunrise). The word east does not seem to have changed much in several thousand years.

PIE *aus* leads to Proto-Germanic *austron* (dawn; also, the name of a goddess of spring and fertility), to Northumbrian *eostre*, and to Old English *Easterdaeg*. In Greek mythology, Eos was the personification of the dawn (known as Aurora in Roman mythology).

According to Bede, an 8th century British monk and scholar (673 – 735 CE), Anglo-Saxon Christians took the name of the goddess Austron for their Mass of Christ's resurrection, now known as Easter. The term *eastre*, used in Old English, came to Middle English as *estre*, and the first known use of the word Easter is before the 12th century.

Other languages use variants of Latin *Pascha* and *Paschalis* to name Easter. *Pascha* comes from Hebrew *pesah*, *pasah* (he passed over) and Aramaic *pasha* (pass over). Old French *paschal* comes from Latin in the 12th century and to English unchanged as paschal in the early 15th century. *Pasche* was an early Middle English term for Easter; however, Easter became the predominant term.

The term Easter egg (originally, *pace egg* from the 1610s—*pace* from *pasche*) is attested from 1825. Easter rabbit is from 1888 and Easter bunny is from 1904. This use of seemingly pagan or pre-Christian customs comes from German immigrants to North America and grew more and more popular after 1900.

Eternity

Have you ever tried to imagine something that is infinite—something that just goes on for ever and ever? When I was a child I used to lay in bed at night and try to imagine the infinity of outer space, stretching my mind as far as I could make it go, and then saying to myself, "It's that much farther again... and then more!" My mind would stretch like a rubber band until it could stretch no more and then it would snap back sending a little frisson of awe up and down my body—like the sense of vertigo when standing on a cliff edge and looking down.

Similarly, when thinking of eternity, I think of time that has no beginning and no end—that is, I try to imagine timelessness. If eternity is timeless in this manner (that is, if there is nothing before or after eternity), would not eternity exist as an eternal here and now present moment rather than as something that happens later in the future? And, if eternity happens later, how do we consider that which 'fills up' or exists in this eternal present moment—aside, of course, from the me who is thinking such thoughts? The mind boggles.

To say the least, the word eternity, like the word infinity, is hard to get my mind around.

The origin of the words eternal and eternity can be found in PIE *aiw* (vital force, life, eternity). PIE *aiw* suggests that it is life itself that which is eternal. From PIE *aiw* emerge similar words in several languages; for example, Gothic *aiws* (age, eternity), Old Norse *aevi* (lifetime), German *ewig* (everlasting), Greek *aion* (age, vital force; a period of existence, a lifetime, a generation; a long space of time; in plural, eternity), and Latin *aevum* (space of time, eternity). From these words comes the English word eon, first seen in the 1640s.

Latin *aevum* is the root of Latin *aeternus* (of great age, enduring, permanent, everlasting, endless) and 12th century Old French *eternité* (eternity, perpetuity) from which, in the late 14th century, emerges the English noun eternity (the quality of being eternal).

Also, in the 14th century the adjective eternal comes to English, from Old French *eternel* (eternal) and Latin *aeternalis* (of great age, lasting, enduring, permanent, everlasting, endless). Since the word eternal came to English it has been used in two ways; first, to mean things or conditions without beginning or end; and second, to mean things or conditions with a beginning but no end. I'll let the philosophers and theologians take over from here.

The use of the word eternal to mean 'infinite time' is from the 1580s. Also, from the 1580s is the use of 'The Eternal' in reference to God.

In brief, to speak of eternity or eternal life, it is as if we are simply saying "Life goes on." Life and the vital forces or energies that create and sustain life are, as far as we can know, eternal. We participate in such eternal life in each present moment.

Ethics, Morals, Virtue

Ethics

The word ethics can be traced back to PIE *swed-yo* and *s(w)e*, words which denote a person's social group (for example: "we ourselves"). Related words include Sanskrit *syah*, Latin *suescere* (to get accustomed), Slavonic *svojaku* (relative, kinsman), Gothic *swes* (one's own), Old Norse *sik* (oneself), German *sein* (self).

PIE *s(w)e* is the root of Greek *ethos* (habitual character and disposition, moral habit, an accustomed place). Ethos can be described as the characteristic spirit of a people in a particular time and place.[91]

From these origins in Greek *ethos*, the word ethics comes to English in the late 14th century as *ethik* (a study of morals), from 13th century Old French *etique* (ethics, moral philosophy), Latin *ethica*, and Greek e*thike philosophia* (moral philosophy). The noun ethics, as the science or study of morals, is from around 1600 as is the adjective ethical; e.g., ethical behavior. Ethics, meaning the moral principles of a person or group, is from the 1650s.

In brief, ethics describes not just the 'what' or content of such moral principles but also more importantly the reasons within a given culture related to 'why' such principles are of value.

---

91   Online   Etymological   Dictionary: https://www.etymonline.com/word/ethos#etymonline_v_11658

Morals

If ethics can be considered in terms of the reasons for behavior, morals can be described in terms of actual proper attributes, characteristics, and behaviors required of a person in society. The English word moral, from the mid-14th century, pertains to good or bad character or temperament according to moral principles. The word moral comes from the 14th century Old French *moral* and from Latin *moralis* (pertaining to manners) and Latin *mos, mores* (one's disposition, mores, customs, manners, morals). The word immorality is from the 1560s.

Latin *mores* has uncertain origins. The Online Etymological Dictionary suggests that the word may be related to the origins of the Old English word *mood* (heart, frame of mind, spirit, courage, arrogance, pride, power, violence) which is related to Proto-Germanic *moda*, Old Saxon *mod* (mind, courage), Old Frisian *mod* (intellect, mind, intention), Old Norse *moor* (wrath, anger), and Middle Dutch *moet*, Old High German *muot*, and German *mut* (courage). However, all these words are also of unknown origin.

By 1630, the word moral is being used in stories of morally good persons; as in the 'moral of the story'. At this time moral referred to the character of a person rather than a physical action.

In brief, morality seems to be about a disposition to act based within an ethical system comprising a set of reasons, rules, or guidelines regarding good and bad behavior.

Virtue

The word virtue has its origins in PIE *wi-ro* (man) and Latin *virtutem*, *virtus* (moral strength, high character, goodness; manliness; valor, bravery, courage (in war); excellence, and worth). From Latin, the word evolves to 10th century Old French *vertu* (force, strength, vigor; moral strength; qualities, abilities). And by around 1200, *vertu* or virtue arrives in English meaning moral life and conduct; a particular moral excellence. In early English translations of the Bible, Wycliffe and others use 'virtue' whereas the King James Version uses 'power'.

In these origins and from these ancient times, we see virtue as the qualities of a 'good man'[92] qualities which, over time, focus increasingly on moral strength. Perhaps it is not surprising to learn that the words virile and virility have the same origin as the word virtue.

In the early 14th century the seven cardinal virtues were identified: the natural virtues of justice, prudence, temperance, fortitude, and the theological virtues of hope, faith, and charity.

The medieval term *vera religio* suggests that religion is a virtue not an organization with a headquarters somewhere; that is, "the virtue of being genuinely or truly religious, of genuinely or truly loving God … God is more important than religion as the ocean is more important than the raft" (Caputo, 2019, 176).

The adjective 'virtual' (influencing by physical virtues or capacities; effective with respect to inherent natural qualities) appears in the late 14th century from Latin *virtualis*, *virtus* (excellence, potency, efficacy).

The notion of virtue in women, especially related to chastity and sexual purity, is from the 1590s.

Virtual, as the sense of being something in essence or capable of producing a certain effect, though not actually or in fact, is from the mid-15th century; e.g., as in the computer sense of "not physically existing but made to appear by software" is from 1959.[93]

In brief, perhaps virtue, with ethics and morals, is a way of describing a person's character.

Evangelist, Evangelize, Evangelical, Evangelism

To be an evangelist or to evangelize is to deliver a message.

---

92   I note the concern for inclusive language here; however, in this case I am following from PIE *wi–ro* (man).

93   Online   Etymological   Dictionary: https://www.etymonline.com/word/virtual#etymonline_v_7821

The word evangelist comes from combining Greek *eu*[94] (good) and Greek *angellein* (announce; from *angelos*, meaning messenger, and the root of the word angel). The Greek words *euangelizesthai* (to bring good news) and *euangelistes* (preacher of the gospel) came to Latin as *evangelista* and later to Old French as *evangelist*.

In early Greek Christian texts, the word evangelist refers to the authors of the four gospels. In classical Greek, the word *euangelion* (the reward of good tidings) *was* the message rather than the messenger.

The English word evangelist, referring to Matthew, Mark, Luke and John, appears in the late 12th century. In the late 14th century, the word evangelist was also used to mean 'an itinerant preacher', a meaning of evangelist that had also been used in the early church.

The verb 'to evangelize' appears in the late 14th century.

The adjective evangelical appears in the 1530s and was used to mean both 'of or pertaining to the gospel' and 'a Protestant'; in particular, a German Protestant. By the mid-18th century, evangelical referred to "a tendency and school of Protestant thought seeking to promote conversion and emphasizing salvation by faith, the sacrifice of Christ, and a strictly religious life". The use of evangelical to describe a person who subscribes to such a school of thought is from 1804 (Online Etymological Dictionary[95]).

The noun evangelism (the preaching of the gospel) comes from the 1620s. The use of evangelism in relation to evangelical Protestantism is from 1812.

The noun evangelization, meaning the action of preaching the gospel, is from the 1650s and later meaning the act of bringing someone under the influence of the gospel is from 1827.

---

94   Greek *eu* (good; from PIE *esu*, also meaning good) is used in many English words; for example, eucalyptus, eugenics, eulogy, euphemism, euphony, euphoria, euthanasia, and others. The opposite of *eu-* is Greek *dys-* (e.g., dysfunctional).

95   http://www.etymonline.com/index.php?allowed_in_frame=0&search=evangelical&search mode=none)

Evil

The word for evil has not changed all that much over the years. However, the meaning and use of the English word evil has evolved and changed.

Evil comes from PIE terms *wap* and *upelo* (bad, evil). From these roots, we see the lineage of the word evil from Proto-Germanic *ubilaz*, Old Saxon *ubil*, Old Frisian and Middle Dutch *evel*, Dutch *euvel*, Old High German *ubil*, Gothic *ubils*, and German *ubel* to Old English *yfel*.

In Anglo-Saxon the word *evil* was used in a similar manner as English words such as bad, cruel, unskillful, defective, harm, crime, misfortune, or disease are now used. *Evilchild* is attested as an English surname from the 13th century.[96]

Old English *yfel* (evil) referred to sin, wickedness, that which is bad, and anything that causes injury, morally or physically. The Oxford English Dictionary tells us that in Old English and older Germanic languages "this word is the most comprehensive adjectival expression of disapproval, dislike, or disparagement."[97] This would seem to indicate that while the term evil was used to describe many unfortunate or unsavoury elements of human behavior, the term did not have the same powerful and emotional connotations as it does today.[98]

In Middle English, the word bad came to be used in place of what had been previously termed as evil in Anglo-Saxon. The word evil began to take on the connotations of moral badness. At this time, the opposite of both words, bad and evil, was the word good.

In brief, in its earliest days, the word evil meant many things that today we might categorize as 'bad'.

It was not until the 18th century that the term evil came to primarily mean extreme moral wickedness. Which raises the question: why not until

---

96   https://www.etymonline.com/word/evil

97   http://www.etymonline.com/index.php?allowed_in_frame=0&search=evil&searchmode=none

98   Other uses of the term include evil as a malady or disease (first seen around 1200) and evil-favored (first seen in the 1520s) meaning ugly. Similarly, the current slang use of the term wicked to mean wonderful comes from the 1920s.

the 18th century? Presumably the reason is not that people were suddenly more evil than before or that wickedness itself had become more wicked.

Perhaps the intensity of learning, debate, and turmoil during the years from the Renaissance and Reformation to the 18th century Enlightenment had heightened the awareness, not just of evil, but of how people perceive evil and of their often conscious choices as participants in and even as agents of evil, choices which have awful consequences. Evil was perceived not just as a force that swirled around people; it was somehow something that people created in their actions. And so, perhaps, people increasingly reached for the word evil to describe how they treated one another.[99]

However interesting, such inquiry goes beyond the etymological limits I have set for myself in these writings. The etymology of the word evil seems simple in contrast to the profound concept and terrible realities of evil itself.

Faith

What is the difference between faith and belief? Have you noticed that these words are often used in everyday conversation as if they have the same meaning? Given these similarities in their usage, what do the origins of the word faith tell us about how belief and faith are different?

The word faith is rooted in PIE *bheidh* (to trust, to endure, to wait), a word which is the root of the Latin words *fidere* (to trust), *fides* (trust, faith, confidence[100], reliance, credence, belief), *fidelis* (loyal), and *fidelitas* (faithfulness). *Fidere* and *fides* are related to words such as fidelity, fealty,

---

99   For example: "By taking the mystique out of evil, Kant removed some of its captivating power. He enabled us to see that evil is not a property of some external demon or deity but a phenomenon deeply bound up with the anthropological condition. With the arrival of Kantian ethics evil ceases to be a matter of abstract metaphysical accounting and becomes instead an affair of human practice and judgement" (Kearney, 2003, 87).

100   The words confident and confidence are from Latin *com* (with, together, nearby, beside) + *fidere* (to trust). The Old Testament Hebrew word for faith is *emunah* (the confidence that a cry for help will be heard); Borg, 2018, p. 21).

infidel (i.e., someone not to be trusted), and Fido[101] (Latin for "I am loyal, trustworthy, faithful"). What experiences might lie beneath these origins of the word faith?[102]

From these Latin origins emerge Old French *fied* and *foi* (faith, belief, trust, confidence). In these Old French words and in Old English *geleafa* (to love deeply), the origin of the word belief, we see that in the years leading to the early medieval period the words faith and belief were perceived as similar. It could be said that people were loyal to what they loved and to that which they held in esteem.

However, in the mid-13th century medieval world, we begin to see the English word faith emerging as a word in its own right, a word different from belief, a word meaning the duty of fulfilling one's trust, a meaning that did not necessarily have a connection with divinity. Faith at that time was simply the duty or need to wait and to trust with confidence and loyalty. Similarly, today we say a 'faithful servant', a 'faithful dog', 'acting in bad faith', or 'if ye break faith with us who die' as in the poem *In Flanders Fields*.

Faith, as the act of waiting in trust and confidence, is related to *bheidh*, another PIE word, meaning 'to wait trustingly'. PIE *bheidh* is related to Old English *bidan* (to stay, to trust, to rely) which is the root of bide and abide (to wait with patience, confidence, and trust)[103], as in the hymn *Abide with me*. 'To bide your time' is to have faith, to trust the process, so to speak.[104]

The word faith began to take on a more overtly religious meaning in the early 14th century when it came to mean the assent of the mind to the truth of a statement for which there is no proof or for which there

---

101   The popularity of the dog name Fido is attributed to the fact that it was the name of Abraham Lincoln's well-known and well-loved dog.

102   For example: to experience the whole of reality "as gracious, nourishing, and supportive of life, to see it as that which has brought us into existence and continues to nourish us… to see reality [in this way] creates the possibility of responding to life in a posture of trust and gratitude. And we're back to faith as trust" (Borg, 2018, p. 26).

103   In its original sense in the 1520s, abide also had a negative connotation: to put up with something; or, more strongly, for example, "I can't abide her presence here".

104   When Jesus said "Oh ye of little faith" (Matthew 8: 26), he was not talking about the disciples' limited understanding of religious doctrine but of their limited confidence or trust.

is incomplete evidence. By the mid-14th century, faith was being used in relation to the Christianity, and by the late 14th century, the word faith was being used in reference to any religion. During this period, 'to have faith' meant to adhere to a particular religious doctrine.

In brief, the origins of the word faith would suggest that it was first used to describe acts of abiding confidently with trust and loyalty. Such loyalty was given to someone or something perceived as worthy of trust and then one acted and lived in faithfulness to this someone or something. Only during the medieval period and later in the Reformation did the word faith come to be used to describe a doctrine or belief that you 'had' rather than something you 'did'.

See also BELIEF.

Fate, Destiny

What is the relationship of fate and destiny? How are they the same? How are they different? What might the origins of these words tell us about this relationship?

Fate

The word fate (one's lot in life; a predetermined course of life) is first seen in late 14th century English. The word fate is from Old French *fate* and Latin *fata, fatum* (prophetic declaration of what is to be, oracle, prediction; that which is ordained; a thing said; things spoken by the gods) and from PIE *bha* (to speak, to say, to tell). Latin *fatum* carried the sense of a curse, something that must inevitably come to pass.

Latin *fata* and *fatum* reflect the Greek word *theosphaton* which carries sense of fate as a life sentence (i.e., in a similar way in which someone is 'sentenced' to prison). Your fate is that to which you are sentenced at birth. As such, fate carries with it a sense of doom and judgment.

By the late 15th century, the word fate was also used to describe both the power that rules and the agency which predetermines events. By the 1580s, the word carried the sense that life was determined by one of the three Fates of Greek mythology (i.e., the goddesses Clotho, Lachesis, and Atropos). By the 1660s fate was used to mean 'that which must be' and by 1768 the word referred to a 'final event'; i.e., your fate is what awaits you at the end of life. In most cases the word increasingly carried the sense of bad luck or bad fortune, particularly in the sense that you were stuck with your fate—there was no escape.[105]

The native Anglo-Saxon word for fate, predating the English word with its French, Latin, and Greek origins, is *wyrd* (fate, chance, fortune) from the Proto-Germanic *wurthiz*, PIE *wert* (to turn, to wind), and PIE *wer* (to turn, to bend). Anglo-Saxon *wyrd* is the origin of the word weird (odd-looking, uncanny), first seen in 1815. Isn't it weird how this word is related to fate!

Destiny

The word 14th century word destiny is from the 12th century Old French *destinee* (purpose, intent, destiny, that which is destined) and Latin *destinare* (to make firm, establish, established by fate, determine); that is, Latin *de* (completely, formally) + Latin *stinare* (to stand). *Destinare* is the origin of the word destination. These words in turn derive from PIE *steno*, *sta* (to stand, to make firm).

Fate and destiny

In sum, fate is what you're stuck with from the beginning of your life. Fate seems inexorable, there are no choices. Fate seems to be about obedience, about submission to the norms of the group or community, or to the will of powers greater than yourself.

Destiny, on the other hand, seems more like a destination—something that you're headed toward. There will likely be many twists and turns on the journey but the destination is the goal toward which you are headed.

---

105   Note that it was during the Reformation of the 16th and 17th century that the meanings of fate were evolving in this way. Perhaps the somewhat negative sense of fate at this time is related to the sense of having your life direction dictated by someone else's gods. On the other hand, it's usually a good thing if your life is directed by your own god or gods or fates.

Sometimes there is a sense of a destiny unfulfilled—a life unexpectedly cut short. Destiny calls or beckons you forward. Destiny is a response to vocation, to a calling, or the sense of a guiding spirit.[106] Destiny seems to be about freedom, individual choices, intentionality, and decisions regarding one's life.[107]

Questions come to mind: How can a person's sense of the fatedness of their life be transformed into a more destinal perspective in which they take responsibility for the direction of their life? What can we say about fate when a person, toward the end of their life, looks back at the choices they've made, and wonders at the forces and powers that made their life in spite of their choices? Can we say that fate is what you see when you look back at life ("It was meant to be," as my mother would say) and that destiny is what you see when you look forward ("Life is what you make of it")? Like that glass that is half-empty or half-full, fate or destiny depends on your perspective.

Font

The word font, in English from the early 14th century, comes unchanged from Old English *font* (a water basin used in baptism), Latin *fons* (fountain), and earlier Latin *fontanus* (a spring). These words are rooted in the PIE *dhen* (to run, to flow).

Font, meaning written letters or characters with a particular face and size of printing type,[108] comes from Middle French *fonte* (a casting) and *fondre* (to melt), Latin *fundere* (to melt, to cast, to pour out) and from PIE *gheu* (to pour out). From such words we have the English word foundry.

---

106   In Plato's account of the Greek myth of Ur, each person is born with a guiding spirit. The Greek term for this guiding spirit is *genius*.

107   The relationship between obedience and freedom is considered in more detail in under the word RESPONSIBILITY.

108   To read a most interesting book on fonts (e.g., Arial, Calibri, Gill Sans, Helvetica, Times Roman and hundreds of others, including Highway Gothic—the font used now on most highway signage in North America), consider: Garfield, S. (2012). *Just my type: A book about fonts*. New York: Penguin.

I can't help but make the connection between the pouring of metal in a foundry and the pouring of water in baptism—both are about creating something new.

Forgiveness

When I was a boy saying the Lord's Prayer as part of my bedtime ritual, I puzzled over the phrase "Forgive us our trespasses as we forgive those who trespass against us." I thought about the "No Trespassing / Keep Out" sign on a neighbour's gate down the street.[109] In church, I heard different words, "Forgive us our debts as we forgive our debtors". When I asked my father what a debt was, he explained that a debt was money or something that you owed to someone. "Hmmm," I thought. My puzzlement remained. I don't remember feeling any more enlightened about the prayer. I didn't owe anyone any money.

Even now when I think about forgiveness, I am puzzled but more curious. On the surface, to forgive seems a good or necessary thing to do. Yet questions arise as I reflect and write. Does forgiveness focus on the giver or the receiver of forgiveness? Is it necessary for the person wronged to forgive? Can someone forgive herself or himself? Does forgiveness require anything of the receiver of forgiveness? If a wrongdoer sincerely expresses remorse and repents, is forgiveness necessary? Does a person only forgive a wrongdoer once or is forgiveness a repetitive act? If debts or trespasses or sins are forgiven, does this mean we are clear of the consequences of our actions?! What exactly is forgiveness, anyway?

Reflecting on such questions is not simply idle intellectual curiosity or speculation on one's moral obligations. People inflict painful even terrible things upon one another. Revenge, punishment, forgiveness are all possible responses. So, why forgive?

---

109   The word trespass came to English around 1300 from Old French *trespasser*. At that time, trespass meant to transgress (i.e., to disobey a command or law), to commit an offense, or to sin. However, by the late 15th century, trespass had more commonly come to mean 'to enter unlawfully'; e.g., as first attested in forest laws passed by the Scottish Parliament in 1455.

What might the origins of the word forgiveness tell us about the act of forgiveness?

Two ancient streams of language development inform and expand our understanding of the meaning and use of the word. One stream is related to the impetus necessary to change your mind about something; the second is related to gifts and giving. Both streams begin in PIE—the first more direct stream to forgiveness takes us through the Germanic languages; the second more indirect stream takes us through Latin.

In the first stream, the Germanic roots of the word forgiveness come from a combination of three word-forms: *for-*, give, and *-ness*.

To begin: *for-*: PIE *pr, pre* (forward, in front of, toward, near, against, through) and Proto-Germanic *fur* (before, in) lead to the Old English prefix *for-* (away, opposite, completely) which indicated either loss or destruction, or loss and completion. For example, something could be destroyed and therefore 'complete'; or, something could be destroyed in order to prepare the way for the completion of something else—like changing a habit or changing your mind about something having seen a new perspective; like the seed is destroyed as the plant grows.[110]

Next, the word-form 'give' comes from Proto-Germanic *geban* (to take, hold, have, give) and PIE *ghabh* (to give and receive).[111] The word 'give' arrives in Old English (specifically, in West Saxon) as *geifan* (to give, bestow, deliver to another; allot, grant; commit, devote, entrust). So, the word forgive, combining *for-* and *giefan*, can be seen, perhaps, as to completely give or to give forward or to give away.

The word-form *-ness* at the end of a word, from Proto-Germanic *in-assu*, denotes an action, quality, or state attached to a word in order to form an abstract noun; i.e., forgiveness.

In brief, in this Germanic language stream, forgiveness is a word that suggests the state or action (i.e., *-ness*) in which something is given or bestowed or entrusted to another person (i.e., *give*) in the hope of enabling

---

110   Some words beginning with this sense of the prefix *for-* include forget, forbid, forlorn, forsake.

111   PIE *ghabh* holds the sense that to give and to receive are two sides of the same coin: you can't have one without the other. PIE *ghabh* is also the root of 'habit'; i.e., to 'hold' onto a way of doing something.

some kind of change of habit or change of mind (an ending and/or a beginning) for that person or, in fact, for yourself as the forgiver (i.e., *for-*).

This combination of word-forms appears in various Germanic languages; e.g., as *fragiban* in Gothic, as *vergeban* in German, and as *fargeban* in Old Saxon. These words, used in the sense of 'to give up the desire or power to punish', lead to the Old English word *forgiefan* (to give, to grant, to allow; to remit a debt, to pardon an offence) and later the Old English *forgiefnes, forgifennys* (pardon, forgiveness, indulgence).

In the second stream of development, the Latin roots of words related to forgiveness have their beginning in PIE *donum* (gift). PIE *donum* comes unchanged to Latin as *donum* (gift) and *donare* (to give as a gift). From these words emerge Latin *donatio* and *donationem* (a presenting, a giving).[112] When Latin *per-* (through, thoroughly) is added to *donare*, the word *perdonare* is created (to give wholeheartedly, to remit), the origin of the word pardon.

By the 11th century, Old French *pardoner* appears (to grant, to forgive). By the late 13th century, the English noun pardon meant a papal indulgence (i.e., a part or all of a person's time to be spent in purgatory after death could be remitted or pardoned—for a fee). Around this time pardon also began to be used as 'to pass over an offence without punishment'.[113]

When the Vulgate Bible was written in the late 4th century, the Latin word *perdonare* was used as a translation of Greek and Hebrew words related to forgiveness. *Perdonare* carries the sense of forgiveness as a gift, something you give someone. During the development of English in the early Middle Ages, the Old English word *forgiefnes* was used when translating Latin *perdonare*. This English word *forgeifnes* (forgiveness) seems a happy meld of the Germanic usage related to giving up the desire to punish with the Latin usage related to forgiveness as a pardon or a gift.

In sum, forgiveness can be seen from two perspectives: first, as a change of mind or heart in the forgiver and, second, as a gift given to the forgiven.

---

112   In Latin *donum* and *donare* we also see the origins of the words donate, donation, donor.

113   The use of pardon in civil law to mean 'a pardon for a civil or criminal offence; a release from penalty or obligation' is from the late 14th century. The use of pardon meaning 'to excuse for a minor fault' is first seen in the 1540s. The verb 'to pardon' (to forgive for offence or sin) is first seen in the mid-15th century.

In the first case, forgiveness represents the forgiver's freedom to choose how he or she will act in relation to a situation of wrongdoing or harm. Through the act of forgiveness, the forgiver, the person who has been wronged or harmed, lets go of the past. Repentance by the wrongdoer in such a case is not necessarily relevant. Forgiveness is not a reward for repentance. Given these two streams, forgiveness does not necessarily mean that the wrongdoer is off the hook (in serious cases of wrongdoing, the wrongdoer may still be subject to criminal or civil justice). In the second case, forgiveness as a gift, wrongdoers are presented with a situation in which they too, if they choose, can look again at the circumstances of their life and the possibilities for transformation.

In the ancient Greco-Roman world, forgiveness, as we now think of it, was not a common concept or practice. People were pardoned rather than forgiven. In the ancient Hebrew world, forgiveness was usually considered something done only by God. In the early New Testament world, admonitions to forgiveness seem more related to the attitude of the forgiver than to the person being forgiven (e.g., Matthew 18:22 – 35).[114] The notion of forgiveness in which the person forgiven is the focus rather than the forgiver and the notion of forgiveness as a bilateral process between the forgiver and the forgiven are relatively modern concepts.

In either case, whether forgiveness is a change of heart or mind or a gift, it would seem that forgiveness is a choice, an act of will, that can release a person from cultural or traditional obligations of revenge or vengeance.[115]

---

114   Depending on which translation of the Bible you read, the wrongdoer should be forgiven either 77 times (e.g., NIV version) or 490 times (i.e., 70 x 7; e.g., NKJV).

115   Some references related to forgiveness:

Armour, M.P. & Umbreit, M.S. (2004). The paradox of forgiveness in restorative justice. In E.L. Worthington Jr. (Ed.), *Handbook of forgiveness*. Retrieved from http://fetzer.org/sites/default/files/images/Parodox_of_Forgiveness_in_RJ.pdf

Boyle, B. (2011, October). Review of the book *Before forgiveness: The origins of a moral idea*, by D. Konstan. *Foucault Studies, 12*, 192 – 195.

Konstan, D. (2010). *Before forgiveness: The origin of a moral idea*. Cambridge; Cambridge University Press.

Visser, M. (2002). *Beyond fate*. Toronto: Anasi.

Zaibert, L. (2009). The paradox of forgiveness. *The Journal of Moral Philosophy, 6*, 365 – 393. Retrieved from http://minerva.union.edu/zaibertl/zaibert%20the%20paradox%20of%20forgiveness.pdf

Freedom

The word freedom, as you might expect, arouses strong feelings. The word freedom has its roots in the joy of being in charge of one's life, the challenges in the midst of the uncertainties and ambiguities of being responsible for one's decisions, and in ancient words for love.

The word freedom comes from Old English *freodom* (the power of self-determination; state of free will; emancipation from slavery). Related Old English words include *freod* (affection, peace, friendship), *freoman* (freeman), and *freo* (wife).

The word freedom comprises two Old English words: *freo* (exempt from bondage; acting of one's own will; noble, joyful) and *dom* (doom; i.e., a judgment).[116] Old English *free* comes from Proto-Germanic *frija* (beloved; not in bondage) which is from PIE *priy-a* (dear, beloved)[117] and PIE *pri* (to love).

The term free will comes from the early 13th century. The concept of freedom as civil liberty, as exemption for arbitrary or despotic control is from the 14th century. The term free of cost; i.e., no charge, no price tag, is from the 1580s.

The Latin word for free is *liberi* from which we get the words liberation, liberal, and liberty.

Fundamentalism

You could say that a fundamentalist is someone who really likes to get to the bottom of things!

---

116   Judgment not necessarily in a negative sense but rather in the decisional sense. A judgment is a decision based on assessment of information; e.g., King William the Conqueror's 'Domesday' Book—a survey and inventory of his newly conquered lands.

117   Priya, a female personal name originating in India from Sanskrit, means 'beloved'; presumably from PIE *priy-a*.

So, what's at the bottom of the word fundamental? Well, in short, bottom is at the bottom of fundamental.

At the bottom of it all is PIE *bhudhmen* (base, bottom, ground) which is the root of Proto-Germanic *buthm*, Old Frisian *boden*, Dutch *bodem*, Old High German *bodam*, and German *boden*—all meaning ground, earth, soil. From these origins come the Old English words *botm* and *bodan* (ground, soil, foundation, lowest part). These terms are the origin of the English word bottom and terms such as 'bottom land' meaning the low-lying fertile soil or ground next to a watercourse.

PIE *bhudhmen* is also the root of Latin *fundas* (bottom), *fundare* (to ground) and *fundamentum* (a foundation). From these Latin roots emerge Old French *fondement* (buttocks, bottom, foundation) which in the late 13th century came into medieval English as *fundament*, a word referring to a person's buttocks. However, this word gradually disappeared from common use. In its place, the English word bottom, meaning among other things, buttocks or posterior of a person, emerged from Germanic roots and is first seen in 1794.

In brief, the word bottom took the low road and the word fundamental took the high road. During the Middle Ages, the Latin words *fundamentalis* (of the foundation) and *fundamentum* (foundation) were part of the language of learning and academic discourse. From this usage, the word fundamental (original, pertaining to a foundation) came into English in the 15th century. Similarly, the word fundamentals, meaning the primary principles or rules of something, is from the 1630s. Yet even today the Germanic roots of the word fundamental persist—in discussion or dialogue we can still hear someone say, "We need to get to the bottom of this."

Most Christian religious revivals since the Reformation have been articulated as attempts to get back to the basics or fundamentals. Most recently, the religious (particularly Christian) use of the terms fundamentalist and fundamentalism have their roots in the late 19th and early 20th centuries.[118] At that time, fundamentalism became the name of an emerging movement in Protestantism based on scriptural inerrancy. At the

---

118   "The term 'fundamentalism' has its roots in the Niagara Bible Conference (1878 – 1897) [at Niagara on the Lake, Ontario] which defined the tenets it considered *fundamental* to Christian belief." https://en.wikipedia.org/wiki/Fundamentalism

Presbyterian General Assembly of 1910, a list of 'fundamentals' was prepared to describe qualities of 'true believers'. In 1918, the World Christian Fundamentals Association was founded. The terms became widespread following the Northern Baptist Conference in 1922.[119]

Over the years, the terms fundamentalism and fundamentalist have gradually become used in relation to other religions; e.g., Islamic 'fundamentalism' is first seen in 1957.

Glory

Glory as a verb, to glorify, meaning 'to rejoice in' comes to English in the mid-14th century. Glory comes from Old French *gloriier* (glorify; pride oneself on, boast about) and Latin *gloriar* (to boast, vaunt, brag, pride oneself). The Old English word used before the 14th century was *wuldor*.

The noun glory comes to English around 1200 as *gloire* (the splendour of God or Christ; praise offered to God, worship) from Old French *glorie* (glory of God; worldly honour, renown; splendour, magnificence, pomp) and Latin *gloria* (fame, renown, great praise or honor). The origins of the noun glory are controversial. Some scholars suggest that Latin *gloria*

---

119   The following quotations are from the Online Etymological Dictionary: http://www.etymonline.com/index.php?allowed_in_frame=0&search=fundamentalism&searchmode=none

"Fundamentalism is a protest against that rationalistic interpretation of Christianity which seeks to discredit

supernaturalism ... The simple fact is that, in robbing Christianity of its supernatural content, [rationalists] are

undermining the very foundations of our holy religion ... Christianity is rooted and grounded in supernaturalism,

and when robbed of supernaturalism it ceases to be a religion and becomes an exalted system of ethics. [Laws,

"Herald & Presbyter," July 19, 1922].

"A new word has been coined into our vocabulary -- two new words -- 'Fundamentalist' and 'Fundamentalism.' They are not in the dictionaries as yet -- unless in the very latest editions. But they are on everyone's tongue. [Address Delivered at the Opening of the Seminary, Sept. 20, 1922, by Professor Harry Lathrop Reed, "Auburn Seminary Record"].

comes from Latin *gnoria* (knowledge, fame) and *gnarus* (known); some disagree. Latin also has *gloriola* (a little fame).

Glory, meaning 'one who is a source of glory', is from the mid-14th century. Glory meaning 'a thirst for glory, vainglory, pride, boasting, vanity' and as a sense of magnificence is from the late 14th century.

The various uses of glory in the Bible are seen in translations of Greek *doxa* (expectation, opinion, judgement, fame) used to translate a Hebrew word meaning brightness, splendour, majesty of outward appearance).

Glory is one of many words beginning with *gl-*, a sound that conveys the idea of sheen and smoothness; for example, glow, gleam, glimmer, glare, glisten, glitter, glacier, and glide (Liberman, 2009, 36).

God

Have you had an OMG experience lately?! Have you been surprised or startled or awakened by something intruding into your consciousness?! A moment of panic or pleasure? An unexpected gift? Hearing bad news? Unexpected beauty? Driving by a traffic accident? Have you ever felt giddy (a word with ancient origins meaning 'possessed by a god')? Such an experience often prompts an involuntary gasp of awareness—an exhalation or inhalation in response to otherness, an experience of being outside or inside yourself in a new way. See also AWE.

Such experiences seem related to the origins of the word 'god'. There are two views of these origins—one is that the word comes from ancient words meaning 'to call' or 'to invoke'; the other is from ancient words meaning 'to pour' or 'to pour a libation'.

In both cases, these suggested origins are rooted in verbs or actions, not nouns or things. Both origins arise from experiences—either from the invocation of an experience or the response to an experience.

In the first case, the word god may come from PIE *ghut* (that which is evoked) and *gheu(e)* (to call, to evoke). In the second case, the word god may come from PIE *ghu* (to pour) and *gheu* (to pour a libation; i.e., to make a sacrificial or ceremonial offering of a liquid; e.g., wine).[120] The sense of PIE *gheu* as the pouring of a libation leads us to Greek *khein* (to pour) and Greek *khute gaia* (poured earth; i.e., a burial mound).

From these PIE terms (*ghut, gheu*) comes Proto-Germanic *guthan* (the spirit immanent in a burial mound[121]). From *guthan* comes Gothic *gub*, Old Norse *guo*, Old High German *got* and German *gott*, and finally the Old Saxon, Old Frisian, Dutch, and Old English word *god*.[122]

The word god from these Germanic origins seems an everyday word. In contrast, words related to god which come from Latin are usually used in more formal or scholarly circumstances (e.g., words like deity, divine) and are derived from PIE *dewos* (god), which in turn came from PIE *dyeu* (to gleam, to shine). PIE *dyeu* and *dewos* are also the origin of words related to sky and day; e.g., Latin *dies* (day) and diary. *Dewos* leads to the Old Persian term *daiva* (demon, evil god), Sanskrit *deva* (shining one), Greek Zeus (the supreme god of Greek mythology), and Latin *deus* (god). PIE *dhes-* (relating to religious concepts), possibly from PIE *dhe* (to set, to put), is the root of Greek *theos*.[123]

In sum, the word 'god' was, perhaps, first just a gasp, a response to those OMG experiences which inspire and even overwhelm, experiences in

---

120   "…god, most authorities think, is either 'one receiving sacrifices' (the preferred derivation) or 'one called upon'. The etymology of god does not bring out the essence of the Godhead but gives a clue to why god is called god" (Liberman, 13).

121   Burial mounds and barrows are found across Europe during the Neolithic and Early Bronze Age periods (approximately 6,000 years ago) coinciding with the development of early PIE languages.

https://www.britannica.com/topic/burial-mound

https://en.wikipedia.org/wiki/Round_barrow

Watkins (cited by the Online Etymological Dictionary): "Given the Greek facts, the Germanic form may have referred in the first instance to the spirit immanent in a burial mound." (https://www.etymonline.com/search?q=god)

On a more recent personal note, I find it hard to walk through 20th century Commonwealth War Graves cemeteries and not be moved by strong feelings of sadness, respect, and, yes, anger.

122   The Old English word *god* probably was closer in sense to Latin *numen* (a nodding or bowing in acknowledgement and affirmation of a divine presence; see NUMEN). The Germanic word *guthan* was a neuter noun; i.e., neither male nor female. However, the gender shifted to masculine after the coming of Christianity. https://www.etymonline.com/word/god

123   "Today we believe that Greek *theos* and Latin *deus* mean 'spirit' and 'shining, glorious', respectively…" (Liberman, 13).

which the ultimate concerns of a person or a people are made manifest. And, in response to such experiences, people act ritually. They pour libations, make sacrifices and thank offerings, and so on in order to recognize and affirm their relationship to such otherness and mysteries which has come into their lives. Words don't just emerge out of nothing. Words are a response to experiences.

Good

The word good, like its opposites, evil and bad, has not changed much since its origins. The word good comes from PIE *ghedh* (to unite, to be associated, to be suitable), Proto-Germanic *godaz* (fitting, suitable), and OE *god* (pronounced 'gode'). Old English *god* had many meanings—excellent, fine; valuable; desirable, favourable, beneficial; full, entire, complete; of abstractions, actions; beneficial, effective; righteous, pious; of persons or souls, righteous, pious, virtuous; and probably originally, having the right or desirable quality.

When speaking of 'good, better, best', the words better and best come from Proto-Germanic *batizo* (superior, excellent) and *bat* (of the highest quality, first, in the best manner).

The origin of good in PIE *ghedh* suggests that something is not necessarily good in and of itself. Given the connotations of to unite, to be associated, and to be suitable, PIE *ghedh* suggests that if and when something unites or enables association or is suitable or useful, then that something can be considered 'good'; e.g., a good meal, a good tool. Given the rare use of the word bad in ancient times, in cases in which something was considered not suitable or useful, perhaps it would simply have been called 'not good' rather than bad.[124]

In the late use of OE *god*, given the many meanings outlined above, the word could mean skilled or expert (as in a good carpenter); fortunate, favourable (e.g., a good omen), or prosperous; and kind or benevolent

---

124   The word bad is rarely seen before 1400. The word evil was more common until around 1700 as the ordinary antithesis of *good*. The word bad has no apparent relatives in other languages.

when referring to people or to God. By the early 13th century, the word good also meant friendly or gracious. By the early 15th century, good was an expression of satisfaction (e.g., a good time). The use of good to mean the good side of something or a good thing is from the 1660s. By the 1690s good was used to mean well-behaved, as in good children.

In brief, the sense of whether something is good or not depends on a person's perception and judgment which is based, for example, on experience, values, reason, and on a capacity for critical thinking. For example, one person may think that a certain book is very good; another person may think that the same book is not worth reading. The word good describes a person's relationship to the book. The book is still the same book.

Today, the opposite of good can be either bad (e.g., failing to reach an acceptable standard) or evil (e.g., morally reprehensible). A cake that is not good is just bad, it is not evil!

Gospel

In its origins, the word gospel comes to modern English from Old English *godspel*, literally 'good story'; from *god* (good)[125] + *spel* (story, message). Old English *godspel* refers to the first four books of the New Testament which tell the 'glad tidings' story and message of Jesus. Old English *godspel* was a translation of Latin *bona adnuntiatio*, itself a translation of Greek *euangelion* (a reward for bringing good news).[126]

Old English *god* had many meanings: excellent, fine; valuable; desirable, favourable, beneficial; full, entire, complete; of abstractions, actions; beneficial, effective; righteous, pious; of persons or souls, righteous, pious, virtuous; and probably originally, having the right or desirable quality. Old English *god* came from Proto-Germanic *godaz* (fitting, suitable) and PIE *gheudh* (to unite, to be associated, suitable). *God* and *godaz* are also related

---

125 Note that the words God and god have a set of origins that are different from the word good. See also GOD, GOOD.

126 See also ANGEL and EVANGELICAL.

to Old Norse *goor*, Dutch *goed*, Old High German *guot*, German *gut*, and Gothic *gops*.

Old English *spel* or *spell* (story, tale, history, narrative, fable; discourse, command) comes from Proto-Germanic *spellam*, a word related to Old Saxon *spel*, Old Norse *spjall*, Old High German *spel*, Gothic *spill* (report, discourse, tale, fable, myth), and German *beispiel* (an example).

Proto-Germanic *spellam* is also the root of *spel* or spell used to mean an utterance, something said, a statement or set of words with alleged magical or occult powers, an incantation, or a charm. The word spell, as in 'to cast a spell', first seen in English in the 1570s,[127] usually indicates a spell which is harmful to the person who is the target of the spell—in contrast to the use of spells or charms or similar magic words for healing, protection, and so on[128]

The word spell, meaning a story, was also used in Old English to mean a doctrine, a sermon, religious instruction or teaching, and the gospel (i.e., a book of the Bible).

And so, back to *godspel* and gospel. As mentioned, the word originally meant 'a good story'; however, given gradual changes in pronunciation and usage of Old English words over the years, the word *godspel* came to mean 'a god story' as well as a 'good story' or 'glad tidings story'.

In contrast to the usual trend of words coming into English from Germanic languages, the Old English word *godspel* (as 'god story') was taken from England back to continental Europe as Old Saxon *godspell*, Old High German *gotspell*, and Old Norse *godspiall*.

By the middle of the 13th century, the word gospel was being used to describe anything as true that came from the Gospel. By the 1640s, the word gospel was being used as an adjective; e.g., "It's the gospel truth." During the 1650s, the word gospel came to mean any doctrine

---

127   Speaking of spells, the 1570s were at the height of the so-called European 'witch craze' which emerged in the 13th century and peaked in the 16th and 17th centuries. Most of the witchcraft trials and executions occurred in the Holy Roman Empire; that is, an area that now comprises countries such as Germany, Netherlands, Switzerland, Austria, and so on. The use of 'spell' may have spilled over from such areas to England and English at this time.

128   Note that the word 'spell' when used to mean 'to spell someone off', 'to rest for a spell', or 'a good spell of weather' has different origins.

maintained as of exclusive importance. The term 'gospel music' is first seen in the mid-1950s.

Grace

Have you ever received a gift? A gift with no strings attached. What is your response? Simply accept it and respond with thanks and gratitude. What else can you do?

The word grace first came to English around 1200 as a verb, as an action. To grace was to give thanks, from Old French *gracier* (to thank). By the mid-15th century, to grace meant to show favor or to lend or add grace to something. Later, in the 1580s, we see the phrase 'grace us with your presence'. Grace is something you do, not just something you have.

The action of grace can be traced back to PIE *gwere* (to favor) and Latin *gratia* (favor, esteem, regard; good will, gratitude). Grace, experienced as a divine quality or gift, has its roots in Old French *grace* (pardon, divine grace, mercy; favor, thanks) and comes to English meaning 'God's favor or help' around 1200. For such a gift, we give thanks. We are grateful.

Grace, as the short prayer of thanks or gratitude said before a meal, comes from the early 13th century.

In the 14th century, in English, to be 'gracious' meant to be filled with God's grace. The sense of gracious meaning merciful or benevolent comes later in the 14th century; i.e., we can act with mercy or benevolence when we are filled with grace.

In secular terms, the use of grace in relation to virtue and its use to describe a pleasing quality of beauty of form or movement is from the mid-14th century. This sense of grace is related to the Three Graces from the mythology of the ancient classical world.[129] By the mid-15th century,

---

129   The Three Graces were three sister goddesses, daughters of Zeus, King of the Gods in Greek mythology. The oldest daughter was Thalia (representing abundance), then Euphrosyne (representing joy and delight), and the youngest was Aglaia (representing beauty and charm). I can't help but think of the fairy tales which begin, "Once upon a time there was a king with three beautiful daughters and the youngest was the most beautiful of them all…".

the term graceful meant not only full of grace but also meant someone or something pleasant or sweet. By the 1580s, the term graceful referred to someone or something with pleasing or attractive qualities.[130]

In short, grace is a partnership between receiving and giving. I receive a gift and I give thanks.

So, how might we talk about the gift of grace? To me, an experience I would name as grace is an unprompted and unheralded upsurge of feeling, a moment in which everything seems to stop. I experience an unconditional affirmation of my life. I cannot evoke or give myself such an experience. Rather, it seems to wash over me like a suddenly large wave rolling over me on the beach or a gust of wind as I turn a street corner. Grace can feel like a sudden and unexpected realization; or, it can be an unobtrusive tap on the shoulder: here, accept this. I need only say yes—a yes without question or qualification—and respond with gratitude.

Gratitude is a sign or indication of grace. Gratitude is both a thank you and an act of grace in itself. As grateful people, we can, in turn, act with grace. We can be instruments of grace for someone else. We can return the favor.

See also GRATITUDE.

Gratitude

Gratitude comes from PIE *gwere* (to favor) and is related to words such as congratulate, disgrace, grace, grateful, gratuity, and ingratiate. See also GRACE.

From PIE *gwere* comes Latin *gratus* (thankful, pleasing), Latin *gratitudinem* (thankfulness), 15th century Middle French *gratitude*, and in the mid-15th century the English word gratitude. By the 1560s, the word gratitude meant thankfulness.

---

130   At this time, we also see the emergence of the term disgrace—to fall from grace or to be out of grace. The sense of disgrace meaning 'to bring shame upon' comes from the 1590s.

Halo

Halo comes to English in the 1560s from Latin *halo* and Greek *halos* meaning the disk of the sun or moon, the ring of light around the sun or moon, the disk of a shield, or the circular path walked by oxen on a threshing floor. The origin of halo is unknown; however, the path on the threshing floor seems the most probable source.[131]

Halo, as the light around the head of a holy person or deity, is first recorded in English in the 1640s.

Halo is not to be confused with words beginning with the prefix halo-; e.g., halogen. Such words come from Greek *hals* (salt or a lump of salt) and from PIE *sal* (salt).

Heathen, Pagan, Gentile

In ancient times, the words heathen and pagan were used as we use words today such as country bumpkin, country cousin, hayseed, hillbilly, redneck, rube, yokel, and so on. Such words often refer in a derogatory sense to people from a rural countryside. Often, the words heathen and pagan are used to describe people who are not like the person who is speaking or writing.

Gentile refers to another culture or nation and is related to genteel, gentry, and gentleman.

Heathen

Heathen comes from ancient words meaning someone who lives on the heath; that is, on the uncultivated or poor soil wasteland areas of rural areas.

The English word heathen comes from the Old English *haeden* (not Christian or Jewish) which comes from the Old Norse *heidinn* (someone inhabiting uncultivated land). The Old English word *haed* (untilled land,

---

131   https://www.etymonline.com/search?q=halo

tract of wasteland), the root of the modern word heath, comes from the Proto-Germanic *haithiz* and the PIE *kaito* (uncultivated land).

Similarly, in the 4th century, Ulfilas (311 – 383), a Christian missionary to the Goths in what is now Bulgaria, used the Gothic word *haipno* (from Gothic *haibi*—dwelling on the heath) when translating the Bible to Gothic from Greek.

Looking at these origins, I get the sense that people of the early church used the term heathen not only to describe someone who was not a Christian but also, perhaps in a somewhat derogatory fashion, to describe someone who had had the misfortune to be born in a poorer part of the countryside. Heathens were people who lived out in the boondocks. Such usage suggests that the early Christians who wrote and used these words were literate and urban.

Pagan

Pagan comes to English in the 14th century from the Latin noun *paganus* (villager, rustic; civilian, non-combatant). The adjective sense of pagan (that is; of the country, of a village), from 15th century English, comes from Latin *pagus* (country people; province, rural district), originally a district marked and limited by its boundaries (from Latin *pangere* meaning to fix, fasten). *Pagus* and *pangere* comes from PIE root *pag-* (to fix, join together, unite, make firm).

Before Christianity, the term *paganus* was Roman military jargon for a civilian or an incompetent soldier. Even in the 2nd century AD, the word *paganus* was still used with no sense or connotation of 'pagan' meaning a non-Christian person. At that time the term pagan meant more where you lived than what religion you followed. However, during the early years of Christianity, the term was used to describe the conservative rural adherence to the old gods; or, to describe people who were not (yet) baptized. Later, the term came to mean anyone who was not a Christian or a Jew (Borg, 2018 ,77).

Pagan was used primarily in 'western' or Roman Christianity. The equivalent term in 'eastern' or Greek Christianity was 'hellene'.

Pagan, as applied to modern pantheists and nature-worshippers, dates from 1908.

Gentile

Gentile has its origins in the PIE *gene-* (produce, give birth, beget) leading to Greek *genos* (race, kind), and Latin *genus* (race, stock, kind; family, birth, descent, origin) and Latin *gens* (race, clan). The Latin *gentilus* means belonging to the same family or clan, a fellow countryman.

In the context of first century Judaism, non-Jews were known as *goyim* (the nations), translated into Greek as *ta ethne* (the nations; related to the word ethnic) or in Latin as *gentilus*. The meaning of *gentilus* later came to mean belonging to a distinct nation or ethnicity. In Judaism, gentiles were simply 'other people' who didn't happen to be Jewish.

In the Roman Empire, the term *gentilus* referred to people of other nations who were not Roman citizens. With the spread of Christianity, *gentilus* came to refer to so-called pagan or barbarian cultures. In St Jerome's 4th century Latin version of the Bible (the Vulgate), *gentilis* was used in this broader sense when translating Greek and Hebrew words referring to non-Hebrew peoples.

Gentilus is also the root of the English word gentle which comes from Old French *gentil* (high-born, noble, of good family), 11th century French *gentil* (nice, graceful, pleasing, fine, pretty), and 13th century French *gentil* (well-born). After the Norman invasion of England in 1066, Gentile was the surname of a noble family in Hampshire.

By the mid-13th century, the Latin *gentilus* had come to English as the adjective *gentile*, meaning noble, kind, gracious. Today we talk of someone being 'genteel'. By the late 14th century, gentile meant someone of a noble rank or birth, a chivalrous person belonging to the gentry (and from which we get the word gentleman).

Even though the word *gentilus* evolved to mean gentle and genteel in English, *gentilus* had also evolved by the 14th century to the English word gentile meaning someone who was neither a Christian nor a Jew. During the Renaissance and Reformation translations of the Bible from Latin to vernacular languages, this 14th century use of the gentile was used when translating the Hebrew terms *goyim* or *goy* (people, nations, usually of non-Hebraic background) into English.

Heaven

There are no certainties with regard to the origin of the word heaven. The etymological dictionaries mention several 'probables', 'likelys', and the occasional 'perhaps'. Having said this, the word heaven seems to come from and be related to words meaning variously a bright and clear sky, shirts, and stones.

The earliest references to the origin of the word heaven are from PIE *kem* (to cover) and the Proto-Germanic *hibin* or *himin*, words also related to Low German *heben*, Old Norse *himinn*, Gothic *himins*, Old Frisian *himul*, Dutch *hemel*, and German *himmel*—all meaning heaven or sky.

From these Germanic roots comes Old English *heofon*, originally meaning sky or firmament (i.e., the dome or vault or arch of the sky). Later, *heofon* meant the home of the Christian God.

PIE *kem* (to cover) is also said to be related to Proto-Germanic *ham-ithjan*, Latin *camisia* (a soldier's shirt or tunic), Old English *cemes* (shirt), and Old French *chemise* (shirt, under tunic, shift) which now refers to a woman's undergarment or a loose straight-hanging dress. The implication would seem to be that heaven covers us.

Another suggestion is that the word heaven derives from PIE *akman* (which at first meant a stone or sharp stone, and which later came to mean the stony vault of heaven or firmament).

The Greek word for heaven is *ouranos* which became the name of the planet Uranus. In Greek mytholology, Uranus was the god who personified the heavens and who was the father of the Titans. One of the Titans was Atlas who was sentenced to uphold the pillars of heaven as punishment for a failed rebellion of the Titans against the Olympian gods.

The Latin word for heaven is *caelum* (also, sky, abode of the gods, climate) from PIE *kaid-slo*, a term related to Germanic words meaning bright and clear; e.g., Old English *hador*, German *heiter* (clear, shining, cloudless) and Old Norse *heio* (clear sky). *Caelum* is the root of the word celestial. The heavens, meaning the solar system or the 'realm of heavenly bodies', is from 1670s.

In brief, the first ancient words related to heaven refer to the sky. Later words describing heaven as the firmament (like a wall or border) or dome of the sky refer to that which separates earth from heaven--the realm of god or the gods. Heaven then, in this context, is no longer the sky but that which is beyond the sky. This is, perhaps, the most that etymology can tell us.[132]

See also HELL and PURGATORY.

---

132   [1] For a fascinating historical account of how a gradual change in the imagining of the separation of heaven and earth came about in the life of the early church, refer to Peter Brown. (2015). *The ransom of the soul: Afterlife and wealth in early Western Christianity*. Cambridge, MA: Harvard University Press. In particular, refer to the section *"Rich and poor: Heaven and earth, 250 – 650 AD"* (pp. 41 – 46) from which the following excerpts are found.

"One cannot but think that, in these Christian communities, there was a congruence between the sense of almost symbiotic bonds between the living and the dead and the bonds between each other that these groups imagined in their own society. The dead were thought to be as close to the living as the living were expected to be close to each other.

We are looking at relations between the living and the dead that reflected a view of the Christian community as a place where social boundaries were relaxed, both in this world and in the next. The other world, like the Christian community, was seen as a place of ease. Pagan burial imagery featured bucolic landscapes and peaceful gardens. Christians picked up this imagery with enthusiasm. It did justice to their own notion of the relaxed and joyful state of the souls of the departed. This bucolic art also echoed a similar sense of relaxation among the living. It summed up a counter-cultural longing for a religious community that avoided, as much as possible, the blatant hierarchies and abrasive differences in wealth and status that characterized the dark 'world' outside the church.

The fact that, by 300 AD, many Christians were already wealthy, cultivated, and even powerful, did not contradict this representation" (41).

"In the course of the fifth and sixth centuries, as we shall see, the distance between heaven and earth seemed to yawn more widely. From the time of Augustine onward, believers were encouraged to be more conscious of the burden of their sins. Their unexpiated sins were increasingly thought to expose them to danger in the other world. Altogether, average Christians felt further away from heaven than ever before. Their souls were imagined to travel more slowly and at ever greater risk—past demons and through flames of fire—toward an increasingly distant heaven.

But in 300 AD, all this lay in the future" (46).

Hell

How did the word hell, which originally meant a hole in the ground, become the name of such a terrible place?

The word hell has rather innocuous origins in ancient words related to covering and concealing—first in PIE *kel* (to cover, to conceal) and later in Proto-Germanic *haljo* (the underworld; or, a concealed place). Hell and hole have the same origins in PIE *kel*—we could say that these words are cousins.[133]

Proto-Germanic *haljo* leads to Old Frisian *helle*, Dutch *hel*, Old Norse *hel*[134], and German *holle*—words which originally were benign or descriptive rather than judgmental when used to describe the abode of the souls of the dead. In the later Gothic term *halja* we see the beginnings of the sense of hell as a place of punishment.

About 725 CE we first see the Old English word *helle*, meaning the nether world (i.e., the abode of the dead) and the place for all souls after death.

Only later in English translations of the Latin, Greek, and Hebrew words and conceptions of the afterlife—for example, the words used in early church Bibles—was the word *helle* also used to describe a place of punishment.

In the ancient world, three Latin terms were related to the afterlife: *infernum*, *hades*, and *tartarus*. *Infernum* referred to a place—the underground or lower regions.[135] *Hades* referred to a Greek god (Haides, the god of the underworld; a word of unknown origin—perhaps meaning literally 'the invisible' according to one source) and to an underworld place for the dead.[136] *Tartarus* referred to the place where the wicked were confined

---

133   To call something a 'hell hole' is redundant—both words mean the same thing (just like the phrase 'head honcho'—again, both words mean the same thing). PIE *kel* is also the origin of cell (i.e., a cell as a micro-organism, a monk's cell, a prison cell), cellar, and other ancient words related to holes, caves, and caverns.

134   Later, in Norse mythology, Hel was the name of the god Loki's daughter who rules over the evil dead in Niflheim, the lowest of all worlds.

135   *Infernum* is also the root of English word infernal.

136   The word Hades came into the English language in the 1590s.

after death. In early Bible translations, *Tartarus* was also used to describe a place for fallen angels.

Ancient Hebrew had two terms for the afterlife: *Sheol*, a neutral term for the abode of the dead (similar to Greek *Hades*) and *Gehanna*, the destination of the wicked—both terms used in early versions of the Bible. *Gehanna* was used to name the 'lake of fire' and the 'fire and brimstone'[137] described in Revelations. *Gehanna* came into English in the 1620s from the Greek *geenna* and the Hebrew *gehinnom* (the place of fiery torment for the dead). *Gehanna* comes from the place name Ge Hinnom ('valley of Hinnom') southwest of Jerusalem where children were reportedly sacrificed by fire to Moloch, a Canaanite god of the ancient world.

When the KJV Bible was translated into English in the early 17th century, the word hell was used not only as the translation of Latin *Infernum* and *Tartarus* but also as the translation of Hebrew *Sheol* (the underworld) and the Greek Hades and *Gehanna*.

Old English *Helle*, as the name of the place for all souls after death, gradually fell out of use as the word hell took its place. The word hell, as used in the KJV Bible, conflated and subsumed all previous meanings seen in the related Latin, Greek, and Hebrew words from the ancient world and described only the place for the wicked after death.

Given these many definitions and interpretations of the word hell over the years, perhaps it is not surprising that there has been considerable controversy, debate, and disagreement about the nature of hell since the beginnings of Christianity. Various translations of the Bible over the centuries have used the term hell in different ways, each translation reflecting its own purpose and understanding.

In addition, during the medieval and Reformation periods, concepts of hell and heaven, devils and angels, sins and virtues were systematically delineated and categorized. For example, during this time hell was described as consisting of four parts:

Inferno: The hall of the damned (i.e., *Gehanna*)

Purgatory: those en route to heaven after a necessary purification period

---

137   Brimstone, now known as sulfur, was often burned in the purification rituals of ancient cultures.

Limbus Patrum (i.e,. limbo of the Old Testament patriarchs awaiting atonement)

Limbo of infants (children who die without receiving baptism)[138]

This conception of hell is best represented by Dante's epic 14th century three-part poem 'The Divine Comedy' (part one: *Inferno*, i.e., hell; part two: *Purgatorio*; part three: *Paradiso*). Several sources suggest that Dante was influenced by similar themes and concepts from Islamic writings.

In another example, in the 16th century, hell was described by Peter Binsfeld as containing seven rooms—one room for each of the seven deadly sins. Each sin was assigned a particular eternal punishment and each room in hell was ruled by a particular devil.[139] Speaking of the devil, another 16th century document identified a different devil for each month of the year.

A cursory review of the literature reveals that there is certainly no shortage of imagination when it comes to creating conceptions of hell.

Hell used to describe a state of misery or to describe a bad experience dates from the late 14th century. Hell used as an expression of disgust is first recorded in the 1670s. Heck as a euphemism for hell is first seen in 1865.

Heresy, Heretic

Heresy came to English in the 12th century and meant a doctrine or opinion at variance with commonly held or established doctrines or opinions.

---

138   The Latin words *limbo* and *limbus* mean an edge or boundary; e.g., the place between hell and heaven (not to be confused with the limbo, a Caribbean dance). The limbo of infants was dropped from official Roman Catholic doctrine in 2007.

139   During the Reformation of the 16th century various writers documented the different punishments in the various rooms of hell that were reserved for each of the seven deadly sins. Each room was presided over by a different devil. For example, the lusty ended up in a room of fire and brimstone (ruled by Asmodai); the gluttons were in a room in which they were force-fed toads, rats, and snakes (ruled by Beelzebub, a Philistine god; from Hebrew ba'al-z'bub, meaning 'lord of the flies'); the greedy were boiled in oil (in a room ruled by Mammon); the sad folks ended up in a room full of snakes (ruled by Belphegor); angry people were dismembered alive (Satan); the envious ended up in freezing water (Leviathan); and the prideful were tortured and broken on the wheel (Lucifer).

Heresy is from Old French *heresie* (heresy), Latin *haeresis* (a school of thought or a philosophical sect), Greek *hairesis* (a choice, a choosing for oneself), and Greek *haireisthai* (to take, to seize). The implication here is that a heresy is not necessarily something wrong, rather just something different. The word sect, one early meaning of Latin *haeresis*, implies this neutrality.

However, the word heresy was used in early Christian writings to refer to sects other than your own; i.e., my orthodoxy, your sect. To call something a heresy implies "I'm right. You're not."

English language Bibles usually use the term sect rather than heresy.

Finally, a heretic is a member of a heresy (or sect). A heresiarch is the leader of a heresy.

See also SECT.

Hermeneutics

You have probably noticed that when four or five people are discussing a controversial or complex topic there can often be eight or ten different ways of talking about it. At a more everyday level, sometimes even two people can have differing views on the best way to cook something: should we follow the recipe exactly or can we improvise?! What seems an obvious explanation of something for one person is not always understood or explained in the same way by another person.

What to do? In the midst of a sea of information and differing points of view, how do we find ways to talk respectfully and meaningfully with each other? Hermeneutics is one response. It something we all do everyday; for example, when we ask "What's he really saying, anyway?" or "Why does the BBC or CNN or Fox or CBC address the same news story in such different ways?" or when we say, "Now I get it... I can see where she is coming from." Even gossip can be seen as a form of hermeneutics—"Who does he think he is, anyway?!"

So, what is hermeneutics? As an academic subject, hermeneutics is the art of interpretation of text and meaning. Hermeneutics is the study of exegesis (the explanation or critical interpretation of a text; the word exegesis came to English in 1619). The word hermeneutics came to English in 1737. A basic premise of hermeneutics is that each person approaches complex material from perspectives based in their particular culture, education, experiences, and so on.

The adjective hermeneutic (from 1670) comes from Greek *hermeneutikos* (of or for interpreting), *hermeneutes* (interpreter), and *hermeneuein* (to interpret secret hidden foreign languages; to interpret into words), or as Kearney states, "*hermeneuein* is to interpret secret hidden messages from the gods" (Kearney, 2016, 241).[140]

Hermeneutics, a word of unknown origin, is believed to come from Hermes, the name of the Greek god of trade, heraldry, merchants, commerce, roads, thieves, trickery, sports, travelers, and athletes in ancient Greek religion and mythology. Hermes, also the god of speech, writing, and eloquence, was considered the emissary and messenger of the gods. In Roman mythology, Hermes was known as Mercury.

Hierarchy

What first comes to mind when you think of hierarchies? Organizational structures? Categories of things organized from simple to complex? I suspect that angels are not the first things that come to mind!

The word hierarchy comprises two ancient Greek words: *heiros* (sacred, filled with the divine, holy) and *arkheim* (to lead, to rule). *Heiros* comes from the PIE root *eis-* (related to words denoting passion or strong feeling, including the words *oistros* [gadfly; a thing causing madness] and eventually the English word ire) and iron.[141] *Heiros* leads to Greek words such

---

140   Kearney states that "hermeneutics is not just about theology ... it was extended to philosophical and historical-cultural understanding generally. But even at the most basic, ordinary level, the way we read between the lines is always according to a certain kind of selection, through a particular grid or filter. That doesn't mean *á la carte* relativism. And it certainly shouldn't mean imposing ideological agenda on persons, texts, or things... At best, hermeneutics is just being responsible for 'where we're speaking from' and, when it comes to religion, recognizing that we all have a particular cut on God, informed by our respective traditions and cultures ... We are born into an historical conversation that precedes us, and we interpret our lives accordingly, by being as responsible and free as we can..." (Kearney, 2016, 241).

141   Why iron? Perhaps this word reflects passions aroused by the discovery of iron tools and

as *hiera* (sacred rites), *hierarkhes* (high priest), *hierarkhia* (rule of the high priest) and, later, Medieval Latin *hierarchia* (ranked division of angels). The word hierarchy comes to English in the late 14ᵗʰ century from Old French *ierarchie*.

In the 14ᵗʰ century the word hierarchy referred to each of the three divisions of the nine orders of angels as outlined first by Dionysius the Areopagite (5ᵗʰ, 6ᵗʰ century CE) and later by Thomas Aquinas (1225 – 1274). In this hierarchy, the lowest level of angels, the level closest to people, is the 'angel'; the second lowest is the 'archangel'; i.e., 'the ruler of angels'. The Old English phrase *heah encgel* was replaced by the English word archangel, first seen in the late 12ᵗʰ century. Given that there are seven higher levels of 'angels' as you move closer to the divine, perhaps an archangel could be somewhat considered like a department head or a shop steward?![142]

In brief, the Greek verb *arkheim* is related to the noun *archon* (the ruler, the chief). Both Greek words are of uncertain origin. However, combining *hieros* and *archon* gives us hierarchy; i.e., rule by the sacred or by the divine.

The use of hierarchy as a ranked organization of persons (in particular, the clergy) or things is first recorded in the 1610s.

---

weapons in the Iron Age of Europe and the ancient Near East (~1200 – 50 BCE). The Iron Age was the final of three periods of the time between prehistory and proto-history; i.e., the Stone Age, the Bronze Age, and the Iron Age.

142   Drawing upon earlier writers of the early church and various New Testament Biblical references, e.g., Galatians 3:26-28, Matthew 22:24-33, Ephesians 1:21-23, and Colossians 1:16, Aquinas developed a schema of three hierarchies, each comprising three Orders or Choirs of angels. I find it interesting that it was only in the 13ᵗʰ century, a period during which logic and rationality were being recovered and used both in the newly emerging universities and the church and society, that someone like Aquinas took the time to construct this schema.

In Aquinas', the first hierarchy, that closest to the divine, comprised in order of decreasing closeness: seraphim, cherubim, and thrones. The second hierarchy, lower than the first, again in decreasing closeness: dominions or lordships, virtues or strongholds, powers or authorities. Similarly, the third hierarchy: principalities or rulers, archangels, angels. Beneath these were the personal guardian angels (see DAEMON).

Holy

In its origins, the word holy is related to wholeness, health, and healing.

Holy has its beginnings in Proto-Germanic *hailitho* and in PIE *kailo*, both of which mean whole, uninjured, of good omen.

There appears to be no evidence of pre-Christian use of the words *hailitho* and *kailo* to mean holy. However, some scholars have suggested that any pre-Christian use of these PIE and Proto-Germanic terms for the word holy would likely have been related to something that was whole or intact, something that was not to be transgressed or violated.

These two ancient terms are also related to the Old English *hal* (hale, whole), as in 'hale and hearty', which is the origin of the word health and related to the Old English *haelan* (to heal). These two terms are also related to Old High German *heil* (health, happiness, good luck)

Later, *hailitho* leads to Proto-Germanic *hailaga*, the origin of Old Norse *heilagr*, Old Frisian *helich*, Old Saxon *helag*, Middle Dutch *helich*, Old High German *heilag*, German *heilig*, Gothic *hailags*, and Old English *halig*—all of which mean holy or sacred. And from Old English *helig*, we have the word holy. See SACRED.

The Latin word for holy is *sanctus*, leading to words such as sanctify, sanctification, and sanctuary. See SANCTIFY.

The word holiday (holy + day), from the 1500s, comes from the earlier 13th century *haliday* and the Old English *haligdaeg* (holy day, Sabbath). In the 14th century holiday meant both a religious festival and a day of recreation; however, by the 16th century these two meanings had diverged to mean different things.

Holy Ghost or Holy Spirit?

In early Christianity, what is now called the Holy Ghost or Holy Spirit in English was known in ancient Greek as *pneuma to hagion* (from *pneuma*, meaning wind, breath, and spirit used in a general sense; and, from *hagion* or *hagios*, meaning sacred or holy). In Latin, the related term *spiritus sanctus* was and is still used.

So, why do we have two different terms in English—Holy Ghost and Holy Spirit—which appear to mean the same thing? What's the difference?

Holy

First, a quick look at the word holy which has its roots in Proto-Germanic *hailitho* and *hailaga*, words which are the origin of Old Norse *heilagr*, Old Frisian *helich*, Old Saxon *helag*, Middle Dutch *helich*, Old High German *heilag*, German *heilig*, Gothic *hailags*, and Old English *halig*—all of which mean holy or sacred. And from Old English *helig*, we have the word holy. See also HOLY.

Ghost

The word ghost has its origins in PIE *gheis* (to be excited, amazed, frightened).[143] Ghost first appears in Old English as the rather undifferentiated and generic term *gast* (soul, spirit life, breath, good or bad spirit, angel, demon) which in turn comes from Proto-Germanic *ghoizdoz* (supernatural being; often with the power to wound, tear, pull to pieces), Old Saxon *gest*, Old Frisian *jest*, Middle Dutch *gheest*, and German *geist* (spirit, ghost). Old English *gast* is related to Old English *gaestan* (to frighten).

In Old English Christian writing, the term *gast* was used as the translation of Latin *spiritus*. These Old English origins appear to be the beginning of what came to be named the Holy Ghost.

However, in the 14th century, the term *gast* began to lose its religious connotations and came to be used in the more familiar modern sense as the disembodied spirit of a dead person; i.e., a ghost. The gh- spelling of ghost, rare in English before the mid-16th century, first appears in the 15th century influenced by the Flemish and Middle Dutch *gheest*.

---

143   PIE *gheis* is not to be confused with PIE *ghos-ti* (stranger, guest, host). From *ghos-ti* come words such as hospice, hospital, hospitality, host, hostel, hostile, and hotel. Note that a stranger can be both a guest and a threat!

Although the term Holy Ghost continues to be used, the term Holy Spirit began to be used more commonly, especially during the Renaissance and Reformation translation of Bibles from Latin into local languages such as English. For example, the King James Version of the Bible uses Holy Ghost and Holy Spirit interchangeably.

Spirit

The word spirit has its origins in *(s)peis*, one of the PIE words meaning to blow or to breathe. From this root come the Latin words *spirare* (to breathe) and *spiritus* (a breathing). In early Latin translations of the Bible, *spiritus* was used to translate Greek *pneuma* and Hebrew *ruach* (both meaning wind or breath).

Latin *spiritus* suggests the breath of life or the breath of god and contains connotations of character, high spirits, vigor, courage, pride and arrogance. The words respiration and inspiration have their roots in *spiritus*. *Spiritus* can also simply mean the blowing of the wind.

During the medieval period, the term *spiritus* or spirit came to have a number of meanings and uses.[144] In general, by 1500, spirit had also come to mean the character or essential principle, nature, or quality of something (e.g., the spirit of the times, team spirit). In the 1580s we see spirit used in the sense of animation and vitality.

---

144   By the mid-13th century, the word spirit, meaning the animating or vital principle in man and animals, came to English from Anglo-French *spirit* and Old French *espirit* (meaning spirit or soul; and, from *espirit* comes the modern French word *esprit*, as in *esprit de corps*).

In the mid-14th century, the word spirit is being used to mean any supernatural immaterial invisible creature or 'ghost' (e.g., an angel or demon or apparition of a dead person). Also, in the mid-14th century, spirit had come to mean a way of thinking and feeling, a state of mind, and source of desire; e.g., in Middle English 'freedom of spirit' meant 'freedom of choice'.

By the late 14th century, spirit was being used to describe divine substance, divine mind, the extension of divine power to people, or god as well as the divine nature of Jesus.

Also, in the late 14th century the term spirit was used in medieval alchemy to describe a volatile substance or distillate. From this use we get our term 'spirits', first seen in the 1670s, referring to alcohol or strong liquor.

In conclusion...

Holy Ghost comes to English via Germanic languages. Holy Spirit comes via Latin and Greek. Holy Ghost was the term originally used in English; however, by the 20th century, as the word 'ghost' evolved to refer to the spirit of a dead person, Holy Spirit came to be the term predominantly used in English translations of the Bible and other theological writings.

Hope

Hope is a word whose origins are unknown. Having said this, the verb 'to hope' appears to be related to Old Frisian *hopia*, Middle Low German and Dutch *hopen*, and Middle High German *hoffen* (to hope). Hope appears In Old English as *hopian* (to have the theological virtue of Hope; to have trust, confidence; to assume confidently or trust that something is or will be so).

Another theory suggests that hope is related to the verb 'to hop' from Old English *hoppian* (to spring, to leap in expectation, to dance, to limp) from Proto-Germanic *hupnojan* (related to Old Norse *hoppa* (hop, skip), Dutch *huppen* and German *hupfen* (to hop).

Yet another source traces the word hope to Latin *spes* (hope) and Old Slavic *speti* (to hasten, to thrive, to mature), words related to Old English *spowan* (to thrive) and Old English *sped*, from *spodi*, words refer-ring to, among other things, realizing one's potential. These words now relate to 'speed' but first they related to old phrases such as "God speed" or "God send you good speed". These words, of course, don't mean that god wants you to go fast but rather to go in 'good hope' or to 'go and thrive' (Liberman, 193).[145]

From early in the 13th century, hope, as a verb, was used in the sense of to wish for or to desire something; "I hope that 'x' will happen." Or, "I have trust and confidence that 'x' will happen."

---

145   Liberman writes, "In English, *speed* means only 'rapidity', without suggesting why one should be in a hurry or what awaits 'the speeder' at the end of the way" (193)!

Hope is about expectation.[146] However, even though hope implies confidence and expectation, hope also implies uncertainty. If something was certain there would be no need for hope.

Hope, as a noun (to have the feeling of 'hope'), comes from Old English *hopa* (confidence in the future; the sense of God or Christ as the basis for hope). By the late 14th century hope was used to refer to 'a thing hoped for' and 'the grounds or basis for hope'.

These proposed origins suggest that perhaps hope is first of all an action, something we do. It could be said that there is no hope without action; that with action comes hope. The action itself is an act of hope. We act with anticipation and expectation.[147]

The adjective hopeful is from around 1200. Hopeful, meaning having qualities which excite hope comes from the 1560s. Hopeful, meaning someone on whom hopes are set, is from 1720. The adjective hopeless, meaning offering no grounds for hope, is from the 1560s, and meaning having no expectation of success is from the 1580s.

And, to conclude, given the various origins of the word, I have to say that I am intrigued and delighted by the image of someone hopping with hope!

Humble, Humility, Humiliation

Humble

Humble and humility comes from PIE *dhghem* (earth). Could we say that someone who is humble is 'down to earth'? PIE *dhghem*[148] is related to

---

146   For example: Marilynne Robinson states, "In New Testament Greek, the word translated as *hope* seems to have meant something closer to *expectation*" or "a felt lack, an absence, a yearning. Robinson also suggests that hope is love projected forward into the future" (Robinson, 2019, 222 - 226). Or, perhaps, "Hope is a memory of the future." (Gabriel Marcel, cited by Kearney, 203, 179).

147   Even getting out of bed in the morning could be considered an act of hope!

148   Among many other words, *dhghem* forms all or part of: bonhomie, bridegroom, camomile, chameleon, chthonic, exhume, homage, hombre, homicide, hominid, Homo Sapiens, homunculus, human, humane, humus, nemo, omerta.

Sanskrit *ksam* (earth), Greek *khthon* (the earth, the solid surface of the earth), and Latin *humus* (earth, soil) *humilis* (low).

The adjective humble (meaning submissive, respectful, lowly in manner, modest, not self-asserting, obedient), from the late 13th century, comes from Old French *humble* and *umble*, from Latin *humilis* (lowly, humble; literally, on the ground), from *humus* (earth) and PIE *dhghem*. By the late 14th century, humble meant lowly in kind, state, condition, or amount, and of low birth or rank.

The verb 'to humble', also from the late 14th century, means to render oneself humble or to bend, kneel or bow. By the late 15th century, 'to humble' meant to lower someone else in dignity.

In Christian usage, the term humble evolved from being a relatively objective and non-judgmental state (e.g., a state of poverty or affliction; e.g., as described in the Old Testament) to being also a relatively subjective state, still related to poverty, but more related to a state which one choses (e.g., "I choose to be humble, empty, without possessions, self-emptying").[149]

The phrase 'to eat humble pie' (1830) is from umble pie (1640s); that is, a pie made from umbles (edible inner parts of an animal, especially deer), considered a low-class food. Umbles is Middle English *numbles* (offal).

Humility

Humility has the same origins as humble. Humility, as the quality of being humble, comes to English in the early 14th century from Old French *umelite* (humility, modesty, sweetness) and Latin *humiliatem, humiliatus* (lowness, small stature, insignificance, baseness, littleness of mind; and in Church Latin, meekness).

Humiliation

Humiliation as an act of humiliating or humbling, abasement, mortification come from the late 14c., from Old French *humiliacion* or directly from

---

149   Borg, 2018, 82 – 83.

Latin *humiliationem, humiliatio* (a humbling, humiliation), from humiliare (to humble), and from *humilis* "humble" (see above).

Hymn

Hymn can claim two possible sources for its origin. Both involve singing and songs of praise.

The earliest source is the PIE *sam* (to sing) which is related to Hittite *ishami* (he sings) and Sanskrit *saman* (hymn, song). The second suggested source is the Greek *hymenaios* (wedding song), from Hymen, the god of marriage in Greek mythology.

Hymenaios may be related to Greek *hymnos* (song or ode in praise of gods or heroes), the word used by translators of the Old Testament for various Hebrew words meaning 'song praising God'. From *hymnos* we have the Latin *hymnus* (song of praise) which evolved to Old French *ymye* and to Old English *ymen* around 1000 CE. And from *ymen* the word hymn evolved.

The word hymnal, dating from around 1500 CE, comes from the Latin *hymnale* and *hymnus*.

People have been singing for a long time. And, of course, people have always had a lot to sing about.

Incarnation

The roots of incarnation are in PIE *(s)ker* (to cut, to scrape, to hack) and Proto-Germanic *sker* (to shear, to cut). From these roots came Latin *carnem, caro, carnis* (a piece of flesh) and *carnaticum* (flesh, the slaughter of animals).

Incarnation is composed of Latin *in* (into, in, on upon) and *caro* (flesh)—Latin *incarnare* means 'to make flesh'; i.e., to make something into flesh. In the Latin of the early church, *incarnatio* and *incarnationem* meant the act of making flesh; especially the act of God becoming flesh in Jesus.

Incarnation came to English from the 12th century Old French *incarnacion* around 1300 as 'the embodiment of God in the person of Jesus'.

In the late 14th century, incarnate was being used as an adjective and in the 1530s we first see the incarnate used as a verb; i.e., to incarnate. The term reincarnation (the fact of repeated incarnation) is first seen in 1829. Reincarnation meaning 'a new embodiment' is from 1854.

What about the flower called a carnation (*dianthus caryophyllus*)? One source suggests that carnation is a corruption of coronation—i.e., the petals of the flower look like a finely-toothed crown. Another source suggests that the name of pink and red-coloured carnations comes Middle French *carnation*, a term used to describe a person's flesh-coloured complexion. By the 1530s, carnation was also used in English to describe the colour of human flesh.

Other words related to incarnation include carnage, carnal, carnelian, carnival, carnivore, and chili con carne. During the time of the Roman Empire, a *carnifex* was a public executioner.

Integrity

Integrity has its roots in PIE *tag*, meaning to touch, to grasp, and to set things right. I am reminded of the children's games in which we hear, "Tag, you're it!", or of being 'tagged' in a social media app. Words such as tactile, tact, and tactics, also rooted in PIE *tag*, are cousins of integrity. Tactile relates to our sense of touch; tact relates to our skill in dealing with people. We touch people in many ways; e.g., physically, emotionally, and so on.

From PIE *tag* comes Latin *tangere* (to touch) and *intangere*; i.e., *in-* (not) + *tangere* (to touch) which lead to the English words tangible and intangible.

From PIE *tag* and Latin *tangere* comes Latin *integer*. The word integer came to English unchanged from Latin. An integer is anything complete and whole in itself; e.g., in mathematics, an integer is a whole number. An integer is something 'untouched'; it just is what it is—nothing is added, nothing is taken away.

Latin *integer* leads to the word integrity (innocence, blamelessness, chastity, purity) which came to English in the 14th century from Old French *integrite* and Latin *integritatem, integritas* (soundness, wholeness, completeness). The use of integrity to mean wholeness or a perfect condition is from the mid-15th century.

So, in this context, what might it mean to say that a person has integrity?

First, we can say that a person has integrity if they appear whole and complete. In colloquial language we say that the person has 'got their act together'. That is, the person seems centered, focused, self-possessed, self-assured, and connected to themselves and to life. The person exhibits a sense of self-acceptance. We might say that the person is who he or she is in and of themselves. There is no moral dimension to this sense of integrity, no good or bad, the person just is who they are. We use words such as whole and holistic to describe this state of being, words which come from Old English *hal* (healthy, hale) and PIE *kailo* (sound; i.e., normal and healthy, uninjured).

Second, we can say that a person has integrity if they act morally and ethically. That is, they have the ability to distinguish between right and wrong and to act accordingly (i.e., to act morally). They have the ability to understand and describe the reasons and rationales why they believe something to be right or wrong (i.e., to act ethically). Words like perfect and perfection are often implied when describing moral and ethical systems; i.e., ethical systems describe the desired ways toward which people to strive to act. These desired ways of acting imply a state of perfection in the sense of being finished or complete with no errors, mistakes, or defects.

It seems to me at times that for some there is too much concern with the latter (being perfect) and not enough concern with the former (being whole).

To conclude, the word integrity suggests that a person is in touch or in tune with themselves and their surroundings. The person exudes an intangible quality that cannot be pinned down or adequately described or grasped. It implies a sense of mysterious and wholeness that is beyond complete comprehension. We sense, or touch (or are touched by) integrity but we can't really explain it or pin it down.

Intuition

The word intuition has connections to security guards and tutors.

First, the word tuition comes from Latin *tueri* and *tuitus* (to look at, to look after, to watch over) and *tuitionem* (a looking after, a caring for, watching over, protection, guardianship). A *tutor* was a guardian or protector; e.g., a night watchman in a neighbourhood. *Tuition* was the money paid to a watchman or guardian for protection. From these Latin roots, the word tuition (protection, care, custody) came to English in the early 15th century via 13th century Anglo-French *tuycioun* and Old French *tuicion* (guardianship).

The word intuition is formed by adding the prefix *en-* (from PIE; in at) to Latin *tueri* to make Latin *entueri* (to look inward, to consider). From this, come the later Latin nouns *intuitionem* and *intuitio* (a looking at, a consideration). By the mid-15th century the word *intuicioun* (insight, direct or immediate cognition, spiritual perception) is first seen in English and later written as intuition. Perhaps intuition could be considered as one's inner security guard or inner tutor!

The word tutor (guardian, custodian) comes to English in the late 14th century from Latin via 13th century Old French *tuteor* (guardian—like a 19th century governess or later, a nanny), private teacher). The sense of tutor as a "senior boy appointed to help a junior in his studies" is recorded from 1680s.[150] Tuition, meaning the meaning money paid for instruction (1828) probably is short for *tuition fees*.

Tutoring, meaning the action or business of teaching students, is from 1580s. The verb 'to tutor' (to teach) is first seen in 1592. As the swirling controversies of the 16th century Reformation and Counter-Reformation unfolded, tutoring as guarding had became more and more to mean the specific guarding or taking care of a student's education and upbringing. A tutor guarded and guided education so that the right things were learned in the right way in order that the student didn't get sidetracked or off track in their learning and inner life.[151]

---

150   https://www.etymonline.com/word/tutor

151   What might explain this shift to teaching as guarding as the 16th century ended and the

So, in sum, when we say that we trust our intuitions, we are saying that we trust some inner watchman or guardian or inner voice. Originally, a tutor was a teacher who guarded a student's education. Today, perhaps, the various roles of a tutor can also be seen through metaphors such as guide, coach, Sherpa, or shepherd.

Jehovah

Consider how often you come across acronyms in daily life. An acronym is a word formed by taking the first letters of each word in a phrase in order to make a shorthand version of these words. Some common examples of acronyms include NATO (North Atlantic Treaty Organization), scuba (self-contained underwater breathing apparatus), SWAT (Special Weapons and Tactics), AIDS (Acquired Immune Deficiency Syndrome), radar (radio detecting and ranging), and so on.

17th began? The 16th century marked the beginning of the 'Age of Discovery' for the English and other Europeans. Explorers, merchants, political and religious dissidents, conquistadores, and other adventurers set off from Europe in order to expand their knowledge, their wealth, and their control over the rest of the world. Also, the 16th century marked the beginning of the Reformation and an explosion of Protestant denominations and sects; e.g., the Amish, Anabaptists, Anglicans, Anti-Trinitarians, Barrowists, Bohemian Brethren, Brownists, Calvinists, Christian humanists (e.g., Erasmus), Congregationalists, Familists (Family of Love), Freewillers (New Fryelers), Huguenots, Hutterites, Lutherans, Mennonites, Presbyterians, Puritans (Conformists), Puritans (Precisionists), and Socinians. Also, during this time began the witchcraze in which thousands were tortured and burned over a one hundred and fifty year period.

By the 17th century, we also see the Adamites, Baptists (i.e., English Separatists; those who split from the German and Dutch Anabaptists), Behmenists, Children of Light, Diggers (True Levellers), Erastians, Fifth Monarchists, General Baptists (Arminian Baptists), Grindletonians, Independents, Jacobites, Levellers, Muggletonians (the last Muggletonian, Phillip Noakes, died in 1979), Particular Baptists (Dippers), Quakers, Ranters, Reevonians, Reformed Puritans, Seekers (Legatine-Arians), Seventh Day Baptists (Sabbatarianists). This was the period of the English civil war, the Roman Catholic Counter-Reformation, religious wars between Catholics and Protestants, Galileo, Isaac Newton, Rembrandt, and the establishment of Harvard University.

Good grief! I think I need a tutor to keep all this straight. Perhaps it's no wonder that the verb 'to tutor' came into being during such times.

The word Jehovah comes from Hebrew YHWH, a set of letters used in early versions of the Bible to represent the principal and personal name of God. The actual name was considered too sacred to utter or write in full. Between the 6th and 10th centuries CE Jewish scholars (the Masoretes) substituted the name Adhonai for this ineffable name representing YHWH.

In 1516, European students of Hebrew transliterated YHWH as Latin *JeHoVa*. The word Jehovah came to English in 1530 in William Tyndale's transliteration of Hebrew YHWH. YHWH was vocalized as Yahweh.[152]

The Hebrew word *Jah*, from the 1530s, is a short form of Jehovah.[153] *Jah* is seen in words such as hallelujah and Elijah. See HALLELUJAH.

In 1869 scholars proposed that YHWH came from the Hebrew verb *hawah* or *hayah* (was, is; i.e., in the sense of 'the one who is, the existing').

The name *Jehovah's Witnesses* (members of Watchtower Bible and Tract Society) is first attested 1933. The organization was founded around 1879 by Charles Taze Russell (1852-1916).

Jesus Christ

Jesus

The word Jesus is the Latin and then English translation of Hebrew *Yehoshua*, later *Yeshua*, (now *Joshua*, meaning 'the Lord, or Jehovah, is salvation') and the related Aramaic *Jeshua*.

Early church documents were written in Greek. The word Jesus was written as *Ihsous*, a word which captures the meaning of Hebrew Yeshua but not the pronunciation. In speech, Jesus was pronounced as *Iesous* (the same pronunciation as Hebrew Yeshua, but without the same meaning— *Iesous* in Greek means healer[154]). *Ihsous* was abbreviated as IHS; *Iesous* was abbreviated as IES. By the 8th century CE, the abbreviation IHS[155] was

---

152   https://www.etymonline.com/search?q=jehovah

153   Sort of like using Bill as a short form of William or using Bob instead of Robert.

154   See 'Christ' below for a description of the relationship of Old English *haeland* as healer to the words savior and Christ. Also: the English name Jason comes from variations of Greek Iesous.

155   Some sources suggest that IHC may be the source of the 'H' in the slang phrase *Jesus H.*

first seen on vestments and stonework inscriptions—a christogram which is still familiar and in use today.

In the 4th century CE, St Jerome amalgamated various versions of the Bible into a standard Latin Bible (the Vulgate, or 'common', Bible) in which *Iesus* was used for Jesus.[156] For almost 1,000 years, the Vulgate was the official Bible of the Roman Catholic church.

During the medieval period, people could and did lose their lives for translating the Vulgate Bible into other languages. For example, John Wycliffe, declared a heretic after his death, used both *Jhesus* and *Jhesu* in his late 14th century translation of the Bible into English. William Tyndale used *Jesu* in his 16th century English translation of the Bible. He was executed by strangulation for his efforts. The original King James Version of the Bible (1611) used *Iesus*; however, subsequent versions used Jesus, the first use of this form of the word in English. *Jesu* continued to be used in English, especially in hymns.

Christ

The title of Christ given to Jesus of Nazareth comes from Greek *khristos* (the anointed; from Greek *khrein* meaning to rub, to anoint) which is a translation of Hebrew *mashiah*[157] (the anointed, of the Lord). From *khris-*

Christ, first seen in 1924. Sounds to me like a slang phrase coined by scholars.

156   *Iesous* came to Latin as IESVS (in the years of the early Christian church, the Roman alphabet contained only capital letters). Lower case letters of the Roman alphabet did not appear until around 800 CE. At that time in the evolution of written Latin, 'u' replaced 'v' and 'j' was created to distinguish the consonant sound from the vowel sound of 'i'. So, Latin *IESVS* gradually evolved into *Jesu, Jesum*, and *Jesus. Iesu* was used in English from the 12th until the 17th century. The use of 'J' to replace 'I' in Latin and in 16th century French did not come to English until the 17th century after which the name Jesus began to be well-established.

In brief, as language and alphabets evolved, scholars and translators worked not only to find the best Latin and, later, vernacular translations of the original Aramaic and Hebrew words but also how to represent the pronunciation of these words.

157   Hebrew *mashiah*, related to Aramaic *meshiha*, is the origin of Greek *messias* and Latin *messias* from which the English word messiah, first seen around 1300 CE, is derived. Even though the early Greek translation of *mashiah* was *khristos*, in Reformation translations of the Bible (e.g., the Geneva Bible of 1560) the word messiah (rather than Christ) was used from which we have our current English form and meaning of the word. The sense of a messiah as a liberator of captive people is attested from the 1660s.

tos comes the Latin *Christus* and the Old English *crist* (from either 675 or 830 CE, according to various sources).

Until the late 12th century in Anglo-Saxon England, Jesus was known by the Old English term *haeland* (healer, savior; i.e., Jesus the healer or savior). Gradually, however, *haeland* was replaced by *khristos* and *crist* (the anointed) which became the preferred descriptive term for Jesus (i.e., Jesus the Christ or, simply, Jesus Christ). Interestingly, this shift in descriptors reflects a shift from describing the actions of Jesus (the healer or savior) to an attribute of Jesus (the anointed).[158]

The pronunciation of Christ with a long 'i' which replaced the short 'i' of Old English *crist* is a result of Irish missionary work in England in the 7th and 8th centuries. The 'ch' of Christ has been used since the 16th century. Capitalization of Christ begins in the 14th century but was not fixed until the 17th century.

The use of the term Christ as an oath is first seen in the late 14th century. The term Christology (the study of Christ) comes from the 1670s. The adjective Christ-like is also from the 1670s.

Jot & Tittle

When was the last time you used the word 'tittle' in a sentence or in speech? You likely use the word 'jot' much more often. Perhaps the only time that many of us see or hear the word 'tittle' is in the KJV, Matthew

---

158   "Words from the original language can be borrowed as religious technical terms into a vernacular, and we have seen many examples, for one religion or another; but the vernacular, with its different hinterland of associations, is capable of illuminating them in various lights. It took Syriac to make Christ a *hmayra*—a hostage human body, offered to God; Saxon to make him *werodes drohtin*—leader of a war band; Nahuatl *toteu-tonatiuh*—our lord the Sun.

Not all those with a religious faith value metaphor: some demand a straight statement of the supernatural from their scripture: some damn all images verbal or figurative. Some such fundamentalists can be found attached to every one of these missionary faiths. Yet ultimately, every religious tradition is far wider, and deeper, and more encompassing of human life. And the human instinct for worship finds people of every persuasion to take up different stances within a broad faith. All human life may be here, somewhere."

Ostler, 2016, 294.

5:18, a reference to something very small but still important in the grand scheme of things.

The phrase 'jot and tittle' provides an interesting example of how something very small can have enormous consequences.

To begin, do you ever worry about ensuring correct spelling when you write? Have you ever considered the consequences of a spelling error? Generally, nothing drastic will happen if you misspell a word. If fact, we often get a chuckle out of other people's spelling errors! Enter 'funny spelling mistakes' into your search engine and you'll see lots of examples.

When thinking about the impact of a spelling error, consider for a moment the vowel 'i'. Originally called a 'jot' (first seen in English in 1500), 'i' has its origins in the ancient Greek word *iota* and in the ancient Hebrew word *yodh*. The word iota, first seen in English in 1542, means a very *very* small amount of something (when we say we're going to 'jot a note', we usually mean a short note in contrast to when we say we're going to 'write a letter' or 'write an essay'). And that little dot at the top of an 'i' is called a tittle, a word first seen in English in the 14th century.

But I digress. I was talking about the impact of spelling errors and the vowel 'i'. The humble jot or *iota* was at the centre of a major controversy at the first ecumenical council of the Christian Church at Nicaea (325 CE) set up to establish consensus among various versions and doctrines of Christianity existing at that time. (Among other things, outcomes of the Council included the Nicene Creed and an agreement on a formula for when Easter would be held each year.)

A major item on the Council agenda was the controversy regarding the doctrine of the nature of the relationship between God and Christ. Many sects held competing views. In particular, the Arians and the Athanasians, each claiming to represent the orthodox view and accusing the other of heresy, had been arguing and fighting (literally) with each other for years.

In brief, the debate was between advocates of the doctrine of "*homoiousias*" and advocates of the doctrine of "*homoousias*." For those of you still reading (!), the Arians believed that Christ was *homoiousias* (of like substance) with God; i.e., Christ was *like* God but *not* the same nature or substance as God. On the other hand, the Athanasians believed that Christ was *homoousias* (of the same nature) as God; i.e., that Christ was *equal* in essence with God, of the *same* substance, and thus that Christ was God. Eventually a vote was taken and the Athanasians won.

By the way, did you catch the difference between these two terms, *homoiousias* and *homoousias*? Look again... you'll see that the humble jot or *iota* is the only difference.

Justice, Mercy

Justice

The word 'just' has its origins in PIE *yewes* (law), a word used in ancient religious practices that perhaps meant 'to make ritually pure'. From PIE *yewes* comes Latin *ious* (sacred formula). Latin *ious* leads to other Latin terms: *lex* (law, especially specific laws rather than a general body of law)[159], *ius* (right, legal right, law), and *iustus* (upright, equitable, just). From these Latin roots we see the 12th century Old French *juste* (just, righteous, sincere), and in the late 14th century we see the English word just (righteous in the eyes of God, upright, equitable, impartial, justifiable, reasonable). The noun 'just' meaning 'a righteous person or persons' is from late 14c.

The word 'justice' comes from Latin *iustus* and Latin *iustitia* (righteousness, equity) and from 11th century Old French *justice* (justice, legal rights, jurisdiction). The Old French word was used in many different senses including uprightness, equity, vindication of right, court of justice, and judge. By mid-12th century the word justice had come to English meaning 'the exercise of authority in vindication of right by assigning reward or punishment' and 'the quality of being fair and just'.

By around 1200 the word 'justice' was being used as a title for a judicial officer. 'Justice of the peace' comes from early 14th century. Justice meaning 'right order, equity' is also from the late 14th century. The expressions 'to do justice to someone or something' and 'to render fully and fairly showing due appreciation' are from 1670s.

---

159   Lex is a word still used in English legal terminology.

Mercy

The origins of the word mercy are unknown. One suggestion is that mercy comes from the Etruscan word *merk* referring to various aspects of marketplace economics (Etruscan is an extinct pre-Latin language of ancient Italy).

In any case, the mercy clearly has its roots in Latin *merx* (wares, merchandise), a word which is also the root of *mercatus* (trading, buying and selling, trade, market) and, much later, the English word market. *Merx* is also the root of the Latin words *mercedem* and *merces* (reward, payment, wages, pay for hire).

In the Latin of the 4th century Vulgate Bible, *merx* was used to mean favor or pity. In the Latin of the 6th century church, *merx* was used to describe the heavenly reward for those who show kindness to the helpless. In this mercantile context, mercy was a transaction: you give something to get something.

By the 9th century Latin *mercedem* had come to Old French as *mercit* and *merci* (compassion, forbearance from punishment; also, reward, gift, kindness, grace, pity).[160] By the late 12th century, mercy had come to English, meaning 'God's forgiveness of offences'. Mercy, meaning 'disposition to forgive or show compassion' is from the early 13th century.

Given such origins, it would seem that mercy can be seen as a reward or as a mutual exchange of something of value as well as an appropriate action under a set of given circumstances.

Considering such market forces, mercy can be seen as an act of generosity. Just as someone can easily be generous with their goods or money when he or she has an abundance of resources so also for a person to show mercy to another indicates not just a willingness but an abundant inner capacity for mercy. We can choose mercy for selfish or altruistic reasons (i.e., I get something in exchange for showing mercy) and for moral reasons (i.e., showing mercy is the right thing to do). In either case, mercy has been shown to another.

---

160   And, in French, *merci* means thank you—perhaps from "Thank you for showing mercy"? Or, perhaps, from "Have mercy on me—for which I will thank you"??

In brief, justice is about the application of general codes of law or the accumulation of various precedents in common law in relation to behaviors which are 'against the law'. Mercy is both generosity to the poor or downtrodden and forgiveness for offenders. Mercy is the result of an individual decision based on specific circumstances.

Justify, Justification

Justify

The verb justify combines Latin *justus* (just) and *justificus* (dealing justly, righteous) and Latin *facere* (to make, to do; from PIE *dhe* to set, to put). The English word justify, from around 1300, meaning to administer justice, and from the late 14th century, meaning to show something to be just or right, come from Latin via 12th century Old Fench *justifier* (to submit to court proceedings). Justify, meaning to declare to be innocent or blameless is from the 1520s; or, considering the circumstance, justify meaning to afford justification is from the 1630s.

The use of justify (to make exact), used in typesetting, is from the 1550s. The use of justification in typesetting to mean adjusting or making exact, is from the 1670s.

See also JUSTICE.

Justification

The noun justification, as the administration of justice, comes to English in the late 14th century from Latin *justificationem, justificare* (to act justly toward, to make just, to justify). Justification, meaning the action of justifying, showing something to be just or right, is from the late 15th century. Justification in the theological sense as an act by which the soul is reconciled to God is from the 1520s.

Questions of who justifies or how something or someone comes to a state of justification, not to mention the theological distinctions between justification and sanctification, have been under discussion for centuries.

What does seem to be commonly understood is that a people cannot easily justify themselves, if at all!

King, kingdom

King

In its origins, the word king is related to several words including gendarme, gender, gene, genealogy, general, generation, generic, genesis, genetics, genitals, genius, genre, genuine, indigenous, and progeny. All these words are rooted in the prolific PIE word *gene* (to produce, to beget, to give birth) and Latin *genus* (race, stock, kind; family, birth, descent, origin).

The Old English word *cyning*[161] (king or ruler) comes from PIE *gene* through the Proto-Germanic *kuningaz* which can mean 'a leader of the people' or 'of noble birth' or 'someone descended from noble birth'. These meanings and implications of *kuningaz* are uncertain and the subject of much debate (related words include Dutch *koning*, Old Norse *konungar*, Danish *konge*, Old Saxon and Old High German *kuning*, and German *konig*).

In Old English, the word *cyning* was used during the so-called Dark Ages as a title for the Germanic chiefs of tribes or clans in what is now England and later used to name the British and Danish chiefs, also in what is now England. Eventually the word *cyning* became the word king.[162]

---

161   Some suggest that Old English *cyning* is related to Old English *cynn* (family; race; kind, sort, rank; nature; gender, sex), the origin of the words kin and kinship. Old English *cynn* comes from Proto-Germanic *kunjam* (family) and related words such as Old Frisian *kenn*, Old Saxon *kunni*, Old Norse *kyn*, and German *kind* (child).

162   The Latin word for king is *rex* from PIE *reg* (to rule, to lead straight, to put right), a word related to many other words among which are Sanskrit *raj* (king) and Old Irish *ri* (king). Latin *regere* (to keep straight, guide, lead, rule), from PIE *reg*, is related to Latin *regalis* (royal, kingly) and 12th century Old French *regal* (royal). The word regal came to English in the late 14th century.

PIE *reg* also leads to the word ruler which not only means someone who rules but also a device for measuring and drawing (or ruling) straight lines. Most of us had a short ruler in our school geometry kits when we were kids.

The word king, as the name of a chess piece, is from the early 15th century. The 'king' playing card is from 1560s. The use of a king in checkers is first recorded in 1820.

Kingdom

The Old English word for kingdom was *cyningdom* and then *cynedom*. Where does the -dom at the end of kingdom come from? From PIE *dhe* (to set, place, put, do) and Proto-Germanic *domaz* (judgment, decree). From these ancient terms comes Old English *dom*[163] (statute, judgment, condemnation, doom[164]). A book of laws in Old English was a *dombec*[165] (i.e., a 'doom book').

The word kingdom used to refer to one of the realms of nature (e.g., the animal kingdom) is from the 1690s. The term kingdom-come, as in the Lord's Prayer, meaning 'the next world' is from 1785.

Lent

The word 'Lent' comes from an ancient compound of words meaning 'long days'; in particular, the days which get longer as spring arrives. The word

---

163   The suffix -dom refers to an abstract state or idea of something; i.e., a kingdom is a judgment or decision about territory as much as it is about the territory itself. Similarly, the words 'freedom' (Old English *freodom*) or 'wisdom' are descriptions of states or attributes of being in which persons are judged or who judge themselves as 'free' or 'wise'.

For example, free + dom is a state or condition based on the judgment or law or statute in which freedom is given. That is, freedom does not exist in isolation—it is not automatic. It exists in relation to or in the context of participation in and obedience to the political laws and cultural norms of the land. Could we say, tongue in cheek, that not only are we called to freedom but we are also condemned (condoomed?) to freedom?!

164   The modern sense of doom as 'fate, ruin, destruction' is from around 1600 and relates to the finality of the Christian Judgement Day.

165   The 'Domesday Book' (sometimes pronounced as 'doomsday') of 1086 was an inventory or compilation of land ownership decisions and judgments created by William the Conqueror after his conquest of what is now England in 1066. A 16th century writer, William Lambarde, wrote that the book was called Domesday because "it spared no man, but judged all men indifferently".

Lent has its origins in Proto-Germanic *langaz* (long) and *tina* (day). Other 'day' words from this period include Gothic *sin-teins* (daily), Slavonic *dini*, Lithuanian *diena*, Latin *dies* (from PIE *dyeu*, to shine).

From these origins related to 'long days', we also see West Germanic *langitinaz* (the lengthening of the day) which is the source of Old Saxon *lentin*, Middle Dutch *lenten*, and Old High German *lengizin manoth*. And from these emerges Old English *lencten* (springtime, spring).

Lent, in pre-Christian times, meant the coming of spring.

In the Christian calendar, Lent is the forty-day period between Ash Wednesday and Easter. In the early 12th century, these forty days before Easter were known as Lenten which was shortened to Lent in the late 14th century.

Lent, traditionally a time for fasting and the giving up or avoidance of luxury before Easter, symbolizes the forty-day sojourn of Jesus in the desert and his resistance during this period to the temptations of the world. Fasting during Lent, a symbolic act by which Christians could participate ritually in the life of Jesus, was also a way to create and give meaning to the reality of fasting experienced by many people (particularly in northern Europe) as food began to run short during late winter and early spring. Fasting became a common ritual act in which all in the community participated regardless of whether they had food or not.

Life

The word life remains unchanged from Old English *life* (the period between birth and death; the history of an individual). The word life comes from the Proto-Germanic *libam* (continuance, perseverance) and from PIE *leip* (to stick, to adhere).

The word afterlife comes from the 1590s.

Litany

The word litany, first seen in English in the 13th century, means a solemn prayer of supplication. A litany is defined as a list of supplications, often repeated, and led by someone in a call and response liturgical format.

Litany comes from Old French *litanie*, Latin *litania*, and Greek *litaneia*, all meaning a prayer or an entreaty. Greek *litanos* is a supplicant.

You might wonder if the words litany, liturgy, and litigation are related. They don't appear to be. Each word has a different origin. Liturgy comes from Greek *leito* (public) and *laos* (people) + *ergos* (work); i.e., liturgy is the work of the people. Litigation comes from Latin *litigare*; i.e., *litem* (lawsuit) + *agere* (to drive); to litigate is to drive a lawsuit.

Liturgy

The word liturgy is rooted in Greek words for people and for work. In its origins, liturgy means the people's work.

Liturgy comes from combining Greek *laikos* (of the people), *laos* (people), and Greek *ergos* (that works), *ergon*[166] (work); i.e., *leitourgia* (literally, 'the work of the people').

Related Greek words include *leito* (public), *leiton* (public hall), and *leite* (priestess). In Greek, a *leitourgos* was a public servant or someone who performed a public ceremony.

The Greek word *leitourgia* (liturgy, public duty, ministration, ministry) is the root of Latin *liturgia* (public service, public worship), Middle French *liturgie*, and the English word liturgy.

In the 1550s the word liturgy referred to the service of the Holy Eucharist. By the 1590s, liturgy meant the formulas for conducting any of

---

166   *Ergon* is the root of ergonomics, the applied science concerned with working effectively and efficiently. Also: *Gaia* ('mother earth) is the origin of 'geo'. So, *geo* + *ergon* = George; i.e., 'earth worker' or 'farmer'!

the divine services of Christian churches. The adjective 'liturgical' comes from the 1640s. The word liturgist is from 1649.

Lord

Bread is pretty important, right? Bread has been called the staff of life. Would it surprise you to learn than the origins of the words lord and lady are related to bread?

During the centuries of the first millenium the language of Western European Christianity was Latin. During this time the Latin word for lord was *dominus* (to rule, dominate, govern). However, in what is now England, most common people did not speak Latin. At that time, the Old English word for a ruler, a feudal lord, or master of a household was *hlaford*.[167]

So, what's the connection between lord and bread?

When the OE word *hlaf* (bread or loaf) and the OE word *weard* (keeper, guardian) were combined, they became *hlafweard*; i.e., a guardian of the bread, the steward of the food supplies (a rather important job I would suspect in those days). From *hlafweard* came OE *hlaford* which by the mid-13th century had evolved to OE *loverd* which in turn became the modern English word lord.

Similarly, the OE *lafdi* or *lavede* (lady) comes from OE *hlaefdige* (mistress of a household, wife of a lord). The word *hlaefdige* means bread-kneader and comes from OE *hlafaeta* (household servant, loaf-eater). The word lady, as a woman of superior position in society, is from around 1200.

In brief, as modern English developed, especially during the time of translations of the Bible, the word lord rather than *dominus* was used.

Other developments related to the word lord include the 14th century verb 'to lord'; i.e., to exercise lordship, to play the lord, to domineer. Lord as an interjection (e.g., "Oh my Lord") also comes from the 14th century. Laird, as a surname (from mid-15th century), is a Scottish and northern

---

167   The PIE word for lord, *poti* (lord, powerful), is the origin of words such as potent (powerful, effective) and possible (that can be done, to be able, having an indicated potential).

English variant of lord. The phrase 'Lord's prayer' is first seen in English in the 1540s. To lord it over someone comes from the 1570s.

See also MASS, Lammas Day.

Love

Love is an ancient word and has changed little since its origins in PIE *leubh*[168] (to care, desire, love) and Proto-Germanic *lubo* (love) and *lubojan* (to love).

Other words related to these roots of love include Old High German *liubi* (joy), German *liebe* (love), Old Norse, Old Frisian, Dutch *lof*, German *lob* (praise), and Old Saxon *liof*, Old Frisian *liaf*, Dutch *lief*, Old High German *liob*, German *lieb*, Gothic *liufs* (all meaning dear, beloved).

Love came to Old English as the verb *lufian* (to love, cherish, show love to; delight in, approve) and the noun *lufu* (love, affection, friendliness).

English has one word for love in all its expressions; however, in the ancient world there were several Greek words describing various expressions and forms of love including *agape* (love of, or care for, everyone; in Latin, *caritas*), *eros* (sexual love)[169], *ludus* (playful love), *philautia* (love of self), *philia* (deep friendship), *pragma* (longstanding love), and *storge* (love that family members have for one another).

Love, meaning a beloved person, is from the early 13th century. Love letter is attested from the mid-13th century. Long song is from the early 14th century. 'To fall in love' is attested from the early 15th century. To be in love with someone is from around 1500. To make love (in the sense of to pay amorous attention to) is from the 1570s. Love affair is from the 1590s. Love seat is from 1904. Love life (one's collective amorous activities; from psychological jargon) is from 1919. The psychological term love-hate

---

168 PIE *leubh* is also the root of the word belief; i.e., to love something intensely.

169 In Latin, the word for erotic or sexual love is *venereae* (from which we get the term 'venereal disease'): How romantic. Also, the Latin name of the Greek god Eros is Cupid: compare the god Eros (one of the oldest of the Greek gods, but always portrayed as a virile young man) with the cutesy infantile Cupids with their bows and arrows that you see on Valentine's Day cards. Seems like something got lost in the translation from Greek to Roman mythology.

relationship is from 1937. To make love as a euphemism to have sex is from around 1950.

Mass

The word mass, now meaning a eucharistic service, comes from Latin *missa* (dismissal) and *mittere* (mission). The word mass likely comes from the Latin words of blessing at the conclusion of a church service; i.e., the Dismissal, "*Ite, missa est*" ("Go, the prayer has been sent" or "Go, you are dismissed"). In Old English, this dismissal was sometimes known as the *sendnes* (send-ness, the state of being sent out).

In this context, the word mass seems as much or more about being sent *out* from church to do the church's mission as it is to be *in* church at a particular service (see also MISSION, MISSIONARY).

Lammas Day

Speaking of masses, have you ever wondered about the long weekend holiday that falls on the first weekend in August? When I was a child, this was called the Bank Holiday long weekend'. I now live in British Columbia where this holiday is known as BC Day.

In its origins, this holiday was known as Lammas Day, a harvest festival that fell sometime in August. Lammas comes from Old English *hlafmaesse* (loaf-mass); i.e., a mass that was celebrated using the first bread made from the summer wheat harvest.

Also, the word *hlaf* (loaf) is the root of *hlafweard* (one who guards the loaves)—the root of the word lord (see LORD). Also, *hlaf* is related to the word 'lady' (from ancient words for bread-kneader) and Old English *hlafaeta* (household servant; literally, a loaf-eater).

Meditation

Did you know that the words meditation and medicine come from the same root word? Both come from PIE *med* (to measure, limit, consider, advise, to take appropriate measures).

From PIE *med* comes Greek *medesthai* (to think about) and *medomai* (to be mindful of) as well as Latin *modus* (measure, manner), *modestus* (modest), *modernus* (modern), *mederi* (to know the best course for, to heal, give medical attention to, to cure)[170], and *medicus* (physician). From PIE *med* we also see the Sanskrit *midiur* (I judge, estimate), Welsh *meddwl* (mind, thinking), and Old English *metan* (to measure), as in the phrases 'to mete out' or 'to dole out'.

More specifically, PIE *med* leads to Latin *meditari* (to meditate, to think over, reflect, consider). Latin *meditationem* and *meditatio* (a thinking over, a meditation) lead to Old French *meditacion* (thought, reflection, study) and to English around 1200 as meditation (used generically at that time to mean devout preoccupation, contemplation, devotions, prayer).[171]

The medieval use of Latin *meditari* (meaning, to meditate) meant to plan, devise, practice, rehearse, study. The English word meditation, meaning discourse on a subject, is from the early 14th century. Meditation, meaning the act of meditating, continuous calm thought on a subject, is from the late 14th century. The English verb 'to meditate', meaning 'to ponder', comes from the 1580s.

---

170   Latin *mederi* is the root of medical and medicine.

171   So how are meditation, contemplation, and prayer different? What might the origins of these three words tell us?

Meditation, in its origins, seems to be about thoughtfulness, mindfulness, study, and reflection. Prayer, in its origins, seems to be about speaking with intention, perhaps on the other side of meditation, with in the anticipation of some expected action or outcome. Contemplation, in its origins, seems to be about being present in a (sacred) space and time that is intentionally set apart from daily activity. Contemplation may include ritual action without necessarily any focus on particular thought or action.

Messiah

The word messiah has its origins in Aramaic *meshiba* and Hebrew *mashiah* (the anointed of the Lord, the anointed king), from *mashah* (to anoint). Similarly, the Arabic word for messiah is *al-masih* (the anointed, the traveller, the one who cures by caressing).

In the early church's Greek translations of Hebrew scriptures, the word *khristos* (see CHRIST) was used when referring to *mashiah*.

The word messiah came to English in around 1300. The use of messiah in the 1560 Geneva Bible reflects the desire to highlight the Hebrew rather than Greek origins of the word.

In the Old Testament, the word messiah was used to describe the expected deliverer of the Jewish nation. The use of messiah in English to mean an expected liberator or savior of (any) captive people is attested from the 1660s.

The adjective messianic dates from 1831, from Latin *messianicus*.

Minister

What's the difference between a minister and a priest? Generally speaking, the word minister is a broad term meaning to render aid or service whereas words like priest, pastor, deacon, bishop and so on refer to more specific roles and responsibilities. Traditionally, the term minister was used in more 'low church' or 'Protestant' Christian denominations whereas priest was used in more 'high church' or 'Anglo-Catholic' settings. Today, however, such terms can be used interchangeably.[172]

The word minister has its earliest origins in words related to small, minor, minus, and to lessen. Later origins of the word are related to serving and service. We can see the 'mini' in minister.

The earliest root of minister is PIE *mei* (small). From this source come the Latin words *minor* (smaller) and *minus* (less), the roots of the English words minus and diminish which appear in the 15th century.

---

172   https://www.anglican.ca/ask/faq/minister-or-priest/

From these roots come the Latin verb *ministrare* (to serve, attend, wait upon) and the Old French *menistrer* (to serve, to be of service, administer, attend, wait on). Perhaps, in this context, to minister is to perform a small or routine everyday service for someone.

In the early 14ᵗʰ century, *menistrer* came to English as the verb 'to minister'; that is, to provide religious service, to perform religious rites. At this time, we see the first use of minister to mean the work or functions as synonymous with the work or functions of a priest.

Later, in the mid-14ᵗʰ century, the English verb minister was also used to mean 'to serve food or drink' and by the end of the 14ᵗʰ century the English word minister was also being used to mean 'to render service or aid'. Both uses come to English from Latin through Old French.

The use of the term minister as a noun (i.e., a person who ministers) also comes from the 14ᵗʰ century. The noun minister is rooted in the Latin *minister* (inferior, servant, priest's assistant—from sense of being subordinate). The related Old French *menistre* meant servant, valet, member of household staff, administrator, musician, or minstrel. The nouns administration and administrator and the verb 'to administer' also come from this period.

The word ministry comes from the Old French *menistere* (service, ministry; position, post, employment) and from Latin *ministerium* (office, service, attendance, ministry).

The use of minister to mean a high officer of the state (i.e., being of service to the Crown) is from the 1620s. Only in 1916 was the term ministry used to name certain departments in the British government.

Miracle

Have you smiled lately? Have you noticed that smiles most often come to us unbidden and unheralded? Something happens and we smile. We see someone smiling and we smile, almost involuntarily. Smiles are infectious. Smiles are little everyday affirmations of life. Consider the state of the human condition without smiles.

A smile is a miracle. Literally.

In its origins the word miracle comes from PIE *smei* (to smile, to laugh). PIE *smei* is related to Sanskrit *smerah* (smiling) and Greek *meidan* (to smile). From these beginnings we have the Latin *smeiros* and *mirus* (wonderful, amazing, astonishing), *mirari* (to wonder at, to marvel, to be astonished; also, to regard, to esteem), and *miraculum* (object of wonder). In the Latin of the early Church, *miraculum* was used to mean a marvellous event caused by God.

The Old English word miracle, from the 12th century, meaning a wondrous work of God, comes from the 11th century Old French *miracle* (miracle, story of a miracle, miracle play) which in turn is from the Latin *miraculum*. The Spanish *milagro* and Italian *miracolo* also come from Latin miraculum.

By the mid-13th century, the word miracle began to be used to mean any extraordinary or remarkable feat without any necessary reference to a deity.

In the 4th century Vulgate Bible, the Greek words *semeion* (sign), *teras* (wonder), and *dynamis* (power) were translated respectively into the Latin words *signum*, *prodigium*, and *virtus*. When the Bible was translated from Greek to English during the Renaissance and Reformation, the word miracle was used for each of these three Greek words.

So, could we conclude by saying that a smile is not only a miracle, but also a sign of wonder and power. Smiles, like miracles, can change things.

Mission, Missionary

The word mission comes from Latin *mittere* (to send). Its pre-Latin origins are unknown. From *mittere* comes Latin *missio* and *missionem*, words which have a number of meanings: the act of sending, a dispatching; a release, a setting at liberty; discharge from service, dismissal.

The notion of a mission as 'a sending abroad' comes from Jesuit activity in the 1590s. The notion of a mission as a sending of people to other countries for political and/or economic purposes (e.g., a trade mission) comes from the 1620s. The use of mission to mean aircraft on a military operation comes from 1929. This sense of mission was also later used to describe spacecraft missions to earth orbit, to the moon, and beyond.

The term missionary, from Latin *missionarius*, usually in the context of a religious mission is from the 1625. The use of missionary as an adjective; e.g., "She was engaged in missionary activity" is from the 1640s.

This sense of mission and missionary was not used in the early church; i.e., the early church did not have 'missionaries' in the sense of the word as it is currently known and used. Rather, the Greek terms *euangelizesthai* (to bring good news), *euangelistes* (preacher of the gospel), and the Latin terms *evangelista* (evangelist) and *docere* (instruction of converts) were used.[173]

Many words have their origin in Latin *missio* and *missionem,* including admission, commission, dismiss, emission, intermission, manumission, mass (i.e., the eucharist), missile, missive, omission, remission, submission, and transmission.

Monk, Friar, Nun

Monk, Friar

The word monk has its origins in Greek *monos* (single, alone) and PIE *men–* (small, isolated). From these roots come the Greek word *monakhos* (monk, solitary) and Latin *monicus* and, later, Latin *monachus* (monk; originally religious hermit). Proto-Germanic *muniko*, from Latin *monicus*, is the origin of Old Frisian *munek*, Middle Dutch *monic*, Old High German *munih*, German *monch*, and Old English *munuc* (used to refer both to men and women). Old English *munuc* evolved to monk.

---

173   "But given the prevalence of persecution in the history of the early church, it is usually believed now that the main channel of new conversions was not the conscious seeking-out of converts, which would have endangered both preacher and proselyte, but a process of conversion by association through networks of friends and relations."

Ostler, N. (2016). *Passwords to Paradise: How languages have re-invented world religions.* New York: Bloomsbury, 124 – 125, referencing R. Stark. (1996). *The rise of Christianity.* Princeton, NJ: Princeton. Also: Stark (1997).

The late 13th century word friar is from Old French *frere* (brother), Latin *frater* (brother) and PIE *bhrater* (brother).[174]

Monks are not the same as friars (e.g., Friar Tuck of the Robin Hood legends). Monks are members of religious communities; e.g., the Benedictines and Cistercians. In contrast, friars are members of mendicant (begging) and wandering religious orders (e.g., the Franciscans).

Nun

The word nun comes from Old English *nunne* (nun, vestal, pagan priestess, woman devoted to religious life under vows) and Latin *nonna* (nun, tutor).

Latin *nonna* (feminine) and *nonnus* (masculine) were first used, particularly by children, as terms of respect for elderly persons. Similar words include Sanskrit *nona*, Persian *nana* (mother), Greek *nanna* (aunt), Serbo-Croatian *nena* (mother), Italian *nonna* and Welsh *nain* (grandmother). From such words comes the word nanny.

Mystic, Mysticism

Would it surprise you to learn that the origins of the word mystic can be traced back to the Sanskrit word *mukah* (dumb, mute)? Perhaps not. Perhaps to be a mystic is to be someone who is rendered speechless by the mysteries in life.

From Sanskrit *mukah* comes Latin *mutus* (silent, speechless) and the English word mute.

Also, from Sanskrit *mukah* comes the Greek words *muein*, *myein* (to close, to shut; in particular to close the eyes or lips).[175] From these beginnings comes Greek *mystes* (an initiated person) and *mystikos* (secret, a mystic) and Latin *mysticus* (mystical, of secret rites).

---

174   PIE *bhratar* (brother) is one of those words close to the heart which have come to English from PIE almost unchanged over the millenia. Bharat is also another name for India.

175   Greek *myein is also the root of myopia (near-sightedness).*

From Latin *mysticus* comes 14ᵗʰ century Old French *mistique* (mysterious, full of mystery) and later the English word mystique (a special quality that makes a person or thing interesting or exciting). And from *mysticus* come the words mystic (a practitioner of mysticism), first seen in the 1670s, and mysticism, first seen in 1736.

Returning to Greek *mystes*, we see that it is also related to Greek *mysterion* (secret rite, doctrine) and Latin *mysterium* (secret rite, secret worship, secret thing), words leading to Old French *mistere* (secret, mystery, hidden meaning) and the English word mystery.

Mysticism is beyond words. It seems more about feeling and affect. Perhaps to be a mystic is to be quietly present to life's mysteries rather than trying to explain them.

Numen, Noumenon, Noesis

I remember lying in bed as a child trying to imagine infinity. I would stretch my mind, like a rubber band, until I felt it was stretched as far as it would go and then I would say to myself, "Infinity is that much farther again, and more." At such moments, I would feel a frisson of awe.

Similarly, at other times, I would wonder, "How can God be everywhere?" At that time, I didn't know enough to have thoughts such as, "If God is everywhere, does that mean God is everything or in everything?" or "If God created everything, does that mean that God is outside of everything?" or "Does everywhere also mean that which is 'outside' of everywhere?" My mind boggles even now.

Similarly, years later, I learned that many ancient cultures struggled with understanding and expressing the concept of 'nothing'. Can nothing be something? If you only attend to your physical senses, there will always be 'something'. Can 'something' exist beyond the perception of these senses? How do you talk about the feeling that there is a 'something' there, but a something that is beyond sensation or description or explanation?

In mathematics, the numeral zero, 0 (from Arabic *sifr*, medieval Latin *zephirum*), was used in some ancient cultures (e.g., Mayan, pre-BCE Mesopotamia) to represent this sense of nothingness, and was used extensively in mid-5th century India. By the 8th century, the numeral zero was being used in China and in Middle Eastern Islamic universities. By the 11th century, zero and other so-called Arabic numerals had replaced Roman numerals as the basis of mathematics in Western Europe.

So, we can talk about nothing in mathematics using zero. How do we think or talk about experiences which are seemingly beyond 'something', experiences seemingly beyond our senses, experiences which seem beyond thought let alone beyond words? How do we talk about the feeling of being part of something larger than ourselves or a feeling of something inside ourselves that is perceived to be other than ourselves? For example, how do we talk of experiences of awe?

How do we keep or hold this sense of the ineffable or the 'other' in mind? Since ancient times people have reported such experiences, often perceived as divine or mystical, for which they seek or create words to describe and later explain.

Words such as numen, numenon and noesis name such experiences. Numen refers to the ineffable or the 'other' perceived as external to us. Numenon refers to the ineffable or the other perceived as within us. Noesis refers to a sense of knowing that is beyond feeling.[176]

Numen and numinous

Numen is defined as a spiritual force or influence often identified with a natural object, phenomenon, or place. Latin *numen* refers to the acknowledgement and affirmation of a divine presence, often perceived as a divine force of an object, place, or phenomenon that inspires awe (e.g., a grove of trees or the movement of the sun and moon (https://www.merriam-webster.com/dictionary/numen).

Numen, a noun, has its origins in PIE *neu* (to nod), Greek *neuein* (to nod), and Latin *neuein*, *nuere* (to nod) and Latin *numen* (divine will, divine

---

176   Could we say that words such as numen, noumenon, and noesis are to philosophy what the number zero is to mathematics? How do such words help us describe and explain nothingness or unknown-ness in the way that zero helps mathematicians?

approval expressed by nodding the head; divinity). *Numen*, literally, is a nod, a nod of acknowledgement or a nod of respect, an affirmation.[177]

Numen, meaning a divine spirit or presiding divinity, comes to English in the 1620s. The adjective numinous (divine, spiritual) comes to English in the 1640s from Latin *numen*. That is, numinous describes something that has spiritual or divine qualities.[178]

Noumenon and noesis

First, how does noumenon relate to the word phenomenon—a word which is likely more familiar to most than noumenon?

First, phenomenon comes from PIE *bha* (to shine), Greek *phainein* (to bring to light, cause to happen, to show), and Greek *phainomenon* (that which appears, that which is seen). A phenomenon is something perceived as outside of ourselves. The word phenomenon (an extraordinary occurrence) comes to English in 1771. The word phenomenology (the study of human consciousness and self-awareness; a looking at yourself from outside of yourself; e.g., "Why did I do that? What was I thinking?")[179] is from 1797.

In contrast, noumenon refers to something that is perceived as something that is 'in mind'; i.e., something in our mind that is perceived by our mind (perhaps the metaphor of 'hunch' or 'gut feeling' may apply). The word noumenon has uncertain origins; however, it is the source of Greek *noos* (mind) and Greek *noein* (to apprehend, to perceive by the mind rather than directly by the senses).[180]

---

177   "How did *numen,* a Latin term meaning "nod of the head," come to be associated with spiritual power? The answer lies in the fact that the ancient Romans saw divine force and power operating in the inanimate objects and nonhuman phenomena around them. They believed that the gods had the power to command events and to consent to actions, and the idea of a god nodding suggested his or her awesome abilities-divine power."
https://www.merriam-webster.com/dictionary/numen

178   Perhaps, just as something 'luminous' emits light, something 'numinous' emits spirit or a sense of the divine.

179   Phenomenology is the study of *how* objects are perceived by consciousness (not the objects themselves). Phenomenology is not so much a 'philosophy' or a doctrine as much as it is a way of thinking about something. https://en.wikipedia.org/wiki/Phenomenology_(philosophy)

180   *Noos* is not the same as psyche (breathe, soul), from PIE *bhes* (to blow, to breathe), Greek

The term noumenon was introduced from Greek by Immanuel Kant (1724 – 1804) in 1796, to refer to 'an object of intellectual intuition'. Kant used this term to identify objects or events that exist independent of human sense and perception; i.e., things which may exist but are unknowable; or, "a posited object or event that is known (if at all) without the use of the senses."[181]

The English word noesis (from 1820) comes from Greek *noesis* (intelligence, thought) and from Greek *noein* (to have mental perception), both from *noos* (mind, thought). The adjective noetic (pertaining to the intellect) comes from the 1650s from Greek *noetikos*.[182]

Noumenon and noesis come from the Greek words *noumenon* (that which is perceived) *and noein* (I think, I mean; to apprehend, perceive by

---

psykhein (to blow), and Greek *psykhe* and Latin *psyche* (the soul, mind, spirit; life, one's life, the invisible animating principle or entity which occupies and directs the physical body; understanding, the mind (as the seat of thought), faculty of reason. In Greek mythology, *psykhe* was personified as *Psykhē*, the beloved of Eros.

Also in ancient Greek *psykhe* refers to a departed soul, spirit, or ghost, and is often represented symbolically as a butterfly or moth. The word had extensive sense development in Platonic philosophy and Jewish-influenced theological writing of St. Paul. Psyche came to English in the 1640s meaning 'animating spirit' and in the 1650s meaning 'human soul.' In English, the psychological sense of "mind" is attested by 1910.
https://www.etymonline.com/word/psyche#etymonline_v_2788

181   https://en.wikipedia.org/wiki/Noumenon
Also, in classic Greek Platonic philosophy, the noumenal related to ideas known to the mind (or the intuition, or imagination?) and the phenomenal related to what could be known through the senses. Rational modern philosophy is now skeptical of such noumenal knowledge which is independent of the senses. Even though the noumenal world may exist, some say it is unknowable. Some even regret this distinction; e.g., "Nietzsche rejected the Kantian distinction between a noumenal and phenomenal world" (https://en.oxforddictionaries.com/definition/noumenal).

182   Borg defines noetic as "a vivid sense of knowing (and not just intense feelings...) -- a nonverbal, nonlinguistic way of knowing marked by a strong sense of seeing more clearly and certainly than one ever has. What is known is 'the way things are' when all of our language falls away and we see 'what is' without the domestication created by our words and categories ... [a direct way of knowing] not mediated through language." And, "...those have such experiences also insist that it is a *knowing*, and not just a feeling; it is a   noetic and not simply a subjective emotional state" (Borg, 2018, 31, 66).

the mind)[183] originate from the word Greek *nous* (perception, understanding, mind, thought).[184] The origins of *nous* are unknown.

In brief, numen relates to what and how the mind perceives of the world outside the body. Noumenon refers to what and how the mind perceives itself. Whether we experience what we would call the divine as an external or an internal force or being, we can do little but acknowledge such an ineffable experience with a nod without necessarily needing to or even being able to explain the experience.

Yet while the numinous is ineffable, beyond words of description or explanation, the numinous calls for 'noetic' responses—responses most effectively seen in the countless imaginative and artful expressions of music, images, dance, and, yes, even words.

Paradise

What do you think of when you think of paradise? Does an orchard or a vineyard or a storage space or a hunting park for aristocracy or a walled garden come to mind?

The word paradise comes from Greek *paradeisos* (meaning a Persian orchard or hunting park) which in turn comes from Avestan[185] *pairidaez* (a walled or enclosed garden). Greek *paradeisos* was used in early translations of the Old Testament in reference to the Garden of Eden and was also used in reference to heaven in early versions of the New Testament (e.g., Luke 23: 43).

Avestan *pairidaeza* is composed of *pairi* (around) and *diz* (to make or form a wall). Greek *paradeisos* is composed of *peri* (around) and PIE *dheigh*

---

183   "A rough equivalent in English would be 'something that is thought', or 'the object of an act of thought'". Wikipedia: https://en.wikipedia.org/wiki/Noumenon

184   A thought: Could we add noesis (of the mind) to the classic nature / nurture paradigm? Is it not the mind in self-reflection which discerns and considers both sides of this nature / nurture debate? Does not noesis play as much of a role in in the development of a self as nature and nurture? Just saying…

185   Avestan, a 15th century BCE language related to Persian, became the language used in Zoroastrian religious scriptures. Avestan is related to the ancient Vedic Sanskrit language of India.

(to form, to build). As an ancient Indo-European language, Avestan *diz* is likely also rooted in PIE *dheigh*.

Páradise, in reference to the Garden of Eden, came to English in the late 12ᵗʰ century from Old French *paradis* (paradise, Garden of Eden) which in turn comes from Latin *paradisus* and Greek *paradeisos*.

The more general sense of paradise as a beautiful, pleasant, or peaceful place that seems to be perfect comes from around 1300.

Parish, Diocese

Parish

The word parish comes from ancient words related to clan and neighbourhood.

In its origins, parish comes from PIE *weik* (clan)[186] which is also the origin of the Greek word *oikos* (house).[187] When you add Greek *para* (near) to *oikos* you get the Greek work *paroikos* (neighbour; that is, a person near your house). Early Christian writers used the word *paroikos* to mean sojourner; that is, a person who was just passing through the neighbourhood on their way to somewhere else (or spiritual sojourners passing through the physical world).

As early Christianity developed and expanded, the word *paroikos* evolved to Greek *paroikia* (diocese or parish) and Latin *parochia* (diocese). From this word emerges 11ᵗʰ century Old French *paroisse*. At this time parish and diocese were more or less synonymous. By the end of the 14ᵗʰ century, the words parish and diocese had differentiated. A diocese was an area containing several churches or parishes governed by a bishop.

By around 1300 we see the English word parish which gradually replaced the Old English word *preostscyr* (priest-shire). At this time a

---

186   PIE *weik* is also the origin of words such as *villa, village,* and *villain.*

187   Greek *oikos* is also the root the word ecumenical, from the Greek *oikoumene* (the inhabited world).

parish meant both a district with its own church and the members of such a church.

The adjective parochial (pertaining to a parish) is seen in the late 14th century. By the mid-15th century we see the word parishioner (from Old English *parishen*). The term parochial school is seen from 1755. The use of parochial to mean limited or narrow or confined to a small region is from 1856. Parochialism meaning a narrowness of character or tendency to be limited to only those things which affect your local area is from 1847.

Diocese

The word diocese, meaning the district and population under the pastoral care of a bishop, comes to English in the mid-14th century from Old French *diocese* and Latin *diocesis* (a province of the Roman Empire under the jurisdiction of a governor). The Greek word *dioikesis* (government, administration; originally, economy, housekeeping) comes from *dioikein* (to control, govern, administer, manage a house), from *dia* (thoroughly) + *oikos* (house) and from PIE *weik* (clan).

An archdiocese, from 1762, is the seat of an archbishop, from *arch-* (chief) + diocese.

Parson, Pastor

Parson

Parson comes to English in the late 12th century from Old French *persone* (curate, parson, holder of church office) and Latin *persona*[188] (person, human being, personage, a part in a drama; i.e., an assumed character).

The early usage of parson is obscure. Perhaps it refers to a person legally holding church property or meaning a 'person of the church'.

---

188   Latin *persona* originally meant a mask or false face of wood or clay worn by actors in a theatre. Latin *personare* meant to sound through (i.e., to speak through the make). The origin of *persona* is not known but some suggest it may come from ancient and extinct Etruscan *phersu* (mask).

Pastor

Pastor comes from words related to the care for animals as well as for the land on which animals graze (i.e., the pasture). Pastor also comes from words meaning shepherd (see SHEPHERD).

The oldest roots of pastor are found in PIE *pa* (to tend, keep, pasture, feed, guard, protect). From these roots come the Latin words *pascere* (to feed, to lead to pasture, to set to grazing, to cause to eat) and *pastorem* (shepherd).

These Latin words are the source of the 12th century Old French words *pastor* and *pastur* (herdsman, shepherd) and from them the mid-13th Middle English *pastour* which was used at that time as a surname.[189] By the late 14th century *pastour* meant a spiritual guide or a shepherd of souls and gradually became the word pastor.

The adjective pastoral (of or pertaining to shepherds) comes from the early 15th century. The use of pastoral to describe an idealized form of country life emphasizing purity and happiness is from the 1580s.

The verb 'to pastor' used to describe one of the roles of a priest or pastor is first seen in 1872.

Passion, Compassion

What does it mean to be passionate? What is your passion? What are you passionate about?

Passion is rooted in Latin *pati* (to suffer, endure) and *passio* (suffering, enduring). When the word passion came to English from Old French and Latin in the late 12th century it referred to the physical suffering of Christ on the cross.

---

189   For example, Mr Pastour, like Mr Shepherd or Mr Mason. The French chemist and bacteriologist who invented the process of pasteurization in the 19th century, Dr Louis Pasteur, has a surname which means pastor.

In both Roman Catholic and Protestant liturgies, Passion Sunday (also known as Palm Sunday) is the day in Lent just before Easter when one of the gospel accounts of Christ's crucifixion is read.

The term passion has evolved to encompass other meanings. In the early and medieval church, the term passion was also used to describe the suffering of martyrs and by the early 13th century the term passion was used to describe suffering in a more general sense.

However, by the early 14th century, the term passion had come to mean strong emotion; in particular, desire. By the 1580s passion was also being used as a term for sexual love and the sense of amorousness. By the 1630s the term passion was being used to mean a strong liking and enthusiasm.

During this period, when describing empathy or pity for the suffering of others, Latin *passio* was used, a translation of Greek *pathos* (from which come words such as apathy, pathetic, pathology, sympathy, and so on).

The word compassion (i.e., Latin *com* + Latin *passio*—to suffer with, to suffer together) suggests a sharing in the suffering of others or to have had similar experiences of suffering ourselves.[190]

So, what does it mean to be passionate about something? We are passionate about those things about which we feel strongly—so strongly, in fact, that we are willing to sacrifice or suffer for such things.

Peace

The word peace, from PIE *pag* (to fasten), is rooted in the notion of a binding together by treaty or agreement. PIE *pag* is the source of Latin *pacem* (agreement, treaty of peace, tranquillity, absence of war) and Latin *pacisci* (to covenant, to agree). Latin *pax* and Greek *eirene* were used by Biblical translators to render Hebrew *shalom* (safety, welfare, prosperity).

From these origins comes Old French *pais* (peace, reconciliation, silence, permission). By the mid-12th century the Anglo-French word *pes*

---

190   In Aramaic and Hebrew, the word compassionate is related to the word *rechem* (womb). In this context, to be compassionate is to be life-giving and life-nourishing (Borg, 2018, 135).

came to English replacing the Old English word *frio* (happiness). By the 1500s we see the modern spelling of peace.

The phrase 'peace of mind' is from around 1200. The sense of peace as 'quiet' is attested by 1300. At this time, the word peace was also used to mean the absence or cessation of war or hostility.

The use of 'peace' as a greeting is from the early 14th century.

Pentecost

Pentecost is related to the number fifty and has its origins in words related to the number five.

PIE *penkwe* (five) is the root of Greek *pente* (five)[191] and the Proto-Germanic *fimfe*—the origin of the English word five.

Pentecost comes from the Old English *pentecosten*, the Christian festival celebrated on the seventh Sunday after Easter. *Pentecosten* comes from Latin *pentecoste* and Greek *pentekoste*, both meaning the fiftieth day, from Greek *pentekonta* (fifty). The seventh Sunday would be seven weeks or forty-nine days after Easter; hence, the celebration of Pentecost on the fiftieth day.

Pentecost or *pentekostos* is the Greek name for the Old Testament Feast of Weeks, a Jewish harvest festival observed on the 50th day following Passover.

The word pentecostal, from Latin *pentecostalis*, is first seen in the 1660s.

Pentecostal, referring to the Christian denomination which emphasizes gifts of the Holy Spirit (described in the New Testament: Acts 2), is first seen in 1904.

---

191   Other words with *pente* as a root include pentagon, pentagram, and pentangle.

Poverty, Chastity, Obedience

Poverty, chastity, and obedience—words with origins in terms meaning 'next to nothing,' 'to be cut off or separated', and 'listening'. How might these origins inform the vows of an intentional religious life?

Poverty

The word poverty has its origins in PIE *pauko* and *pau* (few, little) from which Latin *paucus* (few, little) emerges. From *paucus* comes Latin *paucitas* and *paucitatem* (fewness, scarcity, a small number) and then the 14th century Old French *paucite* and the English word *paucity*. In these origins of paucity, we see no judgment—just a word that describes a condition in which there is not much of something.

However, from Latin *paucus* also comes Latin *pauper* (poor, not wealthy), a word still used in English, and later Old French *povre* (poor, wretched, dispossessed, inadequate; weak, thin). A person is judged a pauper or poor in relation to other (richer) people in their community. From these roots, the English adjective poor emerges in the late 12th century to describe someone lacking money or resources, someone who is destitute, needy, or indigent. The use of the word poor to collectively describe such persons (e.g., the poor will always be with us) also comes from the 12th century. Also, we first see the word poverty, meaning the wretched state or condition of being poor or in misery.

In the 14th century, the word poor was used to describe the inferior or inadequate or scanty quality of something; e.g., poor farmland, a poor harvest, a poorly made product, and so on.

When we think of someone entering a religious order and taking a vow of poverty, we don't usually think of someone choosing to live in misery or in a state of dehumanizing wretchedness. In fact, a religious order provides food, clothing, and shelter to its members—often a much better life than the poor who live in surrounding communities.

Chastity

Chastity, in its origins, is related to words such as cast (both as the verb, to cast; and as a noun; e.g., a cast on a broken arm, caste, and castration. The origin of such words is PIE *kasto* and *kes* (to cut), Latin *carere* (to be cut off from) and Latin *castus* (cut off, separated, morally pure). Latin *castus* also means chaste (to be cut off from faults).[192]

Latin *castus* is related to Latin *castitatem*, *castitas* (purity, chastity) and Old French *chastete* (chastity, purity). By around 1200 *chastete* came into English and was defined by the Church in terms of sexual purity, but not necessarily limited to virginity or celibacy; i.e., a person could be 'chaste' in the context of marriage. *Chastete* eventually became the word chastity.

The adjective chaste, from Latin *castus*, came to English about the same time (around 1200) and was used to mean virtuous and pure, especially in relation to unlawful sexual intercourse (as defined by the Roman Catholic Church).[193] The use of chaste as a noun meaning a 'virgin person' is from the early 14th century. The use of chaste to mean 'sexually pure or innocent' is seen beginning in the 15th century.

The sense of the word chastity as abstinence from sexual intercourse does not necessarily mean that sex, *per se*, is bad or wrong. Rather, given the origins of the words chaste and chastity, we get the sense that a decision to be chaste is a decision to 'cut oneself off' from sexual intercourse, regardless of previous sexual activity (or of no sexual activity), in order to focus on other priorities and purposes in one's life.

---

192   Latin *castus* (in the sense of to be cut off from) is the source of the word castration. Latin *castus* (in the sense of being cut or separated into groups) is the source of the Portuguese word *casta* (breed, race, caste) which was adopted in English as 'caste' and applied to Hindu social groups in India in the 1610s.

193   Perhaps it is not surprising that the word chastity appears around 1200. Although celibacy laws for priests had been declared during the 5th century, it was only during the renewal of Western Europe as it emerged in the 11th and 12th centuries from the so-called Dark Ages that laws regarding priestly celibacy were also renewed and more rigorously enforced; for example, Pope Gregory VII's 11th century decree against clerical marriages and the Second Lateran Council (1139) rule forbidding priests to marry. Perhaps not coincidentally, at this time a major religious movement in Western Europe emerged known as the 'cult of Mary' which is reflected, for example, in the numerous 'Notre Dame' churches and cathedrals built at this time—notably Notre Dame Cathedral in Paris. https://en.wikipedia.org/wiki/Clerical_celibacy_in_the_Catholic_Church

Obedience

To be obedient is not just to hear but to listen; that is, to hear with intention. The roots of obedience are in PIE *au-dh* (to perceive physically, to grasp) and PIE *au* (to perceive). From PIE *au* comes Latin *audire* (to listen, to hear) and Latin *obedire* (to obey, to be subject to, to serve, to pay attention, to give ear: literally, to listen to). Latin *obedire* is formed by combining the Latin prefix *ob* (e.g., toward, by way of) with Latin *audire*.[194]

From these Latin roots comes 12th century Old French *obeir* (to obey, to be obedient, to do one's duty). Old French *obedient* comes unchanged to English as obedient in the early 13th century and by the late 13th century the word obey comes to English. Also, in the early 13th century, the word obedience (submission to a higher power or authority) comes to English from Old French *obedience* and Latin *oboedientia*.

Vows of Poverty, Chastity, and Obedience

In brief then, given the origins of these three words in ancient terms meaning 'next to nothing', being 'cut off or separated', and 'listening', what might we consider in relation to the religious vows of poverty, chastity, and obedience?

Could we consider monastic poverty not so much in terms of having next to nothing but rather in terms of being detached or having a sense of detachment from what you do have? Could we consider chastity not so much in terms of cutting oneself off from something but rather in the sense of a symbolic cutting away of the distractions and attachments in one's life in order to focus more intentionally on what is of ultimate concern? Could we consider obedience not in terms of doing what you're told, but rather in terms of freely and responsibly listening to the voices of necessity?

---

194   PIE *au* is also the root of many later English words such as audible, audience, audio, audit, audition, auditorium, and so on.

Praise

Have you ever heard the words *herian* or *herry*? Have you ever herried anyone? *Herian* is an Old English word for praise. *Herry* is an Old English verb meaning to praise or to commend. These words have long disappeared from common use with the possible exception of Scrabble enthusiasts. *Herian* came from Gothic *hazjan* and Proto-Germanic *hazjana*, ancient words also meaning to praise or to commend.

Eventually Old English *herian* was replaced by *laud*, the Latin word for praise. *Laud* is still in use; e.g., many church liturgies include the *Te Deum Laudamus* ("Thee, O God, we praise"), a hymn written in the fourth century; or, the hymn "All Glory, Laud, and Honor" written in 820 by Theodulf of Orleans and translated to English in 1851 by John Mason Neale. The phrase *summa cum laude* used in graduation ceremonies means 'with great praise'.

Laud, which came to English in the late 14th century at the same time as the word praise, is from Old French *lauder* (to praise, extol), Latin *laudare* (to praise, commend, honor, extol, eulogize) and Latin *laus* (praise, fame, glory), and originally from PIE *leu* (song, hymn, poem). PIE *leu* is also the root of Old English *leod* (song, poem, hymn) and Proto-Germanic *leuthan* (from which derives German *lied*, meaning song). The English word laudable is from the early 15th century and the word laudatory is from the 16th century.

The English word praise comes from words related to price and prize, words related to value and worth.

The words price and prize have their origins in PIE *pret-yo* (to see, to traffic in) and PIE *preti* (to pay back, to recompense). From these PIE roots came Latin *pretium* (price, value, worth, cost) which in turn eventually led through Old French *pris* to the English words precious, price, and prize. Later, from *pretium*, comes Latin *pretiare* and Old French *preisier* (to value highly, to praise). Old French *preisier* is the root of both 'to praise' (to laud, flatter, commend) and 'to appraise' (to determine the value or worth of something).[195]

In the early 14th century, the word praise came to English from Old French *pris*. The verb 'to praise' (to laud, commend, flatter) also came to English around this time from Old French *preisier* (to praise, to value).

In sum, the use of the word praise, particularly as a form of worship specifically directed to God, is from the late 14th century. The use of praise as noun (i.e., praise as a thing in itself) begins in the early 14th century but is not commonly used in this sense until the 16th century. The word laud (praise) has been with us since ancient times.

Pray, Prayer

The word prayer begins in PIE *prek* (to ask, request, entreat). It appears that not much has changed regarding this word either in its form or its usage over the last 5,000 or so years.

PIE *prek* is related to Sanskrit *prasna* (a spiritual question; in particular, a question such as a student might ask of a teacher) and to Old High German *frahen*, German *fragen*, and Old English *fricgan*, all meaning to ask a question. In such a context, a prayer could be perceived as a request or desire for knowledge, understanding, and wisdom.

PIE *prek* is also related to Latin *prex* (prayer, request, entreaty), *precari* and *precare* (to ask earnestly, to beg, to entreat). From these Latin roots we see Old French *preier* (to pray), the source of the early 13th century English verb pray (to ask earnestly, to beg). By around 1300 the verb to pray meant, in particular, to pray to a god or saint.

The old Germanic sense of 'to pray is to ask a question', as seen in Old English *fricgan*, seems to have been gradually replaced by the Latin sense of 'to pray is to ask for a particular outcome', as a supplicant might ask something of a person with the power to grant the outcome.[196]

---

195   Praise, as high approval, is based on such a sense or appraisal of the value and worth of something. On the other hand, an appraisal of something does not necessarily imply approval or praise.

196   The historian Peter Brown describes the sense of prayer as 'asking' in terms of prayer and

The noun prayer, following from the verb 'to pray' and seen around 1300, comes from Old French *prier* (prayer, petition, request). Prayer-book is seen in the 1590s, the word prayerful is from the 1620s, and prayer-meeting is from 1780.

Today there are many different types of prayer in Christianity; for example, confession, penitence and expiation, consecration and dedication, petition and intercession, adoration and praise, and thanksgiving.

In brief, a person in prayer is someone who self-consciously and intentionally speaks what is on their heart and mind.[197] Whether the person speaks in the quiet of their own space or with the 'two or three who are gathered together', the person or persons praying are acting in the anticipation and trust that something will happen as a result of their prayer, that

---

memory; in particular, prayer as an asking to be remembered. Some early Church prayers were requests that their dead family members and friends remember them and speak for them in the afterlife, almost as if people prayed (or asked), in effect, "Could you put in a good word for me before I also go to the afterlife?" To quote Brown at some length:

"What is distinctive about these Christian graffiti [i.e., writings on the walls of cemeteries] is that they reveal that the living prayed intently to be remembered *by* the dead ... But these prayers were not addressed to the great martyrs alone. They were also made to the ordinary dead [i.e., dead relatives, fellow believers] [who] were asked to pray for the living ... The request to the dead for their prayers runs as a refrain through Christian [grave] inscriptions.

"But what exactly was it to 'ask', and, especially, to 'hold in the mind?'" [That is, why would someone ask the dead to remember them?]

"...in the late antique world. To 'remember', to 'hold in the mind', was not to store away a fact: It was to assert a bond; it was to be loyal [i.e., to be faithful] and to pay attention to somebody. Memory was ... a gift to the potentially forgotten dead in the other world ... To forget was an aggressive act. It was an act of social excision that severed links that had previously been established by an equally purposive act of memory. In practice, to remember was to intercede ... the prayers [of intercession] asked for the petitioner to be remembered by the holy dead who, in turn, had the power to mobilize the memory of God ... these graffiti linked memory with intercession."

Brown, 2015, 38 – 41.

197   So how are meditation, contemplation, and prayer different? What might the origins of these three words tell us?

Meditation, in its origins, seems to be about thoughtfulness, mindfulness, study, and reflection. Prayer, in its origins, seems to be about speaking, perhaps on the other side of meditation, with intention in the anticipation of some expected action or outcome. Contemplation, in its origins, seems to be about being present in a (sacred) space and time that is intentionally set apart from daily activity. Contemplation may include ritual action without necessarily any focus on a particular thought or action.

there will be a response, even if the response is no response. And, perhaps, as they continue to pray and live their lives, they become active participants in the response to the prayer. Prayer, as self-conscious intention, becomes self-conscious action. A prayerful person walks the talk.

Preach / Preacher

Have you ever thought about the connection between the positive and negative connotations of preaching? What's the difference between a good preacher and a bad preacher? What's the difference between someone who preaches *to* you and someone who preaches *at* you?

Preach has its origins in PIE *deik* (to point out)[198] and Latin *dicare* (to say).[199] The Latin prefix *prae* (before) was added to *dicare* creating the word *praedicare* (to proclaim: i.e., pro + claim suggests both 'saying before' and 'before saying'). The addition of *prae* suggests that the speaker is standing 'before' a group of people and proclaiming a message. In another sense, the addition of *prae* suggests an emphasis on the reflective thought that the speaker has done before proclaiming the message.

The verb 'to preach' is seen in Old English as *predician* and in the 12th century as *preachen*, from Old French *preechier* (to preach, to give a sermon) and Latin *praedicare*.

The noun preacher comes to English from 12th century Old French *preecheor* (preacher) and Latin *praedicatorem*, *praedicator* (public praiser, eulogist, proclaimer).

The phrase to 'preach to the converted' is recorded from 1867. The use of the slang word 'preach' as the means of address for a pastor or preacher is first recorded in 1968. The phrase 'to preach to the choir' is attested from 1979.

---

198   PIE *deik* is related to other ancient words such as Greek *deiknynai* (to prove), Latin *digitus* (finger), Old High German *zeigon* (to show), and two Old English words: *teon* (to accuse) and *taecan* (to teach).

199   Latin *dicare* is related to words such as dictate, dictator, diction, dictionary.

Preach is a word with both positive and negative connotations. In its positive sense, the art of effective preaching is the thoughtful delivery of a message to a receptive listener. On the other hand, preaching can also be the proclamation of harsh judgments to a potentially defensive listener or writing or speaking in an annoying way about the right way to think or act.

Presence

What does it mean for someone to have presence? I think of a person who fills a room when they enter or someone who speaks with authority, someone to whom we listen when they speak, someone we notice in a crowded room. What does it mean for each of us to have a unique presence?

The word presence has ancient roots in PIE *es* (to be) which leads to Latin *es* and *esse* (to be), Greek *ousia* (being, essence), and Latin *essentia* (being, essence). By 1600, we see the noun essence used to describe an ingredient which gives something its particular character and the related adjective, essential (e.g., essential oils). By the 1650s, essence referred to the general sense of the basic element of anything.[200]

The word presence is grounded in being, in the essential, and, in the quintessential.

First, where does the word quintessential come from? Since ancient times people have sought ways to describe what seems to be the essential nature of something; e.g., the world, human nature, ways of being, and so on. Many of these descriptions comprise sets of four elements or, perhaps, metaphors. For example, the medicine wheel of indigenous peoples describes the world and human nature in terms of the four cardinal directions (north, south, east, west). The ancient Greeks described the world in terms of combinations of earth, air, fire, and water. Hippocrates, a 5th century BCE Greek physician[201], and Galen, a 2nd century CE Greek physician, characterized human illness in terms of the heart, liver, lungs,

---

200   The word essence was used in early English to mean the "substance of the Trinity". https://www.etymonline.com/search?q=essence

201   Hippocrates, for whom medicine's 'Hippocratic oath' is named.

and kidneys, each of which related to one of four bodily humours: black bile, yellow bile, blood, and phlegm, each of which in turn was associated with a personality descriptor; i.e., melancholic, choleric, sanguine, and phlegmatic. Carl Jung, a pioneer of 20th century psychology, used four pairs of characteristics to describe personality and temperament: Introvert / Extravert, Sensation / Intuition, Thinking / Feeling, and Judgement / Perception. And so on.[202]

During the medieval period, people who thought about such things began to feel that there was some mysterious fifth element which held the other four elements together. They felt that this fifth element was some kind of unifying force or energy. This element or essence was considered the ultimate nature of something. In Latin, this fifth element was called the *quinta essentia* (*quinta*; i.e., five). Our words quintessence and quintessential mean the absolute essence or the heart of something; or, something which is of the utmost importance and ultimate concern.

So, how is presence related to essence and quintessence?

The word presence is from Latin *praesse* (pre-being, to be before); that is, from Latin *pre* (before) + Latin *esse* (to be). Latin *praesse* is a word that indicates something being or existing before something else; often before something in time.

---

202   For another example: David Bebbington's 1989 book, *Still Evangelical?*, uses four qualities to define the term evangelical: truth of the Bible as the centre of faith, Jesus's death as atonement for sin, personal experience of salvation, and sharing the gospel in word and deed.

Another example: in 1950 the Vatican officially declared that Mary, the mother of Jesus, had completed the course of her earthly life and was considered to have entered 'body and soul' into heaven. Could this mean that Mary should now be considered 'the fourth' element of the Holy Trinity!? Controversy has existed for many years in both Islam and Christianity regarding the relationship of Mary to the Trinity. And, have you noticed how many other things in life also come in four?! Four-leaf clovers, four suits in a deck of cards, four-stroke engines, four seasons, four gospels, four strong winds that blow lonely, four gospels, four compass points, four-letter words, four horsemen of the apocalypse. Let's not forget fair and square and a square meal! Do you want a real vehicle?! Get a 4x4 with four on the floor!

On the other hand, the Wu Xing conceptual scheme in Chinese philosophy describes the relationship of *five* elements: wood, fire, earth, metal, and water. Also described in Wu Xing are five phases, five agents, five movements, five processes, five steps/stages, and five planets. This scheme is used to explain a wide array of phenomena.

We could continue with trinitarian explanations of the world; e.g., the 'rule of three' seen in writing and storytelling, in the rules of rhetoric, comedy, principles of advertising, and so on.

In contrast to presence (the sense of something existing before something else), the word present comes from Latin *praesentia* (a being present) and Latin *praesentem* (present; at this point in time, not the past or future). In this sense, being present means being here and now.

However, *praesentia* (being present now) also comes from *praesse* (to be before) suggesting, perhaps, that whatever is present now also contains something from the past; that is, suggesting that past and present exist at the same time. For example, we say that 'all my life has brought me to this point'. To be 'present' or to be 'my presence' is to bring my 'essence' with me wherever I go.

The mid-14th century English word presence (the fact of being present) has its origins in 12th century Old French *presence* from these Latin origins. Presence meaning an impressive demeanor is first seen in the 1570s. Presence meaning that a divine or spiritual presence is being felt is from the 1660s.

Consider presence in terms of the sense of 'pre + being'; i.e., *pre + essentia*, or pre-essence or pre-being! Perhaps presence is what we bring with us when we're born, when we come into being. We come fully loaded with presence, with life energy![203]

So, in this context of the quintessential, of presence, and of being present, perhaps this is why when we say, "Take five", we not only mean 'take a break' but we imply "Take some time to get in touch with your real self, take time to get reconnected to who you are." Similarly, at times of success or celebration when we exclaim, "Gimme five!" we imply, "Give me your real self; give me your energy, your creativity, your winning spirit!" In short: Get connected to your essence, to that which makes you *you*: give me some of your essence, your energy, your spirit. Get connected to your being; or, share some of your being with me.

So, what might it mean then to have and to exhibit presence? Among other things, presence is the condition of our being present here and now. Presence implies that something unique about us stands out. Presence is a

---

203   This sense of our essence arriving with us when we're born is seen in the Plato's account of the Greek myth of Ur. In this account, the Greek word for this pre-being with which we are born is *genius* (guardian spirit) from PIE *gene* (to give birth, to beget). And, as you might expect, Greek *genius* is the root of our word genius. If nothing else, this makes me think of parenthood in a different way.

distinguishing bearing or manner; i.e., a quality of poise and effectiveness that enables us to achieve a close relationship with others. Presence carries a sense of attention and intention. We are the life, and the consciousness of that life, that we have been given. People perceive life itself in us.

As in D.H. Lawrence's poem *We are transmitters*, "life flows through us" (Lawrence, D.H. (1969). *Selected poems*. New York: Viking, 105). People see presence in those ways by which we respond to the challenges of life and to the ultimate concerns of our life.

Priest

What do you think of the idea of a priest as the lead-cow?!

This idea, one that can be found when considering the origin of the word priest, and an idea that is as yet unverified, comes from the combination of PIE *pres* or *per* (meaning pre-; before) and PIE *gwou* (cow, ox, bull) or PIE bous (cow). PIE *pres* + *bous* would seem to suggest the cow before the cow? Or the lead-cow? Or, the leader of the cows? *Pres* + *gwou* is said to have evovled into the word priest. Or, *pres* + *bous* could have become the word presbyter. Who knows? I know, it's a stretch, but nevertheless interesting.

Two more substantial and verified suggestions for the origins of priest are found in Greek *presbyter* (elder) and in Latin *praepositus* (person placed in charge).

First, Greek *presbyteros* (elder, senior) and *presbyter* (elder; also the origin of Presbyterian) is the source of the Latin terms *presbyter* (leader of a Christian congregation) and *prester* which in turn lead to Old Frisian *prestere*, Old High German *prestar*, Old English *preost*, and the Middle English *prest* which over time evolved as priest.

Second, Latin *praepositus* (person placed in charge) is the root of the Latin *prevost* (to put one person over others; also the origin of provost), which led to the Old High German *priast*, *prest* (one put over others). In this version, the Old English *preost* comes from Old High German *priast* and *prest*, and then evolves to Middle English *prest* and so on to priest.

So, lead-cow, elder, or the person in charge of others? What do you think?!

Prophet

The word prophet is rooted in PIE *bha* (to speak, tell, say). However, anyone can speak. What is it about the origins of the word prophet that would indicate that such a person speaks with authority?

PIE *bha* is not only the source of the Greek *phanai* (to speak) but is also the source of Latin *fama* (talk, reputation, renown, good reputation). Greek *phanai* is the origin of Greek *prophetes* (interpreter, spokesman of the gods, inspired teacher). Latin *fama* is the origin of the English word fame. So, considering this combination of sources perhaps we could say that a prophet is someone of renown who speaks with authority, even with the authority of the gods.

From these PIE and Greek origins came Latin *propheta* and Old French *prophete*. Latin *propheta* was interpreted in Old English as *witga*, a word with Germanic origins related to wizards and witches. However, by the late 12th century, the word prophet (one who speaks for God, one who foretells, an inspired preacher) was in common English usage. The word prophetess comes from the around 1300.

In translations of the Bible, Hebrew *nabj* (soothsayer) was translated as Greek *prophetes*. In turn, *prophetes* was first translated as Latin *vates* (poet, bard, soothsayer, seer). However, some Christian writers, perhaps uncomfortable with the pagan associations of *vates*, used Latin *prophetes* (the Latin version of Greek *prophetes*). In English, the word prophet meaning a 'prophetic writer of the Old Testament' is from late 14th century."[204]

The word prophecy comes from Greek *prophetes* and Greek *propheteia* (the gift of interpreting the will of the gods) and from Old French *profecia*. The English words *prophecie* or *prophesie* appear around 1200. A prophecy as something spoken or written by a prophet dates from around 1300.

---

204   [1] Online Etymological Dictionary: Prophet.
https://www.etymonline.com/search?q=prophet

The word prophetic appears in the late 15th century.

The use of the English word prophet in relation to Mohammed dates from the 1610s. Prophet has been used in a non-religious sense since 1848.

Proverb

In its origins the word proverb means 'words put forward'. The dictionary defines a proverb as "a brief popular saying (such as 'Too many cooks spoil the broth') that gives advice about how people should live or that expresses a belief that is generally thought to be true" (Merriam-Webster). The word proverb comes from the combination of 'pro' and 'verb'.

The prefix pro- is rooted in PIE *pro-* and *per-*, both meaning forward or through. From PIE *pro-* comes both Greek *pro-* (before, in front of, sooner) and Latin *pro-* (on behalf of, in place of, before, for, in exchange for, just as).[205]

The word 'verb' has its origins in PIE *were* (to speak). From this root comes the Latin word *verbum* meaning 'a word'.[206] By the 12th century, the Old French *verbe*, from Latin *verbum*, had come more specifically to mean a 'verb' (i.e., a verb is a part of speech which expresses action or being)—a word first seen in English in the 14th century.

In Old English, the Old Testament Book of Proverbs was called the *cwidboc*—from a combination of *cwide* (speech, saying, proverb, homily) and *boc* (book); however, this word eventually gave way to stronger Latin and French influences. *Cwidboc* was replaced by the English word proverb

---

205   A common modern usage of 'pro-' in terms meaning "in favor of, favoring" (e.g., *pro-independence, pro-fluoridation*, pro-life, pro-choice, etc.) was not in classical Latin and is attested in English only from the early 19th century.

206   Note that in a phrase such as "in the beginning was the Word", the word Word is a translation of the Greek word *logos*, a philosophical and theological term related to reason, to Greek *sophia* (wisdom), and to the concept of a 'go-between' connecting the divine and human, spirit and matter. On the other hand, the Latin word *verbum* refers to ordinary common 'words' and does not have the same meaning as Greek *logos*. In spite of this ancient distinction, in English the same word, 'word', is used in reference to both 'words' in general and 'the Word'. In brief, "In the beginning was the Word" refers to *logos* not *verbum*. See also WORD.

which comes from Latin *proverbium* (a common saying, old adage, maxim) and 12ᵗʰ century Old French *proverb*. The first version of the word proverb appears in English in the 13ᵗʰ century Old Testament *Boke of Prouerbyys*. By the 14ᵗʰ century, the word proverb had emerged. The adjective proverbial appears in the early 15ᵗʰ century.

Proverbs are memorable words of wisdom, stated in everyday terms, often with humour and wit. Such proverbs are 'put forward' or 'carried forward' in individual and cultural memory because of their connections to feeling and emotion.

Psalm

Psalms are songs. Psalms are meant to be sung. In its origins, we can see that a psalm is a song that can touch and move us. Psalms are poetry.

Psalm comes from Greek *psalmos* (song sung to a harp) and *psallaein* (to play on a stringed instrument). These Greek words have their origin in PIE *pal* (to touch, feel, shake, strike softly).[207] Greek *psalmos* became Latin *psalmus*, Old French *psaume*, Old English *psealm* and *salm*, and later the word psalm.

Psalmist is first seen in English in the late 15ᵗʰ century and comes from the Middle French *psalmiste*, the Latin *psalmista*, and the Greek *psalmistes*—all meaning to sing psalms.

A psalter is a book of psalms. Psalter comes from Old English *saltere* and *psaltere*, Latin *psalterium* (the songs of David), and Greek *psalterion*.

A psaltery is an ancient stringed harp-like instrument of the zither family played by plucking the strings (not to be confused with the 19ᵗʰ century bowed psaltery, a stringed triangle-shaped instrument played with a bow). Psaltery, a word from the beginning of the 14ᵗʰ century, comes from Old French *psalterie* (12ᵗʰ century), Latin *psalterium* and Greek *psalterion* (both meaning a stringed instrument), and from Greek *psallein* (to play on a stringed instrument).

---

207   Related words include Latin *palpare* (to touch softly) and the modern English word palpate (to examine by touch).

Pulpit

The word pulpit comes from Latin *pulpitum* (a raised structure on which preachers stand; a scaffold or stage or platform for actors). Before that the origins of the word are unknown. In Middle High German the word pulpit was borrowed from Latin and is perhaps related to the current German word *pult* (desk).

Pulpit meaning the preachers or ministers generally (e.g., the message from the pulpit) is from the 1560s.

The word pulpiteer (i.e., a professional preacher) is first seen in the 1640s.

The term 'bully pulpit' was coined in 1904 by US President Theodore Roosevelt in relation to the power of his office as a conspicuous position that provided an opportunity to speak out and to be listened to.

Purgatory

The word purgatory has its origins in PIE *ag* (to drive, draw out or forth, move), Latin *purigare* from *purus* (pure) + *agere* (to set in motion, drive; to do, perform), and Latin *purgare* (to cleanse, make clean, purify—especially of the body, free from what is superfluous). From these Latin roots comes 12th century Old French *purgier* (wash, clean; refine, purify morally or physically), Anglo-French *purger*, and around 1300 the English verb *purge*.

The noun purge (that which purges) is first seen in the 1560s. A purgative or act of purging is from the 1590s. Purge, in the political sense, is from 1730.

The word purgatory, first seen around 1200, comes from Old French *purgatore* and Latin *purgatorium* (a term coined by St Bernard, 1090 - 1153).

Purgatory, as a part of Roman Catholic doctrine, has a long history. In brief, "Purgatory is the state of those who die in God's friendship, assured of their eternal salvation, but who still have need of purification to enter into the happiness of heaven."[208] In this context, purgatory could be considered as a transitional process or a state, not a place.

Purgatario is the second part of Dante Alighieri's (1265 – 1321) poem *Divine Comedy;* the first part being *Inferno* and the third *Paradiso*. The poem outlines Dante's imaginative version of the afterlife.

Reconciliation

Have you ever argued with someone? Have you ever participated in a debate? Have you ever listened to people arguing or listened to a debate? Voices are raised. The temperature rises.

The word reconciliation has its roots in such heated exchanges and in ancient words meaning 'to shout (or call) together'. The word reconciliation emerges from the desire to resolve conflict by talking rather than by fighting.

Reconciliation is rooted in PIE *kele* (to shout) and Latin *clamare* (to cry out, shout, proclaim).[209]

Latin *clamare* leads to *calare* (to call) which in turn leads to *concilium* (council), a combining of Latin com- (together) and *calare*—a *concilium* is a group of people who talk together.[210]

From Latin *concilium* come *conciliatus* and *conciliare* (to bring together, unite in feelings, make friendly), words which lead to English conciliate. And so, add a re- (again) and you have *reconciliate* (to bring together again; regain; win over again, conciliate) first seen in English in the mid-14th century from Latin *reconciliare* and 12th century Old French *reconcilier*.[211]

---

208   https://en.wikipedia.org/wiki/Purgatory

209   From these roots we also have the English verb 'to claim', first seen around 1300, meaning to call, call out; to ask or demand by virtue of right or authority. *Clamare* is also the root of 14th century clamor, acclaim (to acclaim, 14th century; acclaim 1667), and acclamation (1540s).

210   The word council comes to English in the 12th century from Latin *concilium*, Old French *concile* (assembly; council meeting; body of counsellors) and Anglo-French *cuncile*.

211   The use of reconcile in terms of balancing a financial statement, is from the late 14th century. 'To become reconciled' is from the 1660s.

And from the verb reconcile, we also see in the mid-14th century, the noun reconciliation from Latin *reconciliationem* and *reconciliation*.

In the 1540s we see the verb 'to conciliate' come to English from Latin *conciliatus* and *conciliare* (to bring together, unite in feelings, make friendly) from *concilium*.

The Sacrament of Penance and Reconciliation (commonly called, the Sacrament of Confession, Reconciliation or Penance) is one of the seven sacraments of the Catholic church.

Reconciliation does not simply or superficially mean that people can become friendly again after a disagreement: more importantly reconciliation has the sense that the people who have been involved on different sides of a difficult situation can work together to create for themselves a new or transformed relationship to that situation in which harm is repaired, relationships are restored, and trust is rebuilt; e.g., as seen in restorative justice mediations.

Rector

The word rector comes from PIE *reg* (to move in a straight line; to direct in a straight line, to lead, to rule; also, the root of regal), Latin *regere* (to rule, guide), and Latin *rector* (ruler, governor, director, guide). The word rector appears in English in the late 14th century.

The word rector was used by the Romans to refer to both governors and god; however, by the 18th century the term referred only to clergymen and college heads.

A rectory, from the mid-15th century, referred to the benefice (i.e., the revenue from an endowment) of a rector; from 14th century French *rectorie* and Latin *rectoria*. The use of rectory to mean the residence of a rector is from 1849.

The word director is related to rector and comes from Latin *dirigere* (*dis-* = apart + *regere* = to direct, guide, keep straight). That is, a director is be someone who is set apart to be the leader.

Redeem, Redeemer, Redemption

The 14th century English word redemption is rooted in Latin *emere* (originally meaning, to take; later meaning, to buy, gain, procure) from PIE *em* (to take, to distribute). The Latin word *redimere*, meaning to buy back or to redeem, was formed by adding the suffix *red* to *emere*.[212]

The word *redimere* is related to Latin *redemptionem* and *redemptio*, words which mean, depending on context, a buying back, releasing, ransoming, or bribery. From these Latin origins come 12th century Old French *redemcion* and 14th century English redemption, words meaning at that time the deliverance (or 'buying back') from sin. In this sense of the word redemption, a commercial transaction became a metaphor for the theological interpretation of a spiritual experience. And, of course, the English word redemption still means to buy back or exchange something; e.g., when we redeem coupons or gift cards when making a purchase at a store. However, it should be noted that in the theological sense, even though you can redeem your coupons at the store, a person can't redeem themselves![213]

The verb 'to redeem' came to English in the early 15th century from Middle French *redemer* (to buy back) and also from Latin *redimere*. The theological sense of 'to redeem' meaning to deliver from sin and spiritual death is from the early 16th century.

The use of 'to redeem' meaning 'to make amends for' is from the 1520s. The sense of 'to redeem' meaning to make good a promise or obligation is from 1840.

The noun 'redeemer' also comes to English in the early 15th century and is used in the Christian sense to describe or name Jesus. Redeemer replaced the earlier word *redemptor*.

---

212   Just as in English when 'an' is used before a word beginning with a vowel (e.g., an apple) so also In Latin, when a root word began with a vowel, the prefix 'red' was used instead of 're'.

213   "Redemption is not something that can be willed ... redemption exceeds the limit of human potentiality." (Critchley, 2014, 205).

Religion

The word religion has its origins in Latin. Three sources have been suggested.

One suggestion is Latin *religiens* (careful, the opposite of *negligens*—not careful; i.e., negligent). Another suggestion is that the word religion comes from *relegere* (to go through again); in particular, to read again (*re* meaning again plus *legere* meaning to read[214]).

However, the primary and most popular source of the word religion is its connection with the Latin *religare*[215] (to bind fast); in particular, *religare* meaning to place an obligation on; and, meaning the bond between humans and gods. In this context, the word religion is as much about community as it is about religion. Religion, from *religare*, is a binding together of groups of people who share common beliefs, values, and god(s).

The Latin word *religionem* as "respect for what is sacred, reverence for the gods; conscientiousness, sense of right, moral obligation; fear of the gods; divine service, religious observance; a religion, a faith, a mode of worship, cult; sanctity, holiness"[216] also reflects this notion of religion as community. In the 5th century CE, Latin *religionem* was also used to mean monastic life in community.

Paradoxically, in the ancient world there was no word for religion as we currently use the word; that is, "there were no organizations with empire-wide oversight over religious practices—no religious authorities who transcended particular localities ... ancient religion was less about what one thought and more about what one did" (Ehrman, 2018, 78).

By the early 1200s, the English word religion, from the Old French *religiun* (piety, devotion, religious community) and the 11th century Anglo-French *religion*, was used to mean a state of life bound by monastic vows as well as the conduct of life which indicated a belief in a divine power. At that time (and now), the term 'religious' (from Anglo-French *religius* and Old French *religious*) was used to describe a person, often a member of a

---

214   Among other words, *legere* is also the root of lecture, legend and legible.

215   The Latin *ligare* (to bind) is also the root of the word ligament, from PIE *leig* (to bind).

216   Online Etymological Dictionary: https://www.etymonline.com/search?q=religion

religious order or community, who was devout, pious, and imbued with or expressive of religious devotion.

In English, religion meaning a particular system of faith is first recorded from around 1300. Religion and religious, meaning the recognition and allegiance to unseen higher powers, is from the 1530s, the early years of the Reformation. During this time, Protestants formed themselves into various, often competing, Christian denominations or 'religions'.

Repentance, Penitence

Repent, repentance

The word repent has had a long and winding path through the centuries meaning different things to different people at different times.

Consider three sources leading to our understanding and use of the terms repent and repentance: Hebrew and Greek sources, Latin sources from PIE, and Germanic sources from PIE. These sources reveal three ways of considering repentance.

To begin, the Hebrew word for repentance is *shub* (return); that is, to repent is to return or to reconnect with that which you have turned away from either inadvertently or by intention. Similarly, the Greek word for repentance is *metanoia* (a change of mind, to come to your senses), from *meta* (beyond) + *neos, nous* (mind).[217] In early Greek versions of the Bible, the meaning of repent came to mean not only to change your mind but also to be sorry for past actions; in brief, to have not only a change of mind but also a change of heart.[218]

---

217   Borg, noting that the Greek word for repentance is *metanoia*, states "to repent is to go beyond the mind which you have, the mind you have gotten from your culture". Borg also reminds us that "the Hebrew word for repentance is *shub* (return)…[i.e.,] to repent is to return … to repent is "to begin the journey of return from the separated self to a new self in God … to repent is to reconnect" (Borg, 2018, 235). In this context, repentance can be considered a re-alignment or a re-centering. Also, in this context, Borg suggests that the word repent means not so much about a turning away from sin as much as a turning toward a new relationship with God (Borg, 2018, 73; in reference to Mark 1.15).

218   "…the real meaning of metanoia … may have begun by meaning 'change your mind' but

Second, the words repent, repentance, and repentant are rooted in PIE *kwoina* and *kwei* (to pay, to atone, to compensate). PIE *kwoina* leads to Greek *poine* (blood money, fine, penalty, punishment) and to Latin *poena* (punishment) and *poenalis* (pertaining to punishment).[219]

Latin *poena* is related to Latin *poenitire* (to make sorry) and to the later medieval Latin *penitire* (to regret). Note the distinction between *poenitire* and *penitire*. The former is something done *to* a wrongdoer whereas the latter is something done *by* the wrongdoer.

By the time *penitire* (to regret) had come to 11th century Old French, a Latin prefix *re-* (again) had been added to form the Old French *repentir* (i.e., to regret again) from which the English verb repent appears around 1300. The noun repentance is first seen in English around 1300 from 12th century Old French *repentance* (penitence) from Old French *repentir*.

During the medieval period we see in this distinction between Latin *poenitire* (punishment) and *penitire* (regret) a gradual shift from the Latin sense of repentance as external punishment to a sense of personal regret and change of mind.[220]

Third, another sense of repentance as regret comes from PIE and Proto-Germanic sources. The English word regret comes from Proto-Germanic *gretan* (to weep) and is not found in other European Romance

---

very clearly meant to repent of, or to be sorry for past actions (and not just in Christian Greek)" (Ostler, 249 - 250).

219   Latin *poenalis* is also the root of the words penal, penitentiary, and so on.

220   Repent is an example of a word which can have quite different meaning depending on the translation of original sources. For example, in Jerome's translation of the Vulgate Bible from Greek to Latin, the Latin verb *paenitet* ('penitence repents me of my sin'; i.e., by being penitent I repent) was changed to *paenitentiam agite* ('to do penance'). The word penitence "began to change its meaning: no longer 'to be sorry,' but 'to show your regret by doing penance' and mortifying the flesh ... suggesting a link (otherwise hard to defend) with *poena* (punishment).

Erasmus (1466 – 1536), one of the greatest scholars of the Renaissance and Reformation, when reviewing the Vulgate Bible in light of original Greek texts, proposed a different translation for Matthew 3:2 ("Repent, for the kingdom of heaven has come near", NIV Bible). His translation of Greek *metanoia* suggests that repent should be translated as 'change your mind' or 'come to your senses'. This Reformation translation or understanding of the meaning of 'repent' as 'change your mind' is distinct from the more traditional view of 'repent' as 'be sorry for past actions' which had been evolving for the thousand years of the Vulgate Bible. That is, Erasmus suggests that repent be translated in terms of its original meaning rather than what had come to be the meaning as reflected in the Vulgate Bible (Ostler, 2016, 49 – 250).

languages. *Gretan* is the origin of Old Norse *grata* (to weep, to groan) and Old English *graetan* (to weep).[221]

Also, the PIE word *krew* (to push, fall, break) is a source of Proto-Germanic *hreowan* (to regret, repent, grieve), Old High German *riuwan*, and the English word *rue* (regret). The sense emerging from this sense of repentance as regret (and grieving) suggests repentance as an interior crisis related to the awareness of wrongdoing and to the expression of a willingness to turn from wrongdoing to righteousness and to embody a change of mental and spiritual attitude toward wrongdoing.[222]

In brief, the three sources for the word repent suggest meanings related to a change of mind and heart (Greek), punishment (Latin), and regret (Proto-Germanic). Repentance has its roots in ancient words meaning external accountability and punishment for wrongdoing. However, by medieval times, the meaning of repentance had shifted from such external social pressure to a more internal sense of regret and remorse for one's wrongdoings.

Penance, penitence

During the early centuries of the Church, penance was a public act or a conversion. Penance was a change of mind, a dramatic break with the past and a desire to lead a different life; in particular, to show this change in public as a guarantee of future behavior in adherence to the Christian values which had been chosen. Later, for example during the development of monasteries in the 5th and 6th centuries, penance became more of a private and daily activity, the ongoing routine of intentionally living a life centered in Christian values.[223] Contrary, perhaps, to current popular imagination, penance for the early church was not punishment.

---

221   The verb regret (to look back with distress or sorrowful longing; to grieve for on remembering) came to English in the late 14th century from Old French *regreter* (to long after, bewail, lament someone's death; ask the help of) and from Proto-Germanic *gretan*.

222   The medieval distinction between repent and regret, seen in modern languages, is not seen in more ancient languages.

223   Brown, P. (2015). *The ransom of the soul: Afterlife and wealth in early Western Christianity.* Cambridge, MA: Harvard University Press, 124 – 131, 259.

The word penitence is rooted in Latin *paene* (nearby, almost) and Latin *paenitere* (to cause or feel regret). *Paenitere* originally meant the feeling that something was unsatisfactory or not enough, feeling badly about something, not just a wrongdoing, but not living up to one's potential or vocation. The implication seems to be 'try harder next time'. This feeling of *paenitere* leads to sense of being penitent, from Latin *paenitentia* and *paenitentum* (penitent). The word penitence came to English around 1200 from 11th century Old French *penitence*.

Penance, meaning a religious discipline or self-mortification as a token of repentance and as atonement for some wrongdoing, comes to English in the late 13th century from 12th century Old French *peneance* and Latin *paenitentia*. The adjective penitential is from around 1500.

The early 15th century word penitentiary (a place of punishment for offences against the church) comes from Latin *penitentiarius* (of penance). The modern use of penitentiary to mean a house of correction (correction implying a change of mind, a change of heart) is from 1806. At that time, a penitentiary was an asylum for prostitutes. The shortening of penitentiary to 'the pen' is attested from 1884.

In sum, repentance is a change of mind and heart. Repentance is an inner decision expressed in regret or remorse in relation to wrongdoing and/or to separation from self, others, and to one's god. Penance is the outer expression of repentance—penance is an action performed by the penitent. We 'do' penance. Our actions are intended to atone and to repair the harm of the wrongdoing.

Responsibility

When I was growing up I remember my mother saying from time to time in exasperation to no one in particular (although I think my dad may have been in the room), "Why doesn't anyone take more responsibility around here? Why do I have to do everything myself?"

I remember that one of my mother's admonitions to me as the eldest child was that I be responsible. She didn't say "Be good." She said, "Be responsible—be an example to your brother and sister." At the time though, all that my child's ears heard was, "Be good." Only as I grew older did I begin to get a sense of what being responsible might mean.

Responsibility has its origins in words related to marriage and to offering drinks to the gods.

Responsibility has its origins in Latin *respondere*, a word comprised of *re-* (back) and *spondere* (to pledge or to promise solemnly). From *spondere* come the words spouse and sponsor; i.e., *spondere* implies a pledge made by a sponsor or a promise made between spouses. To be *re*-sponsible is to return or go back to or to be reminded of our pledges.

Spondere, in turn, comes from Greek *sponde* (the chants performed during the libations or drink offerings to the gods) and PIE *spend* (to pour a libation for the gods, to engage oneself in a ritual act). The word responsibility comes from the pouring of a libation or drink to the gods as a symbolic act of offering yourself to the gods.

The first appearances of words related to responsibility illustrate its evolution of usage and meaning: response (14th century), responsible (as answerable, 1590s), responsible (as accountable for one's actions, 1643, the time of the English civil war between Cromwell's republicans and the monarchy), responsible (as reliable, trustworthy, 1690s), to respond (1719), and responsibility (the condition of being responsible, 1787, the time of the American and French revolutions). Responsibility meaning that for which one is responsible comes from 1796; e.g., being responsible for one's actions, for one's daily work, and so on.

In brief, the word responsibility evolved during the turmoil of the 17th and 18th centuries as old social systems declined and new ones came into being; e.g., the diffusion of various Protestant denominations during the Reformation and the political revolutions of the Enlightenment. In this context, responsibility, particularly in terms of the awareness of one's social responsibilities and of one's conscience, seems to be a relatively modern word.[224]

Modern education systems are rooted in such a context of responsibility. As children and young adults grow older they are expected to become

---

224   "Thus, answerability or responsibility consists in hearing and assuming the call, in wanting to have a conscience" (Critchley, 2014, 194).

more responsible for their own learning. But, to become responsible for their learning as adults, they are obliged to learn certain things and to develop certain skills as children. This is the case whether learning occurs in school or in more informal learning environments like a sports field or a church or a home.

Even when learning how to prepare a meal or play a sport or play a musical instrument there are certain things they have to learn. If she or he wants to be a welder or a nurse there are certain things they need to know. Yet in daily life and in the work place they will be continually confronted with unique situations needing solutions which they have to figure out for themselves.

This relationship between responsibilities for learning and obligations for learning reflect a paradox which, in short, suggests that in order to become responsible adults who are capable of making informed decisions about their lives and their participation in a modern society children need to learn certain worthwhile things. For example, they must learn fractions or study history or a catechism whether or not they like fractions or history or memorizing the catechism. Society obliges children to attend school, public or private, so as to ensure or encourage that they become free and autonomous adults who can function effectively in the world.

The notion of developing responsibility for oneself and for one's learning raises provocative questions related to religious education. For example, is religious education actually education or is it indoctrination? Such questions, interesting as they may be, are beyond the scope of this writing.

In sum, responsibility has come to imply living and acting in the creative tension which exists between obedience (e.g., to the gods or to fate or to the state) and freedom (i.e., free to think and act for oneself), between doing what's needed and doing what's wanted, between constraints and possibilities. Responsibility has to do with being both obedient and free at the same time.

Righteousness

The word right has several meanings; for example, to be correct, to be straight, not bent, a right angle (90°), to be right-handed, and others. These meanings come from Proto-Germanic *rehtan*, from Old Saxon and OHG *reht*, and first of all from PIE *reg* (move in a straight line, to rule, to lead straight, to put right). PIE *reg* also leads to Greek *orektos* (upright; i.e., erect) and Latin *rectus* (straight).

The meaning of right as correct or morally correct comes to Old English as *riht* (morally correct; just, fair, good, fitting) from Old Saxon *reht*. The word righteous, from the 16th century, comes from Old English *rihtwis* (right-wise; i.e., wise, meaning 'in the same manner'[225]). The word righteousness, from Old English *rehtwisnisse*, combines the terms right (correct, doing the 'right' action), -wise, and -ness (a condition of something).

Righteousness, meaning 'right in the same manner', implies a social context or culture in which one acts 'rightly' in order to be in line with other people of the society. Someone who is 'out of line' is not on the 'straight and narrow', so to speak.

For example, in Old Testament Hebrew, the term *zedaqah* (righteousness) is a response to *ze'aqah* (the cry; i.e., the cry of the poor for justice; or, the cry of a plaintiff). In this context, righteousness is an act of justice granted by the powerful to the weak.[226] Later, in the early Christian church, the word righteousness came to be used in relation to the giving of alms by the wealthy to the poor.[227]

The word unrighteous comes from the early Reformation of the 1520s. The word self-righteous is first seen in the 1680s.[228] Righteous, from jazz slang, meaning genuine or excellent, is from 1942.

---

225   Not the same use of wise as is used in regard to wisdom; rather wise as used in a word such as likewise.

226   "…most often in the Bible the word 'righteousness' means 'justice'. It doesn't mean some kind of individual rectitude…" (Borg, 2018, 169).

227   Brown, 2012, 79 – 80.

228   Borg suggests that in many cases today the term righteousness or self-righteousness has connotations of "keeping your moral shirttails clean, avoiding being stained by the world … [in that

In sum, the word righteousness not only describes the inner qualities of a person's character but also the 'right actions' (e.g., ensuring justice) which follow from these qualities of character which are in line with a prescribed or expected set of social values and mores.

Rite, Ritual, Ceremony

Rite, Ritual

The words rite and ritual have the same origins as the word arithmetic. Who would have thought that these words would be related to one another?

When I was young, I heard a woman say that going to church was "just a ritual", as if to say, boring or a waste of time. For her, every Sunday service seemed to be more or less the same—same prayer book, same pages, same words, same prayers. It seemed as though she wanted each Sunday service to be a novel experience, just like her favourite television programs. I remembered her as I began to think about the words rite, ritual, and arithmetic and what these words might have in common.

The origins of the words rite and ritual are somewhat mysterious which is perhaps appropriate given the meaning of these words. Etymological dictionaries suggest that rite and ritual may come from PIE *re(i)* (to count, to number, to reason). PIE *re(i)* may also be the origin of Sanskrit *riti* (a way, a custom) and Latin *ritus* (a religious observance or ceremony, custom, usage, rite).

It is not a mystery that the word rite came to English in the early 14th century from Latin *ritus*. The word ritual, used as an adjective, came to English in the 1560s from Middle French *ritual* and Latin *ritualis* (relating to religious rites) and Latin *ritus*. The use of ritual as a noun was first seen in 1649.

So, what's the connection between rite, ritual, and arithmetic? Latin *ritus* is related to Greek *arithmos* (number) and Old English *rim* (number). *Arithmos* comes from PIE *re(i)* and is the origin of the word arithmetic.

---

sense] In many ways, compassion is the opposite of righteousness" (Borg, 2018, 136).

Arithmetic is predictable and unchanging. There are no surprises. In arithmetic, 1+1 always equals 2. We don't worry about arithmetic being the same all the time. Like arithmetic, rite and ritual (for example, baptism or the eucharist) have a prescribed and stable nature; however, unlike arithmetic, they do evolve and change (or disappear).

Rite and ritual are representations of meaning; however, unlike the logical unfolding of arithmetic, rite and ritual are expressed in dramatic forms. When we attend a play; e.g., *Hamlet*, even thought the script is always the same, the script and the staging will be interpreted in different ways. In such a play, we perceive an expression of something that is meaningful about human life—we don't attend this play in order to learn about the history of Denmark.

The origins of rite and ritual suggest that early peoples looked for ways to represent and symbolize their sense of the meaning of life's mysteries in such dramatic and heartfelt ways. In contrast, philosophy and theology which came later, provide more rational or doctrinal explanations of meaning.

Rite and ritual are about meaning. Rite and ritual are like windows—they are transparent—they work best when we don't see them but see through them. The relative sameness of rite or ritual is what allows them to be transparent.

Like a play or a drama, in rite and ritual we put ourselves into a situation with the intention of experiencing mystery and meaning. Participating in a ritual is participating in sacred time just like entering a church is entering a sacred space. Participating in a ritual is an act of faith.

Ceremony

Rite and ritual are part of a ceremony or ceremonial event.

The word ceremony was introduced into English in the late 14th century as *cerymonye* by John Wycliffe (1320 – 1384), the translator of the first English language Bible.[229] *Cerymonye* comes from Old French *ceremonie* and from Latin *caerimonia* (holiness, sacredness; awe; reverent rite, sacred

---

229   Such vernacular translations of the Bible were banned or considered heretical during the 14th century.

ceremony). Ceremony, like rite and ritual, is a word with obscure origins, possibly from Etruscan.

The adjective ceremonial, meaning belonging to (religious) ritual, first seen around 1400, comes from Latin *caerimonialis* (pertaining to ceremony) and from *caerimonia*. The adjective *ceremonius*, meaning full of show and ceremony, from the 1610s, also comes from Latin *caerimonius* and *caerimonia*.

See also SACRAMENT.

Sacrament

Sacrament (and sacred) come from PIE *sak* (to sanctify) and from Latin *saceres* and *sacer* (sacred, dedicated, holy, accursed)—the roots of Latin *sacrare* (to make sacred, consecrate, hold sacred, immortalize, set apart, dedicate). These ancient words suggest that things are not necessarily sacred in and of themselves, rather, we make them sacred through our actions and commitments.

During the Roman Empire, a *sacramentum* (a consecrating) was not just a religious rite but possibly a life or death commitment to something. For example, in the Roman legal system, a *sacramentum legis actio* was a sum of money deposited, like a bond, in a legal procedure to ensure that the party depositing the money was acting in good faith. If you did not act with integrity and good faith in the courts, you could lose your deposit (or worse). Similarly, a *sacramentum militare* was an oath of allegiance which a soldier pledged upon entering the army—in this sense, the person was putting his life on the line as a deposit. The person was dedicating or consecrating his life to the Empire.

In a pre-Christian religious context, a *sacramentum* was an oath rendering the swearer as 'given to the gods'. To take an oath of consecration was to make a commitment to the gods. In the early church of the Roman Empire, a *sacramentum* was a form of initiation into Christian community.

The Latin word *sacramentum* (a consecrating), from *sacrare*, is a translation of Greek *mysterion* (secret rite or doctrine), from Greek *mystes* (one who has been initiated) and *myein* (to close, to shut—perhaps from the sense that only initiates were allowed to see or hear sacred rites; *myein* is also the root of mute). Greek *mysterion*, referring to 'the secret counsel of God', was translated as *sacramentum* in the 4th century Latin Vulgate Bible.

Sacrament came to English around 1200 from Old French *sacrament* (consecration, mystery) and referred to the eucharist as well as to 'an outward and visible sign of an inward and spiritual grace'. The sense of a sacrament as 'a holy mystery' is from the late 14th century.[230]

See also CEREMONY, MYSTICISM, RITE, RITUAL

Sacred, Profane

Sacred

Sacred has its roots in the desire of ancient peoples to make or to consider something sacred. The word sacred has roots in PIE *sak* (to sanctify), a word which seems little changed from its present form. Another source suggests that sacred comes from PIE *shnk* (to make sacred, to sanctify), a word which appears related to Hittite *saklai* (custom, rites).

PIE *sak* is the root of Latin *sacer* (sacred, dedicated, holy, accursed), *sacrare* (to make sacred, consecrate, hold sacred, immortalize, set apart, dedicate), and *sancire* (to make sacred, confirm, ratify, ordain). From these PIE and Latin roots, come 12th century Old French *sacrer* (to consecrate, anoint, dedicate) and, in the late 14th century, the English word sacred (to make holy).

These origins indicate that a person or object is not sacred in itself; rather, persons, places, or objects are perhaps, first, felt to be sacred, and later *made* sacred, perhaps through ritual acts. People decide what is holy and what is not.[231]

---

230   Traditionally, in the Christian church, the seven sacraments are baptism, penance, confirmation, holy orders, the eucharist, matrimony, and the anointing of the sick (extreme unction).

231   For example: "Sacredness is realized in the act of intention because reality is communicative and the mind is made, grace assisting exquisite effort, to experience its meaning" (Robinson, 2019, 294 – 295).

A question arises: why would something be considered sacred in the first place? What is it that would give someone pause for reflection—that is, "This experience is not just something ordinary, there is something extraordinary or mysterious going on here." To consider something sacred is to acknowledge a sense of awe and mystery that surrounds that being considered sacred, something that is perhaps beyond rational explanation.

An Old English word for sacred was *godcund*. The concept of the 'sacred heart' of Jesus as an object of religious veneration is from 1765. The term 'sacred cow' (an object of Hindu veneration) is from 1891. The use of 'sacred cow' as someone or something that must not be criticized is from 1910.

See also SAINT, SANCTIFICATION, SANCTIFY, SANCTUARY.

Profane

The word profane combines PIE *per* (forward, before, in front of; the root of Latin *pro*) and Latin *fano, fanum* (temple; from PIE dhes, a root of words for religious concepts). The Latin words *profanus* and *pro fano* mean 'out in front of the temple' or 'not admitted to the temple'.

The verb 'to profane' comes to English in the late 14th century from Old French *profaner*, Latin *profanare* (to desecrate, render unholy, violate), and Latin *profanus* (unholy, not consecrated).

The adjective profane (un-ecclesiastical, secular) comes to English in the mid-15th century from 12th century Old French *profane* and Latin *profanus*. The sense of profane as 'unholy, polluted' is from around 1500. The word profanity (foul language or the act of profaning the name of the Lord) comes around 1600.

See also SECULAR.

Saint

The word saint, like the word sacred, traces its roots back to PIE *sak* (to sanctify).

From PIE *sak* comes Latin *saceres, sacer, sacrare* (sacred, dedicated, holy, accursed), words which lead to the English word sacred. Note the surprising use of 'accursed' as an early definition of these words leading to 'sacred'. Perhaps in contrast to the consideration of saints as somehow 'perfect' people, I suspect most saints may perhaps have humbly described themselves not so much as accursed but as highly imperfect and unworthy of such saintly veneration.

Latin *sacrare*, related to Latin *sancire* (to consecrate), is the root of Latin *sanctus* (holy, consecrated), Old French *saint* and *seinte* (a saint, a holy relic), Old English *sanct* (saint). By the early 12th century we see English word saint.

The word saint was originally used as an honorary title or a term of respect for a canonized person (that is, the use of St. or Ste. was similar to the use of Dr. or Rev. as prefix to someone's name). However, by the 1300s, the word saint was no longer just a person's title—the person *was* a saint. The use of the word saint meaning a person of extraordinary holiness is from the 1560s.

The word sainthood comes from the 1540s. The adjective saintly comes from the 1620s.

See also SACRED.

Salvation

The word salvation, in its origins, means wholeness, to be made whole, and to be made safe.

In its origins, the word salvation is rooted in PIE *solwos* and *sol* (whole), words which are also the origins of Greek *holos* (whole), Latin *solidus* (solid), and Sanskrit *sarvah* (uninjured, intact, whole).

PIE *solwos* and *sol* lead to Latin *saluber* (healthful), *salus* (good health), *salvus* (uninjured, in good health, safe). Latin *salvus* is related to Latin *salvare* (to make safe) from which we see Old French *sauver* (to keep safe, to protect, to redeem). By 1200 we see the English verb 'to save' (to deliver from danger, to rescue from peril, to bring to safety, to prevent the death of). At this time, we also see 'to save' in the theological sense of 'to deliver from sin or its consequences, to admit to eternal life, to gain salvation'.

The word salvation, in the sense of 'the saving of the soul', comes to English around 1200 from Old French *salvaciun* and Latin *salvationem* and *salvere* (to save).

Around 1300 'to save' was also used to mean to reserve for future use, to hold back, and to store up instead of spending. By the late 14th century 'to save' also meant to keep possession of. The non-religious sense of salvation is first seen in the late 14th century.

The Salvation Army was founded by Rev William Booth in 1878. In sum, does the word salvation imply being saved *from* something or *for* something? Given the roots of the word salvation in words related to wholeness, to be made whole, and to be made safe, perhaps we could say that salvation, in its religious context, implies experiencing the wholeness of our life, warts and all, and, in gratitude, we act accordingly.

Sanctify, Sanctification

Sanctify

The verb sanctify combines Latin *sanctus* (holy) and *facere* (to make, to do); that is, sanctification means to make something holy. Latin *facere* has its roots in PIE *dhe* (to set, to put). Sanctify comes to English in the late 14th century as *seintefie* (to consecrate) from Old French *saintefier* and Latin *sanctificare* (to make holy).

By around 1400, the English word sanctify (to render holy or legitimate by religious sanction) was being used to conform with Latin *sanctificare*. By the early 1600s, sanctify also meant 'to render worthy of respect'.

Sanctification

The noun sanctification, the process of becoming holy or acquiring sanctity, comes to English in the 1520s from Latin *sanctificationem* and *sanctificare* (sanctify).

Questions of who is entitled to sanctify or of how something or someone comes to a state of sanctification, not to mention the theological distinctions between justification and sanctification, have been under discussion for centuries. What does seem to be commonly understood is that a people cannot sanctify themselves![232]

See also HOLY, SAINT.

Sanctuary

A sanctuary, as a building or place set apart for holy worship, comes to English in the early 14th century. Sanctuary has its origins in Anglo-French *sentuarie*, Old French *saintuaire* (sacred relic, holy thing; reliquary, sanctuary), words that suggest a sanctuary is also a place where sacred or holy objects are kept. In turn, these words come from Latin *sanctuarium* (a sacred place, shrine, a private room; e.g., a room or space inside a church building) from Latin *sanctus* (holy).

Since the time of Constantine and by medieval Church law, fugitives or debtors enjoyed immunity from arrest in certain churches. This sense of sanctuary as 'immunity from punishment' is seen in English in the late 14th century; however, exceptions were made in cases of treason and sacrilege.

The general (non-ecclesiastical) sense of sanctuary as a 'place of refuge or protection' is attested from 1560s; as 'land set aside for wild plants or animals to breed and live' it is recorded from 1879.

Interestingly, the word sentry (1610, originally a watchtower) may be a shortened version of sentinel (from *centrinel*, 1590s) or perhaps a shortened version of sanctuary (when used as a shelter for a watchman). https://www.etymonline.com/search?q=sentry

See also HOLY, SAINT, SANCTIFICATION, SANCTIFY.

---

232   "The sanctification of the individual—not the love of humankind in the abstract, which would be much easier, much less irksome, but of the singular neighbour, as encountered—implies to writers [and to anyone, for that matter] who embrace it radical human equality and dignity" (Robinson, 2019, 253).

Satan

Satan begins in the Hebrew verb *satan* (to show enmity to, to oppose, plot against) from the Hebrew root *s–t–n*[233] (one who opposes, obstructs, or acts as an adversary). In early versions of the Bible, *satan* is used to describe an adversarial role rather than to name a character. In the 6th century BCE, Hebrew writers used the term 'the satan' to name any of the angels sent by God to obstruct or hinder human activity.[234]

From these Hebrew roots emerge Greek *Satanas* and Latin *Satan* (used only in the Vulgate Old Testament). In the Greek Septuagint, Hebrew *satan* was translated as *diabolus* (slanderer, one who throws something in the path of another) which in turn later became the English words devil and diabolic. See DEVIL.

By the 12th century Satan had become part of Old English as a proper name given to the supreme evil spirit in Christianity. In the King James Version of the Bible (1611), the word Lucifer[235] is used in reference to Satan (e.g., Isaiah 14:12); however, the name Satan remains more commonly used.

In Peter Binsfeld's categorization of demons and devils, published in 1589, Satan is just one of the seven devils in hell, each assigned to a separate room, one for each of the seven deadly sins.[236] Binsfeld assigns Satan to the room designated to those tormented for the sin of wrath. Wrath, or anger, is perhaps the most potent and even most potentially destructive

---

233   Can, perhaps, s-t-n or STN as Satan can be read in a similar fashion as YHWH came to be read as Yahweh and later as Jehovah? See JEHOVAH.

234   Pagels, E. (1995). *The origin of Satan*. New York: Random House.

235   Lucifer: from Latin *lux* (light) + Latin *ferre* (to carry); i.e., to carry light or light-bringer. In ancient times, lucifer referred to the morning star or perhaps a falling star (KJV Bible Isaiah 14: 12 "How art thou fallen from heaven, O Lucifer, son of the morning"). https://www.etymonline.com/search?q=lucifer

236   The devils assigned to the seven deadly sins were, in order from bad to worst: Asmodeus (lust), Beelzebub (gluttony), Mammon (greed), Belphegor (sloth), Satan (wrath), Leviathan (envy), and Lucifer (pride). Some of these names have become ordinary words in English—mammon, leviathan, lucifer.

emotion. Perhaps this is why the name Satan has stuck in our collective memory more than the names of other devils.

From the word Satan, other English words have evolved. In the 1550s, the term satanist was applied to various Protestant sects by their enemies. In the 1560s we see the use of satanic to describe someone's disposition. Satanic is seen in 1667 in John Milton's poem, *Paradise Lost*. Satanic, meaning diabolical, is seen in 1793. William Blake used the phrase "dark satanic mills" in a poem published in 1808; better known today as the hymn *Jerusalem* put to music in 1916. In the 1820s and 1830s, the term satanism was used by critics in relation to the work of the English poet Lord Byron. In 1895, satanism was used to mean the worship of Satan, particularly in France where it was reputed to be active. Satan worshipper is first seen in 1896.

Saviour

The word saviour comes to us from two sources, one secular and one religious.

First, the secular use of saviour comes to English in the 14th century—a saviour is someone who delivers or rescues someone or something from peril. Saviour comes from Old French *sauveour* and Latin *salvatorem, salvator* (saver, preserver) and *salvare* (to save).

The religious use of saviour comes from Greek *soter* (saviour). The word soteriology refers to the academic study of salvation and, in particular, to the study of Jesus as saviour.

When referring to Jesus, early Old Saxon versions of the Gospels used the term *heliand* (healer)[237], not saviour, from Proto-Germanic hailjan (to make whole), a word which is also the origin of Old Norse *heila*, Old Frisian *hela*, Gothic *hailjan*, Dutch *helen*, and German *heilen*. These words all have their origin in PIE *kailo* (whole, uninjured) which is also the origin of the words hale and health; e.g., 'hale and hearty'. Old Saxon

---

237   Ostler, 2016, 143.

heliand later became Old English *haeland* (healer, healing) and *haelan* (to cure; to save; to make whole, sound, well).

As Christianity spread and took form in early Britain, Greek *soter* and Latin *salvator* (saviour) gradually replaced these earlier terms meaning healer.

In brief, the word saviour embraces not only the notion of 'being saved' but also of 'being healed'.[238]

As the English language developed, particularly as French and Latin words overtook Old English after the Norman invasion of 1066, the word saviour came to be used in both secular and religious contexts. 'Saviour' is the original English spelling. 'Savior' is the later American spelling.

Scripture

The word scripture has its earliest roots in PIE *(s)ker* (to cut, to scrape, to hack) and later in PIE *skribh* (to cut, to separate, to sift). These PIE words lead to Greek *skariphasthai* (to scratch an outline, to sketch) and Latin *scribere* (to write).

Latin *scribere* is related to Latin *scriptus* (to write), Latin *scriptum* (a writing, book, law, line mark), and Latin *scriptura* (an act or product of writing; e.g., the writings contained in the Bible, a passage from the Bible). By the early 14th century, the word Scripture (the sacred writings of the Bible) was seen in English. By the mid-14th century, the word scripture was being used to mean any piece of writing, an act of writing, and written characters.

Latin *scribere* also leads to Old French *escrit* (piece of writing, written paper, credit note, IOU, deed, bond) and, by the late 14th century, to the English word script (something written).

The adjective scriptural is first seen in the 1640s.

Script, meaning handwriting, is first seen around 1860. The theatrical use of script (short for manuscript) is first seen in 1884.

---

238   Tillich, 2005, 43.

Sect, Cult

Was early Christianity a sect or a cult?

Sect

The word sect comes from PIE *sekw* (to follow; *sekw* is also the root of the word sequence) and Latin *secta* (literally, a way, road, beaten path; manner, mode, following, school of thought). Later, Latin *secta* came to mean a religious group or sect in philosophy or religion. From these sources comes Old French *secte*, *sete* (sect, religious community). By the mid-14th century we see the English word sect (a distinctive system of beliefs or observances; party or school within a religion). By the 1570s, sect meant a separately organized religious body. People may have joined such a religious body because it had a certain sects appeal.

Cult

The word cult comes from PIE *kwel* (revolve, move round; sojourn, dwell) from which comes Latin *colere* (to cultivate, to till; to inhabit; to frequent, practice, respect; tend, guard). From *colere* comes Latin *colonus* (husband-man, tenant farmer, settler in a new land) and *colonia* (settled land, farm, landed estate). *Colonia* is also the root of the word colony.

Also, from Latin *colere* comes Latin *cultus*. Originally *cultus* meant tended, cultivated. Later, the meaning included care, labour; cultivation, culture; worship, reverence. From Latin *cultus* come words such as agriculture, horticulture, and so on, as well as the word culture.[239] In the early 17th

---

239   Culture, from Latin *cultura* (the tilling of land, act of preparing the earth for crops), came to English in the mid-15th century from Latin *colere*. Culture meaning the cultivation and promotion of growth in plants is from 1620, a meaning transferred to fish, oysters, etc., by 1796. Culture referring to production of microorganisms in a suitable environment is seen in 1880.

The word culture used in reference to the cultivation and refinement of the mind through education and systematic improvement is from around 1500. The word culture, in this sense, however, was not common before the 19th century except when used as a metaphor borrowed, for example, from agriculture. Culture, meaning learning and good taste, the intellectual side of civilization, is from 1805.

century the word cult comes to English from French *culte*. At that time the word meant worship or homage (a meaning now obsolete). By the late 17th century the word meant a particular form or system of worship. And, by the end of the 17th century, the word cult was rarely used.

However, the word cult was revived in the mid-19th century and used non-judgmentally with reference to ancient or primitive systems of religious belief and worship, especially the rites and ceremonies employed in such worship. And, cult, meaning the devoted attention to a particular person or thing, is from 1829 (https://www.etymonline.com/search?q=cult).

Sect or Cult?

In brief, in the first years of the early church, it could have been or could be considered a sect; i.e., a branch of Judaism. However, even if Christianity began as such a sect, it soon became a cult, both in the context of its Judaic roots and the larger context of the Roman Empire. However, it is not likely that the term cult would have been used at that time except in the most general sense of some state of mind and heart that is being cultivated.[240]

Originally the terms sect and cult simply described different groups of people without any intended negative connotations. Today, however, these two terms *do* have negative connotations—they are associated with new or unpopular religious movements and as such the terms are avoided by scholars.[241]

Culture, meaning the collective customs and achievements of a people, is from 1867. https://www.etymonline.com/search?q=culture

240   Stark differentiates sects and cults. He suggests that sect movements occur "by schism within a conventional religious body when persons desiring a more otherworldly version of the faith break away to 'restore' the religion to a higher level of tension with its environment ... cult movements, on the other hand, are not simply new organizations of an old faith; they are new faiths, at least new in the society being examined ... cult movements violate prevailing religious norms and are often the target of considerable hostility" (Stark, 1997, 33).

Stark also states that some current sociological studies "identify churches and sects as the end points of a continuum based on the degree of tension between the group and its sociological environment. Sects are religious groups in a relatively high state of tension with their environment; churches are groups in a relatively low state of tension" (Stark, 1997, 25). Stark says that such terms and concepts are "*names, not explanations*". The naming of experience does not necessarily explain it.

241   https://www.encyclopedia.com/environment/encyclopedias-almanacs-transcripts-and-

When considering the growth of the early church, terms such as sect or cult can only be used with hindsight based on current word usage and on historical and sociological analysis. Whether Christianity could be considered a sect or cult depends on how these terms are now currently used. Perhaps, instead, with such hindsight and using current terminology, could the early church be called a 'new religious movement'?

Secular

Two theories outline possible origins of the word secular: one is related to being connected and a second to the sowing of seeds.

First, the word secular is said to come from Proto-Italic *sai–tlo* and from PIE *sai* meaning to tie or to bind, particularly in the sense of the links or ties that bind and connect one generation to another.[242] A second theory suggests that the word secular comes from PIE *se* (to sow), as in to sow seeds. This second theory may also be related to the Gothic term *mana-seps* (mankind, world; literally, 'the seed of men').

These early meanings of secular suggest enduring concerns for connection and continuity with past generations and for the growth and development of subsequent generations. To be secular is to be part of the flow of one generation to another. To be secular is to be in the world both now and into the future. To be secular is to be part of community and culture.

From these PIE origins come Latin *saeculum*[243] (age, span of time, race, generation) and *saecularis* (of an age, occurring once in an age). Later, Latin *saecularis* came to mean worldly. From Latin *saecularis* came Old French *seculer* and, by around 1300, the word secular came to English with several connotations; e.g., living in the world, something belonging to the state, something or someone religious but not belonging to a religious order.[244]

---

maps/cults-and-sects

242   PIE *sai* is also related to sinew. Interestingly, a theory for the origin of the word religion suggests that it also comes from ancient words meaning 'to bind together'.

243   Latin *saeculum* is also the origin of French *siècle* (century) and *fin de siècle* (the end of the century, or perhaps more metaphorically, 'the end of an age').

244   For example, deacons and priests were considered secular clergy, unlike monastics or

At that time the word secular described religious people who lived 'in the world'—people who lived as part of the seemingly natural order of things. In contrast, members of members of religious communities (i.e., 'the religious') had symbolically put themselves outside the world. They were people who chose to stand intentionally apart from or in a detached relationship to the natural order of things. Being secular (i.e., being a lay person, deacon, or priest in a local church) and being 'the religious' (i.e., a monk or nun living in a monastic life) were simply two different ways of being religious. The assumption or lived reality at that time was that everyone was religious in some way.

However, over time, the word secular has come more commonly to describe someone or something that is not religious. The verb 'to secularize' (i.e., to secularize property or offices or to remove something from the control of a religious body) is from the 1610s. From 1711 'to secularize' come to mean 'to become worldly'. In 1706 the term secularization was used to describe the conversion of something (e.g., church property) for secular purposes. The use of 'to secularize' in terms of education and other social institutions is seen from 1846.

Secularism, the doctrine that "morality should be based on the well-being of people in the present life, without regard to religious belief or a hereafter" is from 1846. Also, from 1846, we see the first use of the term secularist, one who rejects all forms of religion based on revelation. From 1851 the term secularist also referred to one who maintains that public education and civil policy should be conducted without the introduction of a religious element.[245]

The use of the word secular in reference to humanism and the exclusion of belief in God from matters of ethics and morality is from the 1850s. The term secularization was in general use by 1863.

Today, the term secular has taken on a somewhat oppositional tone— to be secular is to be *not* religious. That is, you are either religious or secular but not both. However, we now see the retronym non-secular (or

---

members of a religious community. Secular clergy work in the world whereas monastics have removed themselves from the world.

245   https://www.etymonline.com/word/secularism#etymonline_v_37732

nonsecular; from around 2000).[246] The implication of non-secular is that a person can be less concerned with religious beliefs or doctrines and more concerned with living in ways that reflect and embody the values of a religious life, a life called by some as one of 'religionless faith' (e.g., Caputo, 2019, Critchley, 2012; Kearney & Zimmermann, 2016, Rollins, 2015).

In such a context, could we say that the secular and non-secular are partners, each twisted around each other—that one cannot exist without the other? Or even that the secular and the religious are partners. They are connected. They are the seeds from which each other grows. The lived reality is that both share the same world.[247]

Sepphoris

Sepphoris is not really a word about religion—or is it?

Some time ago, I read a magazine article[248] in which the writer described his experiences in Sepphoris, today known as Tzippori, a village in central Galilee in the modern state of Israel.

The site of Sepphoris has been inhabited for 3,000 years or more. During the first century BCE, when most of the Middle East was under the jurisdiction of the Roman Empire, a Jewish king, Herod the Great, occupied Sepphoris on behalf of the Romans. In 4 BCE, during a revolt against Roman rule, Sepphoris was burned to the ground and its inhabitants sold into slavery. Later, Herod's son, Herod Antipas, rebuilt the city and established his rule from there.

During the first century CE, Sepphoris prospered and developed. Sitting astride the crossroads of the west-east road linking the port of

---

246   https://en.wiktionary.org/wiki/nonsecular

247   "The secular mind is a concrete expression of a changing transcendence and used religious truth to form itself, as much as did the official ... ecclesiastical discourse. Furthermore, the conflicts that constantly pit emerging secular expressions against orthodoxy or dogma should really be seen as so many internal conflicts which set opposing interpretive options of divine difference against each other" (Gauchet, 1997, 59).

248   Robert D. Kaplan. (January 2000). Israel now. *Atlantic Monthly*. Retrieved 8 Dec 2018: https://www.theatlantic.com/magazine/archive/2000/01/israel-now/304700/

Haifa and Jordan, and the north-south road linking Damascus, Jerusalem and Egypt, Sepphoris was a major centre of trade and commerce. The city sat on a height of land commanding the surrounding territory—an ideal site for a fortress and military base. Sepphoris became a major centre of Jewish learning and spiritual life. In the 12th century, a Crusader castle was built at Sepphoris.

From the time of Herod Antipas until the decline of the Ottoman Empire at the end of World War One, Sepphoris thrived as a cosmopolitan centre of culture and commerce with a multicultural population of 30,000 or so living in relative harmony. Following the Arab-Israeli War of 1948, the Palestinians of Sepphoris were displaced and moved to refugee camps.

I read this magazine article with routine interest until my attention was jolted. With a gasp and dramatic halt I stopped reading. "Well, I'll be damned," I thought, "who knew!" The writer had just described one of the suburbs of ancient Sepphoris—the village of Nazareth—at the bottom of the hill upon which Sepphoris stands.

In that moment, my Sunday School understanding of Nazareth and Jesus was dramatically transformed. Contrary to what I had learned as a child and which I had not thought very much about since, Jesus was not from a rural village out in the middle of nowhere, he was a child from what today we might call 'the suburbs'. He would have seen the world coming and going past his doorstep.

When Sepphoris was being re-built by Herod Antipas it is quite conceivable that Joseph, and even Jesus, were employed there as craftsmen. Some records and traditions from the time suggest that Mary, the mother of Jesus, may even have been born in Sepphoris.

The basic facts and stories which I had learned as a child had not changed. What changed was that I now see these facts and stories within a much broader and, to me, a more meaningful perspective.

Sermon

The word sermon has its origins in words that remind me of the phrase 'getting your ducks in a row'. The word sermon also has origins in words related to protection and keeping watch.

The word sermon comes to English as *sarmun* in the early 1200s when it meant a discourse on a text of scripture. In turn, *sarmun* comes from 10th century Old French *sermon* (speech, words, discourse, homily) and Latin *sermonem* (continued speech, conversation, common talk, rumor; learned talk or discourse; and, originally perhaps, a stringing of words together).

These words have their roots in PIE *ser-mo* (to line up) and PIE *ser* (to protect). Whereas *ser-mo* leads to sermon, PIE *ser* leads to Latin *servare* (to guard, to keep watch), Old High German *gi-sarwi* (armor, equipment), and Old English *searu* (art, skills; wile, deceit).

In addition to sermon, the PIE root *ser* can be seen many English words such as assert, conserve, to desert (to leave one's duty), dissertation, exert, insert, observe, preserve, reserve, reservoir, sorcerer, and sort.

In sum, a sermon is an orderly arrangement of words intended to provide a frame or context holding knowledge or information within some perspective, or to ensure that that the 'right' information is watched and guarded, or that listeners are inspired by a particular message.

Shepherd

Did you know that shepherds have a distant connection with hockey players?

The word shepherd comes from the Old English word *sceaphierde*: *sceap* meaning sheep and *hierde* meaning herd. There are very similar words in German and Dutch; e.g., Middle Low German and Middle Dutch *schaphirde*, Middle High German *schafhirte*, and German *schafhirt*.

Sceap (sheep) is related to other northern European words for sheep; e.g., Old Frisian *skep*, Middle Low German *schap*, Middle Dutch *scaep*, Dutch *schaap*, Old High German *scaf*, and German *schaf*. However, the most ancient origins of the word sheep are found in the PIE origins of ewe; i.e., *owi* (from which comes Latin *ovine*). *Hierde* (herd) comes to English through similar northern European languages from its origins in PIE *kerdh*, meaning a herd or group. The word shepherd comes to English before the 12th century.

When, for example, Psalm 23 states, "the Lord is my shepherd", what might be implied by this metaphor in terms of the role of a shepherd?

Shepherding usually involves working in isolated rural areas, often highland and mountain areas unsuitable for farming. Shepherds live a migratory life, away from home and family, moving sheep from highlands to lowlands on a seasonal basis as well as moving sheep from pasture to pasture and to markets. Shepherds work on the margins of society, not only geographically, but socially. In some societies, shepherds were buried with a tuft of wool in their hand so as on arrival in heaven they could prove their occupation and be excused for missing Sunday church!

Traditionally, shepherds have had a unique role and social status. They usually work alone or with other shepherds. Because of this solitary life and of the mobility inherent in their work, shepherds have enjoyed high levels of responsibility, autonomy, and status. Landowners entrusted shepherds with their sheep for seasons at a time. In the medieval past, shepherds were often used as messengers because of their ability to come and go more independently than other workers. At that time, shepherds were often seen as what today we would call independent contractors, persons with a higher status than farm labourers and other workers who were constrained by more traditional social or feudal roles and structures.[249]

In brief, a shepherd was a person given a high degree of freedom, autonomy, and responsibility with regard to his work and who was answerable only to his employer.

Other related terms include shepherdess, from shepherd + -ess, first seen in the late 14th century, and the verb 'to shepherd', first seen in 1790, meaning 'to herd sheep'. The metaphoric sense of 'to shepherd' as 'to watch

---

249   For example: "There is no element of feudal bondage in the relations between [employers and employees; i.e., shepherds]". Ladurie, E.L. (1978). *Montaillou: A portrait of life in a medieval village; Part 1.4, The shepherds*. (B. Bray, Trans.). London: Penguin, 73.
And: "Mobility itself, as we have seen [pp. 67 – 68], takes with it a high degree of status" (Cunliffe, 2013, 96).

over or to guide' is first recorded 1820. Shepherd's pie is first recorded from 1877. A crosier, the symbol of a bishop's pastoral role, is based on the shepherd's hook-shaped crook or staff.

So, what's the connection of shepherds and hockey players? In medieval French, the shepherd's crook or staff was called a *hoquet* from which we get the English word hockey. A hockey stick is a curved or hooked stick like a shepherd's crook.

Sin, Guilt, Shame

I once saw a neighbour rap his young child on the side of the head for misbehaving. "Born in sin," he said to me, somewhat guiltily, as if feeling the need to justify his action. This memory comes to mind as I sit down to write about the origins of the words sin, guilt, and shame.

Sin

Is sin something that we are or something that we do? Or both? What can we learn from the origins of this word?

The word sin has complex origins in two PIE words related to being and existing: *es* (to be) and *es-ont* (becoming, being, existence; in particular, that which is fundamentally real or true).

First, PIE *es* is the origin of Latin *esse* (to be, that which is) from which comes the word essence (the ultimate nature of something, not just its existence). In addition, Latin *esse* is the root of Latin *sons* and *sontis* (guilty); however, these are not the origins of the English word guilt—more on this in a moment.

Second, PIE *es-ont* is the root of Proto-Germanic *sundjo* (sin; 'it is true'). The related Gothic term is *sunja* (truth). What might we imply from this phrase 'it is true'? Perhaps, a non-judgmental statement that the ultimate nature or essence of something is that it is what it is. In Hittite, another language with PIE origins, we see a confessional statement related to the word sin translated as 'it is being'.

Proto-Germanic *sundjo* leads to the Old Norse word *sannr* (truth) and the Old Norse phrase *vero sannr at* (to be found guilty of). Old Norse *sannr* is also the origin of the Old English word *sooth* (truth, justice), as in the old phrase 'for sooth'.

What are we to make of these ancient origins of the word sin?

First, what is the connection between sin and ancient PIE words related to essence and truth? In these ancient words we see perhaps the shadows of a truth about existence; that is, sin (and guilt) are part of the essence of who we are; i.e., "to be truly the one [who is guilty]."[250] So, what is it that is real or true? What is it in life that might arouse such feelings of sin and guilt? And perhaps shame?

I would suggest that feelings of unease come *before* ideas of sin. Perhaps such ancient PIE words are related to the feelings of unease or discomfort a person may have felt when he or she had the sense of not being true to their essence or essential self, of not living up to expectations of self or others, or when he or she felt separated or even alienated from self or others or one's god, not that they would necessarily have had such thoughts in the moment. Rather, such a feeling or feelings would come *before* thoughts or explanations of the feelings; that is, people would experience disconnections from others or from self and such feelings of unease would arise. If so, perhaps these early origins of the word sin seem to suggest that they were states of being (or feeling) long before they were an idea or concept; that is, "I feel this way" comes before "They is why I feel this way" or "This is what I would call it when I feel this way."

Second, it seems that only in the later evolution of the meaning of the word sin that we see suggestions that sin is about actions as well as a state of being. For example, Proto-Germanic *sundjo*, Gothic *sonja*, and Old Norse *sannr* are roots of German *sunde* (sin), a word used to describe a transgression, trespass, or offense. From these origins comes Old English *synn* (sin) meaning a moral wrongdoing, injury, mischief, enmity, feud, guilt, crime, offence against God, misdeed. This Old English noun *synn* is

---

250   Online Etymological Dictionary: sin
http://www.etymonline.com/index.php?allowed_in_frame=0&search=sin&searchmode=none

the source of the Old English verb *syngian* (to commit sin, transgress, err). And from Old English *synn* and *syngian* we have the English word sin.

Some sources suggest that Old English *synn* was used when translating Greek and Hebrew versions of the Bible. For example, Old English *synn* was used when translating the Hebrew word *hata* (to go astray) and the Greek term *harmartia*, a term which has its origins in archery meaning to miss the bull's eye, but nevertheless hitting the target; or, even to miss the target entirely.[251] In this context, sin can be seen as either an inadvertent error or a wilful wrongdoing.

During the years of the early church, many scholars and theologians wrestled with defining and describing both the idea and the experiences of sin. To name but a few—Marcion of Sinope, Valentinus, Justin Martyr, Origen, St Anthony the Great of Egypt, Pachomius the Great, St Basil the Great of Caesarea, Martin of Tours, St Augustine of Hippo, Pelagius, John Cassian, St Benedict of Nursia, St Columban, Gregory of Tours, and Pope Gregory I the Great—not to mention the writers of the New Testament. In the midst of debate and controversy, Augustine's writings on sin and original sin eventually became the standard view on the subject; in particular, the metaphorical notion of sin as an ongoing state of debt and obligation, not just as instances of wrongdoing.[252]

Some early church scholars listed and categorized sins in the same way that other aspects of the world were listed and categorized; i.e., the seven deadly sins.[253]

---

251   However, other sources suggest that this use of an archery reference may have been obsolete by the time the early Christian church was formulating its doctrines and translations of biblical and other texts. Nevertheless, today the word *harmatia* is used, particularly in a literary context, to describe the tragic flaw in a character that leads to his or her downfall.

252   "This was the view of the relation between sin [as debt] and almsgiving that Augustine advocated after centuries that had already witnessed 'The slow but sure penetration of the metaphor of sin as debt into every aspect of Greek- and Latin-speaking Christianity'."
Brown, P. (2015). *The ransom of the soul.* Cambridge, MA: Harvard University Press, 98; citing Anderson, G. (2009). *Sin: A history.* New Haven, CT: Yale University Press, 9 and 135.

253   An early Christian writer, Evagrius Ponticus (345 – 399) listed eight of humanity's evil thoughts or faults: gluttony, fornication, avarice, pride, sadness (despair), wrath, boasting (vainglory), and acedia (dejection, spiritual lethargy). His pupil, John Cassian (360 – 435), a theologian and pioneer of western Christian monasticism, revised this list and arranged them from least problematic to most problematic: gluttony, lust, avarice, sadness (despair or despondency), anger, spiritual lethargy, vanity,

In brief, the word sin, describing a basic element of the human condition, comes to us through Germanic languages related to the ancient PIE word *es* (to be). The relatively recent notion that a sin is something we do seems a long way from its ancient origins in the understanding that sin is a state of being, part of the essence of human nature and human reality.

Guilt

Usually, we feel bad about doing wrong or making a mistake or not living up to expectations. Such feelings arise in the experiences of our imperfections. In spite of the fact that we all know that 'nobody's perfect' there is often an irrational sense that we should or ought to be perfect or at least be better than we are now. These feelings of unease or guilt in relation to what is termed sin are first of all, as suggested in their origins, about states of being. Being imperfect is just objectively (and non-judgmentally) the way we are and it is natural to feel uncomfortable about this.[254]

The origins of the English word guilt are unknown. The word is first seen in Old English *gylt* (crime, sin, fault, moral defect, failure of duty, financial penalty) and Old English *gyltig* (guilty). One view suggests that *gyltig* comes from Old English *gieldan* (to pay for, a debt related to money). One writer notes, "In both Dutch and German, the word for debt

---

and pride.

Pope Gregory I the Great (540 – 604) revised and condensed Cassian's list, identifying seven 'deadly sins' (again, from bad to worst): lust, gluttony, sadness, avarice (greed), wrath, envy (new to the list), and pride (pride combined with vainglory).

Later, the sin of sloth replaced that of sadness. It was no longer a sin to be sad! Each of the seven deadly sins is matched with one of the seven cardinal virtues; i.e., self-control, temperance, generosity, zeal, kindness, love, and humility.

During the 16th century, various writers documented the different punishments in hell that were reserved for each of these sins. For example, the lusty ended up in fire and brimstone, the gluttons were force fed toads, rats, and snakes, the greedy were boiled in oil, sad (or slothful) folks ended up in a room full of snakes, angry people were dismembered alive, the envious ended up in freezing water, and the prideful were tortured and broken on the wheel.

https://en.wikipedia.org/wiki/Seven_deadly_sins

254   A wise counsellor might suggest that we be more concerned with being 'whole' than with being 'perfect'.

also means guilt."[255] This seems related to Augustine's notion of sin as debt, as noted above. However, other sources suggest that this etymological connection between guilt and *gieldan* is "inadmissable phonologically."[256]

In any case, by the 14th century, the word guilt referred to the state of a moral agent resulting from the commission of a crime or offence either wilfully or by consent. To plead 'not guilty' of an action or wrongdoing comes from the 15th century. Guilty, describing the person who is guilty, comes from the 1540s. Guilty, meaning 'of conscience, feeling' (i.e., a guilty conscience), comes from the 1590s. The term 'a sense of guilt' is from the 1680s. To 'plead guilty' in a court of law comes from the 19th century, even though the Oxford English Dictionary states that, technically, 'guilty' is not a plea but a confession (that is, a person who confesses is not pleading or asking but telling or admitting). In religious terms, one pleads for mercy or forgiveness following a confession of wrongdoing.

This use of the word guilt during the 16th and 17th centuries Reformation suggests that guilt is related to the growing sense of the individual in relation to society and of a personal responsibility for one's actions (i.e., "I did 'x' and feel bad about it"; rather than, "I was born a sinner and can't help myself.")

In brief, guilt is a feeling related to something we have done. Guilt is about what we have done not about who we are.

Shame

How are guilt and shame related? Can we say that shame is feeling bad about feeling bad? Is shame a response to guilt? Is shame the only response to guilt?

The word shame comes from Old English *scamu, sceomu* (feelings of guilt or disgrace; confusion caused by shame, disgrace, dishonor, insult, loss of esteem or reputation; shameful circumstance, what brings disgrace; modesty; private parts). Shame is also from Proto-Germanic *skamo* which is assumed to be from PIE *kemen* (sky, heaven) and from PIE *skem, kem* (to

255   *The Economist*, 30 April 2016, p. 47.

256   Online Etymological Dictionary: guilt (noun). https://www.etymonline.com/word/guilt#etymonline_v_14358

cover; i.e., to cover oneself in relation to shame; a shroud). Such ancient origins suggest that shame is both open to the heavens, open for all to see, and yet is also something that is covered or something to be covered.[257]

The ancient Greeks differentiated two types of shame: *aiskhyme* (disgrace, dishonor; i.e., bad shame) and *aidos* (modesty, bashfulness; i.e., good shame). Other cultures and traditions seem to relate to shame in different ways; e.g., shame as a something you feel in relation to your own life or shame as the feeling that you have also shamed others around you.

Consider the differences between guilt and shame. Guilt focuses on our awareness that our actions have hurt someone; e.g., "I acted badly regarding others. I feel badly about this". On the other hand, shame reflects a judgment; e.g., "I am a bad person" or "You should be ashamed of yourself." Guilt can be productive or creative in that it engenders self-reflection, remorse, and resolve in relation to avoiding future harm to others. On the other hand, shame can lead to self-destructive behavior and future disconnection from self and others. Guilt is something that people can do nothing about (it is what it is) whereas shame is something that they can try and deal with (I can, often with help, decide who I will be in this situation).

There are many ways to think about how to move beyond shame. Concepts such as forgiveness, reconciliation, self-respect, resilience come to mind. However, we're getting a bit beyond etymology at this point!

In brief, in contrast to sin and guilt which are inescapable parts of the human condition, shame can be addressed and transcended. Our life situation may be the same as before but we can move or be moved beyond shame.

To conclude

In the origins of these word sin, guilt, and shame, we see three things: first, sin is a state of being, a condition of being human; second, guilt is the feeling or feelings (e.g., remorse, anxiety, sadness, anger) associated with

---

257   Wiktionary: heaven. https://en.wiktionary.org/wiki/heaven#English

this state of being; and, third, shame is one way we respond to this sense of guilt (often the first way we respond).

Perhaps, by recognizing that, yes, sin and guilt and shame are, in fact, inescapable parts of life we can at least move or be moved beyond being trapped by feelings of shame. These realities will never go away but we can face them with courage.

Soul, Psyche

Words in the English language related to soul come to us on a variety of paths. Soul, as used in Christianity, comes to English via Greek from Gothic and Germanic languages. In contrast, the Greek and Latin word related to soul, *psyche*, is often used in scientific and medical terms and is related to Greek and Latin (and Hebrew) words related to breath and breathing.

Soul

The word soul comes from Old English *sawol* (spiritual and emotional part of a person, animate existence; life, living being) and from Proto-Germanic *saiwalō* (source also of Old Saxon *seola*, Old Norse *sala*, Old Frisian *sele*, Middle Dutch *siele*, Dutch *ziel*, Old High German *seula*, German *Seele*, Gothic *saiwala*). Before that, the origins of the word soul are uncertain.

Some sources suggest that the word soul may be rooted in Germanic *sailian* (binding); in particular, the binding of a corpse so as to restrain the deceased person's return as a ghost. Another suggestion is that the Proto-Germanic word *saiwalo* may be from Proto-Germanic *saiwaz* (sea; or, from the lake). In the ancient world of northern Europe, the sea (or lake) was believed to be the stopping place of the soul before birth and after death or the dwelling place of souls. The word soul, from such Germanic sources, suggests that conceptions of soul (e.g., "a substantial entity believed to be that in each person which lives, feels, thinks, and wills") may be more rooted in ancient tribal memory than in more recent theological doctrine based on words from Greek and Latin (https://www. etymonline.com/search?q=soul).

Most Indo-European words for soul and/or spirit also refer to supernatural spirits. Many have a base sense of an appearance or apparition such as Greek *phantasma*; French *spectre*; Polish *widmo*, from Old Church Slavonic *videti* (to see); Old English *scin*, Old High German *giskin* (originally appearance, apparition), related to Old English *scinan*, Old High German *skinan* (to shine). Other concepts are seen in French *revenant* (literally a 'returning' from the other world), Old Norse *aptr-ganga* (back-comer), and Breton *bugelnoz*, literally night-child. See also SPIRIT.

Soul meaning the spirit of a deceased person is attested in Old English from 971. Soul, as a synonym for person, individual, human being (as in every living soul), dates from the early 14th century. Soul-searching, as an adjective, is from the 1620s; soul-searching, as a noun, is attested from 1871. Soul, as the individual human soul, is from the 1650s.

In recent times, soulmate is from 1822 and soulful (full of feeling) dates from 1860. In 1900, William James, the philosopher, used the term soul in a spiritual or romantic sense in reference to aspects of one's inner life. In psychology, the use of soul in the sense of 'mind' comes from 1910. For a more recent description of soul, I offer the following excerpt from Marilynne Robinson.[258]

Soul, as an attribute instinctively felt by Black persons in the United States and used as jazz slang, comes from 1946. Other related terms include soul brother (1957), soul food (1957), soul music (i.e., gospel music often using 'girl' in place of 'Jesus'), and soul sister (1967). Soulful, as an expression or characteristic of Black feeling, is first seen in 1964.

---

258   "Science tells us we have no souls. And science gives us no name and no way of accounting for the phenomenon of self-awareness that makes our thoughts, doubts, dreams, memories, and antipathies so interesting to us, and our frustrations with our faults and failures so acute. Granting that 'the soul' as an idea might be culturally particular enough that it gives self-awareness a character not intrinsic to it. The classic soul is more ourselves than we are, a loving and well-respected companion, loyal to us uniquely, entrusted to us, to whom we entrust ourselves. We feel its yearnings, its musings, as a truer and more primary experience of ourselves than our ordinary consciousness can offer. Traditionally souls are spoken of as saved or lost, being the immortal part of humankind, even though they are also thought of as unoffending, indeed as offended against when we misuse worldly agency" (Robinson, 2019, 267).

Psyche

The word psyche is from Latin *psyche* and Greek *psykhe*[259] (soul, mind, spirit; life, one's life, the invisible animating principle or entity which occupies and directs the physical body; understanding, the mind as the seat of thought, faculty of reason; also ghost, spirit of a dead person, often represented symbolically as a moth or butterfly). Greek *psykhe* is akin to *psykhein* (to blow, cool) from PIE *bhes* (to blow, to breathe).[260]

In early Greek translations of the Bible, Latin *psyche* was used when translating the Hebrew word *nephesh* (life, vital breath).[261] When the Gothic missionary Ulfilas (ca. 311 – 383) translated the Bible from Greek to Gothic, he used *saiwala* for the Greek word *psykhe*. And so, as noted above, these Gothic and later Germanic words, rather than the related Latin or Greek words, evolved to become the English word soul.

The Greek and Latin words for soul became more used in the evolution of words related to science and academia. The word psyche came to English in the 1640s meaning an animating spirit and in the 1650s meaning the human soul. Psychology, from Latin *psychologia* (the study of the soul), is a term coined in the 1650s by Philipp Melanchthon, a colleague and collaborator of Martin Luther in the development of Lutheranism.

---

259   In Greek mythology, the story of Psyche is one of those "once upon a time there was a king who had three beautiful daughters and the youngest was most beautiful of them all" stories. She was born a mortal human but following her marriage to Eros, the god of sensual love and desire, she became immortal—the only human to do so. The marriage of Eros and Psyche can be considered a metaphor for the marriage or unity of body and soul.

260   PIE *ane* is another term meaning to blow or to breathe. From PIE *ane* come the Latin words *anima* and *animus* with meanings related to living being, soul, (rational) mind, mental powers, passion, courage, and desire. Also, from PIE *ane* comes the Old Irish word *animm* (soul). *Ane* is the root of many other words related to life—e.g., animal, animate, animism, and so on.

261   The word psyche was used in Platonic philosophy and in the Jewish-influenced theological writing of St. Paul. In the Jewish-Alexandrine Pauline, and Neo-Platonist psychology, the psyche is in general treated as the animating principle in close relation to the body, whereas the pneuma (as representing the divine breath breathed into man), the nous, and the Logos stand for higher entities. They are the more universal, the more divine, the ethically purer. By this more explicit separation of the intellectual and ethical activities from the physiological the conception of the mental or psychical (in the modern sense) was at length reached. ["Dictionary of Philosophy and Psychology," J.M. Baldwin, ed., London, 1902]. https://www.etymonline.com/search?q=psyche

Psyche is the root of words such as psychologist (1727), psychology, as the study of mind (1748), psychiatry (1846), psychic (1872), psychomotor (1873), psychopath (1885), behavioral psychology (1890s), and so on. Psyche, in the psychological sense meaning mind, is attested from 1910.

Finally, the Online Etymological Dictionary suggests that distinguishing *soul* from *spirit* is a matter best left to theologians.

Spirituality

The word spirit has its origins in *(s)peis*, one of the PIE words meaning to blow or to breathe. From this root come the Latin words *spirare* (to breathe) and *spiritus* (a breathing). In early Latin translations of the Bible, *spiritus* was used to translate Greek *pneuma* and Hebrew *ruach* (both meaning wind or breath).

Latin *spiritus* suggests the breath of life or the breath of god and contains connotations of character, high spirits, vigor, courage, pride and arrogance. The words respiration and inspiration have their roots in *spiritus*. In Latin, *spiritus* can also simply mean the blowing of the wind.

During the medieval period, the term *spiritus* or spirit came to have a number of meanings and uses. In general, by 1500, spirit had also come to mean the character or essential principle, nature, or quality of something (e.g., the spirit of the times, team spirit). In the 1580s we see spirit used in the sense of animation and vitality.

The Germanic word for spirit, *geist*, has its roots in PIE *gheis* (to be excited, amazed, frightened) which is also the root of the English word ghost. The German word *zeitgeist*, from 1871, has been borrowed by English to mean the spirit of a place or of a particular time or era.[262]

The late 14th century word spiritualty (from Old French *espiritualte*, Latin *spiritualitatem*) referred to the quality of being spiritual. The term was also used in the 15th century to refer to the clergy.

---

262   And, speaking of spirit (*geist*), the German word for enthusiasm is *begeisterung*. The English word enthusiasm comes from Greek *en* + *theos*; i.e., to be possessed by the divine, or to be full of life, to be lively.

The early 15th century word spirituality[263] meant both the clergy and things pertaining to the church. By the early 16th century, the word meant the quality of being spiritual—the use of the term which is most common today.

See also HOLY GHOST OR HOLY SPIRIT.

Temptation

Have you ever tried out something to see whether you like it or not? For example, we 'try on' clothing before purchase. Or, have you ever tested something (e.g., the battery in your wristwatch) or have you ever been tested (e.g., a math test or a blood test)? Have you ever tried to convince someone of something or tried to influence someone to do something? Has someone ever tried to convince you to do something? Have you ever attempted something?

All of these actions—trying, testing, influencing, attempting—are from Latin *temptare*, meaning to feel, to try out, to try to influence, to test. The word *temptare* is contentless in the sense that anything or anyone can be tried or tested. *Temptare* is the origin of the word temptation.

In the Bible the word temptation primarily denotes a trial in which a person has a free choice of being faithful or unfaithful to God; only secondarily does it signify allurement or seduction to sin. The Hebrew words for temptation include *massa*, from *nasa*, meaning to put to the test; and, *bahan*, meaning to test metals. Hebrew uses other words meaning to entice or lure to evil, including *hit'a*, *hesit*, and *niddah*. Similarly, in classical Greek, the original words related to temptation first referred to a 'testing' and only later to the seduction of evil.[264]

---

263   Note that the words spiritualty and spirituality are but one set of many such pairs of words with similar spellings. Others include realty/reality, luxuriant/luxurious, and so on. Eventually, it seems, one word comes to be predominant—in this case, spirituality seems to be winning.

264   http://www.encyclopedia.com/religion/encyclopedias-almanacs-transcripts-and-maps/temptation-bible

Current understandings of old words for temptation, for example, Hebrew *nsh* and Greek *peirazo, peirasmos*, as well as Latin *temptare*, have led to translations in terms of testing (e.g, loyalty-testing), proving (e.g., proof-testing; i.e., show me), trying (e.g., convincing by logic or evidence), and tempting (e.g., enticing to wrong-doing, allowing someone to be enticed).[265]

In church history, the word temptation comes to English from Old French *temptacion*. In the 13th century this word was used to mean the experience or state of being tempted; i.e., of being tested. In particular, at that time, the word was used to mean the act of 'enticing' someone to do wrong. To tempt meant to allure or seduce or entice toward evil or sin or wrongdoing.

By the 16th century (the time of the Reformation), the word was used to name that which tempts a person to sin. The translation of the King James Version of the Bible (1611) uses the word temptation to mean both the sense of a testing or trying, and of an enticement to evil.

Today temptation is generally defined as a strong urge to have or do something. Also, temptation is defined as that something that causes a strong urge to have or do something, especially something that is bad, wrong, or unwise. Temptation carries the sense of risk, of taking a chance, of 'trying it', or 'going for it'. The secular use of temptation in terms of 'testing' is rare, even obsolete.[266]

Testament, Testimony

Testament

Testament comes from Latin words *testis* (a witness to the making of a will) and *testari* (to make a will).[267] These words originate in PIE *tris* (three) and PIE *tristi* (a disinterested third person who is a witness; e.g.,

---

265   https://www.studylight.org/dictionaries/hbd/t/temptation.html

266   https://www.merriam-webster.com/dictionary/temptation

267   To die 'intestate' is to die without having made a will.

a witness to a will). By the 13th century, the word testament had come to English from Latin *testamentum* (a last will disposing of property, the publication of a will).

Latin *testamentum* is from Greek *diatheke* (covenant; will [the legal document], testament), both from Hebrew *berith* (covenant). In the Latin Vulgate Bible *testamentum* put the emphasis on 'testament' rather than 'covenant'.

By the time that the Bible was translated into English in the 14th century both *testamentum* and *diatheke* were used for the translation of covenant. Also, by this time, *testamentum* had also come to refer to the legal terms 'will' (as in 'last will and testament') and 'testimony'. Confusion can be seen in English translations of the Bible at this time; e.g., Wycliffe's translation uses both 'covenant' (from Greek *diatheke*) and 'testament' (from Latin *testamentum*). For example, are we talking about the 'New Testament' or the 'New Covenant'? Over time, 'New tTestament' became the predominant term (https://www.etymonline.com/search?q=testament).

In brief, perhaps, if a will is a person's last wishes regarding their estate, perhaps, in a similar fashion, a testament could be considered as a person's last word on something.

See COVENANT.

Testimony

Testimony is first seen in English in the late 14th century, from translations of Latin *testimonium* used in the Ten Commandments of the Vulgate Bible. Around 1400, testimony was also being used to mean the proof or demonstration of some fact, evidence, or piece of evidence. By the early 15th century, testimony was the legal testimony or sworn statement of a witness.

Testimony came to English via 11th century Old French *testimoine* and Latin *testimonium* (evidence, proof, witness, attestation). As with Latin *testamentum*, Latin *testimonium* comes from Latin *testis* (a witness).[268]

---

268   There is debate over whether the word testimony is related to testes and testicles, particularly given various references in the Bible to the swearing of oaths when euphemistically 'grasping the thigh' or 'loin' of another person; Genesis 24: 2, Genesis 47: 29, Leviticus 7: 33). Latin *testis* (a testicle; also,

Trinity

As you would expect, the word trinity comes from words meaning three. In particular, the earliest source of the word trinity comes from the PIE word for three—*trei*, the source of Proto-Germanic *thrijiz* which in turn is the source of other words for three— Old Saxon *thria*, Old Frisian *thre*, Middle Dutch and Dutch *drie*, Old High German *dri*, German *drei*, Old Norse *þrir*, Danish *tre*, and Old English *þreo*. PIE *trei* is also the source of Latin *tres* (three) and *trinus* (three at a time, threefold, triple).

From these origins come Latin *triad*, *trinitatem*, and *trinitas* and then the 11th century Old French *trinité* (Holy Trinity—i.e., the Father, Son, and Holy Spirit constituting one God in Christian doctrine[269]). The word trinity comes to English in the 13th century.

As Christianity spread across Europe we see related words such as Irish *trionnoid*, Welsh *trindod*, and German *trinitat*.

True / Truth

True

When you think of something being 'true', what comes to mind? What might the origins of the words true and truth tell us?

The word true has origins in PIE *deru* or *dreu* (to be firm, solid, steadfast); perhaps ultimately from PIE *dru* (tree; e.g., in the sense of as 'steadfast as

---

a witness) is related to Greek *parastatai* (testicles) which comes from *parastates* (one who stands by; i.e., a witness). Most current sources now discount this connection between testes and testaments as a modern invention. However, speaking anecdotally, I know of cases reported of juvenile offenders in the justice system using the phrase 'to swear on your balls' meaning that what's being said is absolutely true—i.e., the risk of being caught in a lie could have serious consequences.

The origins of the word test are not related to the origins of testament and testimony.

269   "While researching ancient cultures of the Caucasus, French linguist Georges Dumezil (1898 – 1986) ... discovered tripartite structures in most Indo-European peoples. The Holy Trinity of Christianity may also be an echo of deep, Indo-European belief systems" (Pujol, 2019, 17).

an oak'). The word true also comes from Proto-Germanic *treuwaz* (having or characterized by good faith)[270]; a word related to Gothic *triggws* (faithful, trusty; e.g., being 'true' to your word). These words come to Old English as *trow* (to confide, trust, believe) through Mercian *treowe* and West Saxon *triewe*.

These origins would seem to suggest that something is 'true' because we 'trust' or 'have faith' that it is true. Over time, Germanic languages, including English, introduced distinctions between truth as 'fidelity' or 'faithfulness' and truth as 'factuality' (i.e., to assert, to affirm based on evidence).

The usage of the word true has developed and expanded over the centuries: true, meaning consistent with facts, is first recorded around 1200; true, meaning something real or genuine or not counterfeit is from the late 14th century; true, meaning something conforming to a certain standard is from around 1550.

True love comes from Old English *treolufu*. The phrase 'to come true' (e.g., dreams that come true) comes from 1819. True/false, as a type of test, is from 1923.

The verb 'to true' in the sense of to agree or to make consistent with a certain standard comes from 1841 (i.e., to make true in position, form, or adjustment; e.g., to make something level or square or balanced or concentric, and so on).

So, again, when you think of something being 'true', what comes to mind? Does being 'true' depend on having facts or having faith? It depends.[271]

---

270   The modern German word *treu*, from these Proto-Germanic origins, still means faithful.

271   In brief, philosophers tell us that there are three types of truth: 1) truth as a 'correspondence' (i.e., the connection between a belief and a fact or between an assertion and reality; e.g., Victoria is the capital of British Columbia); 2) truth as 'coherence' (i.e., one truth is related to another truth, as in mathematical or scientific truths; e.g., $a^2 + b^2 + = c^2$); and, 3) truth as 'pragmatic' (i.e., experience, however defined and justified by reasonable people, tells us that something is true; e.g., the glass is half-empty, the glass is half-full; or, two versions of a traffic accident—one from an uninvolved witness and one from the driver of the vehicle); or, neo-pragmatic: "the neo-pragmatic approach is designed to avoid the problems—for example, 'relativist' problems—facing correspondence theories of truth while still preserving truth's objectivity" (https://plato.stanford.edu/entries/truth-pragmatic/).
Also, Picard, M. (2013). *The bedside book of philosophy. From Plato to Paradoxes: Thinking through the ages.* London: New Burlington Books, 40 – 43

Truth

Not surprisingly, the word truth has similar origins to the word true. The word truth emerges from Old English *trow*, from (West Saxon) *triewo* and Mercian *treowo* (faith, faithfulness, fidelity, loyalty; veracity, the quality of being true; pledge, covenant) and from *triewe* and *treowe* (faithful).

The Middle English word for truth is *trewbe*, a word related to the words troth (loyalty, honesty, good faith; loyal or pledged faithfulness, one's pledged word) and betrothal (the act of promising to marry someone). *Trewbe* comes from Old English *treowthe* (the quality of being believable).

The use of the word truth in the sense of 'something that is true' is first recorded in mid-14th century. Truth, meaning accuracy or correctness is from the 1560s. The usage of 'truth' as the opposite of falsehood is also from the 16th century (perhaps not coincidentally the time of the Reformation).

It is interesting to note that whereas English has the verb 'to lie' (i.e., to deceive or to tell an untruth), there is no verb for 'to tell the truth'. We may lie but we don't truth!

Virgin Mary, The

Virgin

The word virgin may have its origins in PIE *wiz-ga* and *weis* (to turn, to twist) which may in turn be the origin of several Latin words: *virgatus* (made of twigs), *virgate* (shaped like a rod, stick or wand)[272]; *virga* (the young shoot of a new plant), and *virgo*[273] or *virginem* (maiden, unwed-

---

272   *Virgate* was also an early English measure of land area. The term 'verge' refers to the edge or margin of a land area. We also speak of being 'on the verge' of something; e.g., "I was on the verge of quitting." Virgate is related to the more recent use of the term 'rod' as a measure of land. A verger was an officer of the early church who carried a verge (a rod which was a symbol of authority).

273   Virgo, the astrological sign, is related to ancient Babylonian fertility myths (related symbols include the furrows in a field, ears of grain, stalks of wheat), to the Greek goddesses Demeter (goddess of wheat and agriculture) and Astraea (goddess of innocence, purity, justice), and the Roman goddess Ceres (the origin of the word cereal).

ded girl or woman; and, *virgo,* used as an adjective, means fresh, unused; e.g., virgin olive oil). From these Latin sources comes Old French and Anglo-French *virgine* (virgin). By around 1200 the word virgin came to English, meaning an unmarried or chaste woman noted for religious piety and having a position of reverence in the Church.[274]

Virgin, meaning a young woman in a state of inviolate chastity or a chaste man, is from around 1300. The word virginity, which came to English at this time, referred to a person's state of virginity or innocence. At this time, virgin meant not just someone who had not experienced sexual intercourse. Virgin also figuratively meant someone pure or untainted—figurative in the sense of a focused or single-minded life of chastity lived in devotion to religious ideals regardless of the person's prior sexual history.

By the 1550s the term virgin was being used primarily in the more literal sense of sexual innocence rather than in the more figurative chaste sense of the word.

The use of the term virgin to mean a naïve or inexperienced person is attested from 1953.

Mary

Mary is an English personal name with origins in ancient times. The earliest references to the name Mary are suggested by ancient Egyptian word-forms such as *mry* (beloved) or *mr* (love). However, the Hebrew name Miryam is the most common source of the name Mary. Miryam has various meanings, including *mrr* (bitterness, perhaps from myrrh), *mry* (rebelliousness), and *sha mrih* (wished-for child). The equivalent name in Aramaic, the main language of the Middle East at the time of Jesus, is Maryam.

---

274   The word virgin is commonly used in Biblical translations of Hebrew *almah* (young woman) and Greek *parthenos* (a maiden, a woman who has never had sexual relations, a woman beyond puberty but not yet married). The famous Parthenon monument in Athens is named for the virgin goddess Athena--the goddess of wisdom, courage, inspiration, civilization, law and justice, strategic warfare, mathematics, strength, the arts, crafts, and skill. In Greek mythology, Athena's symbol was the owl. The scientific term parthenogenesis means reproduction without fertilization. The term also refers to reproductive modes in hermaphroditic species which can self-fertilize.

The early Greek New Testament used Mariam for Mary. The early Latin New Testaments used Maria. These Christian names for Mary are first attested in Greek writings from the 3rd century CE onwards. The 12th century is noted for the dramatic growth of the so-called cult of Mary or cult of the Virgin—seen, for example, in the predominance of Marian pilgrimages at that time and the building of cathedrals dedicated to 'Our Lady', most notably Notre Dame cathedral in Paris.

From these ancient roots come the Old English names Maria and Marie, the origin of the present English name Mary.

See also ANGEL, ANNUNCIATION.

Vocation

Vocation comes to English in the early 15th century from Old French *vocacion* (call, consecration; calling, profession), from Latin *vocationem*, vocation (a calling, a being called), and from Latin *vocare* (to call). All these words come from PIE *wekw* (to speak).

The use of vocation in the early church usually meant a calling to be priest or nun or some other role in the church. The more general sense of vocation as one's occupation or profession is first attested from the 1550s.

PIE *wekw* (to speak) is the source of many words such as: advocate, avocation, convocation, epic, equivocal, evoke, invoke, provoke, revoke, vocabulary, vocal, vociferous, voice, vouch, vowel, and others.

Will

The verb 'to will' comes from PIE *wel-* (to wish, to will), the source of many other related words; for example, Sanskrit *vrnoti* (chooses), Avestan (old Persian) *verenav-*(to wish, will, choose), Greek *elpis* (hope), and Latin *volo, velle* (to wish, will, desire). The English forms of 'will' come from PIE *wel-* via Germanic sources.

Old English *willan, wyllan* (to wish, desire; be willing; be used to, be about to) comes from Proto-Germanic *willjan* (source also of Old Saxon *willian*, Old Norse *vilja*, Old Frisian *willa*, Dutch *willen*, Old High German *wellan*, German *wollen*, Gothic *wiljan* (to will, wish, desire) and Gothic waljan (to choose).

Old English *willian* also means 'to determine by an act of choice'. From the mid-15th century, *willan* also meant 'to dispose of by will or testament'.

In sum, ancient uses of the verb 'to will' reveal several connotations: to wish, to choose, to hope, to desire, as well as to be willing, and to be about to do something. To say, "I will do 'x'" can range from a firm "I WILL do it" to "I choose to do it" to "I desire to do it" or "I'd be willing to do it". Note that 'to will' can be both a command and an intention on the part of the speaker. To ask someone "Will you do this task?" is not a command but a request or an intention—the onus of 'being willing' to do the task is on the person being asked. On the other hand, to say, "You will do 'x'" is a command.

The use of will as a noun comes from Old English *will, willa* (mind, determination, purpose; desire, wish, request; joy, delight) from Proto-Germanic *wiljon* (source of Old Saxon *willio*, Old Norse *vili*, Old Frisian *willa*, Dutch *wil*, Old High German *willio*, German *wille*, Gothic *wilja*)—all meaning the 'will' or 'wish' to do something.

Whether will is used as a verb or noun, it seems remarkably unchanged in form and usage from culture to culture and from the ancient past to the present.

Will meaning the "written document expressing a person's wishes about disposition of property after death" is first recorded late 14th century.

The phrase 'free will' is from the early 13th century. The phrase 'good will' comes from Old English *godes willan* (state of wishing well to another). Good will meaning 'cheerful acquiescence' is from around 1300. The word willingness is from the 14th century. Good will, in the commercial sense of a degree of favor enjoyed through patronage of customers is from the 1570s. The phrase 'will power' is from 1847.

When discussing the Reformation and emergence of the modern moral order, Taylor states, "Rather than passively accepting his own nature, man [*sic*] began to process of actively remaking himself. Crucial to this was the understanding of the will as an agent of moral change…" (https://www. giffordlectures.org/books/secular-age).

Wisdom, Wise, Wit

Have you ever wondered where phrases like "She's a whiz at math" or "I'm at my wit's end" come from? 'At my wit's end' doesn't mean that I don't have any jokes left. Whiz and wit have their origins in wisdom.

What's the difference between wisdom and wise? Wisdom is something that we have or can have. Being wise is something that we are or can be. We have wisdom; we act wisely. Wisdom tends to be collective and cultural; being wise tends to be individual and personal. As wise ones, we participate in and contribute to the wisdom of our tradition, our culture, and our community.

Wise and wisdom

Wisdom is from Old English *wis* (wise) and Old High German *wistuom* (wisdom). Wise, a word older than wisdom, is from Old English *wis* which in turn is from the Old High German *wisa* (manner), Proto-Germanic *wissaz* and *wittos*, and PIE *weid*[275] (to see; i.e., to see in the sense of to know—e.g.,"I see what you mean"). PIE *weid* is possibly from or related to Sanskrit *veda* (I know), to Greek *eidos* (form,) and to Greek *idein* (to see; from *idein* we get the word idea; i.e., "Ahh, now I see… I get the idea").

Could we say at this point that it is not enough just to have wisdom, but that to be wise, wisdom needs to be seen to be believed?

What might we 'see' in a wise person? Presumably we see a person who embodies and exhibits a sense of purpose and meaningfulness as characterized by knowledge (accumulated learning and understanding from observations and reflections upon experiences of the world), insight (the ability to keenly discern inner qualities and relationships), sound judgment (good sense), positive affect or attitude (attentiveness or readiness; a feeling

---

275   PIE *weid* is also, among many other English words, the root of our word video.

or emotion toward knowledge or situations), and a willingness and ability to act wisely (to act with intention; to apply and act on their knowledge).

Wisdom is seen not just in outward behavior but is also seen in a person's self-possession or presence. It is as if we see in such people a centeredness from which moral perception and moral behavior flow. Such people are attractive. We are drawn toward such people and such wisdom.

In brief, perhaps we could say that being seen as wise is related to how we are seen to feel and act on the basis of what we know.

See also CHARACTER, PRESENCE.

Wit

We speak of people who, in stressful situations, have their wits about them. We speak of people who are witty. Wit is another Old English word related to Old High German *wizzi* (knowledge) and Old English *witan* (to know). OE *witan*, in turn, emerges from PIE *wid* (to know).[276] Ancient peoples of northern Europe talked of the 'five wits' to describe knowledge and situations not related to the five senses. These five wits comprised common wit (i.e., humor), imagination, fantasy, enumeration or estimation, and memory (https://en.wikipedia.org/wiki/Five_wits).

Today, wit implies mind, memory, reasoning power, intelligence, [common] sense (i.e., using one's senses), ingenuity (mental soundness, mental capability, resourcefulness), acumen (astuteness of perception or judgment; e.g., 'business acumen'), and imaginative perception.

Wit also means a talent for banter and witticism: the ability to think and talk on your feet, to respond in the moment with insight and humor. We admire the person who seem to effortlessly come up with the right clever or witty remark at the right moment. Such people have the ability to connect seemingly disparate things so as to illuminate or amuse.

In short, wit is a lovely old word that encompasses intelligence and humor. Wit is not just what you know but more importantly it is how you

---

276   Priests of ancient Britain were known as druids; literally 'wise oaks'. An ancient name for oak is *drus*; and so, *drus* + *wid* gives druid. Here also we have another allusion to the metaphor of tree as knowledge.

show what you know and how you engage your knowing with delight and affection when with other people in the immediacy of a given situation.[277]

Witness

Wit comes from PIE *weid* (to know, to see)[278] and through Proto-Germanic *wit*[279] to Old English *wit* (understanding, intellect, sense; knowledge, consciousness, conscience).

The word witness is composed of wit and –ness. The term –ness is a word-forming element denoting action, quality, or state which helps form an abstract noun (e.g., tender + ness = tenderness; mindful + ness = mind-fulness; and so on). The term –ness comes from Old English *-nes(s) and* Proto-Germanic *in-assu*. Witness means the state or quality or action of seeing and knowing. See WISDOM, WISE, WIT.

---

277   Other related words include:

inwit: a medieval English word meaning 'knowledge of the inner self' or 'knowledge within'; a word which was eventually replaced by 'consciousness', a word with Latin roots

unwitting: unknowing

witness: someone who knows because they 'saw' (Greek *idein* = to see). See also WITNESS.

wizard (from the 15th century): a wise or very skillful person, a philosopher or sage; from the Middle English *wysard* and from Old English *wis* (wise). During the medieval period, the line between philosophy and magic was often blurred; however, by the 1550s and the advent of the Reformation, wizard was increasingly used to describe someone who worked with only with magic and the occult. During this period, hundreds of wizards and witches (mostly witches) were tortured and burned.

And, on that happy note, from wizard we get whiz (from 1914; e.g., he's a whiz at math).

278   PIE *weid* is also the root of the words such as idea, video, vision, and wizard. Related words in other languages include Sanskrit *veda* (I know); Greek *oida* and Doric *woida* (I know); Greek *idein* (to see); Gothic, Old Swedish, Old English *witan* (to know); Gothic *weitan* (to see); English *wise*, German *wissen* (to know); Lithuanian *vysti* (to see); Bulgarian *vidya* (I see); and, Polish *widzieć* (to see).

279   Proto-Germanic *wit* is related to PIE *weid-* (to see, metaphorically 'to know'), Gothic *unwiti* (ignorance), Old Saxon *wit*, Old Norse *vit*, Danish *vid*, Swedish *vett*, Old Frisian *wit*, Old High German *wizzi* (knowledge, understanding, intelligence, mind), German *witz* (wit, witticism, joke), and Old English *witan* (to know).

The noun witness first appears in Old English as *witnes*, meaning a person who testifies or an attestation of facts about an event from personal knowledge.

The verb 'to witness' comes to English around 1300 meaning to bear testimony. In the early 14th century 'to witness' meant to affix one's signature and by the 1580s 'to witness' also mean to see or to know by personal presence. The Christian use of the term witness, from the late 14th century, was used as a translation of the Greek *martys* (martyr).[280]

Witness is related to other words such as memory, video, vision, wisdom, wise, and wit.[281]

Word

A word to the wise as we begin: the following item on the origins of the word word describes various words for word. So, in a word, when I write the word word I am not stumbling over my tongue although I may seem a bit wordy. You have my word for it.

So, here we go. The English word word has its origins in PIE *wer, were, werdh* (to say, to speak). In the beginning, a word was an action rather than a thing.

From PIE *wer* emerges Proto-Germanic *wurdan* (the source of Old Saxon and Old Frisian *word*, Dutch *woord*, Old High German and

---

280   In its origins, the word martyr is related to the origins of the word memory. In this context, the words witness and memory can be said to be distantly related. We tend to 'remember' more vividly if there is an affective or emotional connection to what we have seen that is being remembered, such as is usually the case of 'martyrdom'.

The meaning of martyr as witness can be seen as both a noun and a verb—the martyr is a witness and the martyr witnesses. The martyr is a witness who both provides and is the testimony to their faith ("look at me and what I am willing to die for"). From the point of view of the observer, the observer recognizes the strength of faith of the martyr ("I see your self-sacrifice—I may not believe or accept your faith but I see that you believe in it").

Also, whether a martyr is perceived as a revolutionary or a witness or a terrorist or a mentally-deranged person depends on the point of view of the observer / witness (or storyteller).

281   Wit, meaning "ability to connect ideas and express them in an amusing way" is first recorded 1540s; that of "person of wit or learning" is from late 15c. See also WISDOM, WISE, WIT.

German *wort*, Old Norse *oro*, and Gothic *waurd*), and the Old English word *word* (speech, talk, utterance, statement, news, report word). The word word came to Old English from these origins with two meanings: first, speech, talk, utterance, report; and, second, a promise (e.g., she kept her word). In oral cultures, before literacy was common, 'to keep your word' was as important to social cohesion as later signed legal documents.

However, things get more complex when we examine the word Word as used in the New Testament Gospel of John. The word Word does not refer to words as such but rather to the concept of *logos*[282] which for early Greek philosophers was fundamental to understanding and explaining Creation.[283] The word *logos* referred to reason in terms of the controlling principle of order and knowledge in the world and to reasoned discourse or argument about the nature of creation and the world.

Theologians of the early Christian church, drawing from the work of Greek and of Hellenistic-Judaic scholars, used the term *logos* (the divine or eternal present in all things and at all times) to describe Jesus as the manifestation of such divine wisdom and presence in a particular person at a particular time and place. For these writers, Jesus embodies or is the *logos* incarnate, manifest in the creation, governance, and redemption of the

282   Greek *logo* comes from PIE *logo*, *leg* (to collect, to gather; to speak; i.e., in the sense of to gather words, to pick out the words); that is, *logos* is the logical use of words. In ancient Greek, the word for word was *lexis*; the word *lexikos* meant 'of words'. From these roots comes the English word lexicon (a book of words; e.g., a dictionary or a glossary of terms in a technical manual). Both *logos* and *lexis* derive from the Greek verb *lego* (to count, tell, say, speak). Again, as with the PIE origins of word, actions often precede things. Other words related to *logos* include analog, apology, dialogue, logarithm, logic, logistics, trilogy.

283   "The *logos* had indeed been fundamental to Creation for some Greek philosophers from the beginning. For Heraclitus [6th – 5th century] ... everything came about according to the *logos*, which was equivalent both to fire, and to harmonious balance of things" (Ostler, 2016, 73).

world.[284] These and later theologians used various words when translating Greek *logos* to Latin.[285]

During the late medieval period and Reformation, when translators of the Bible into English were looking for a way to translate Greek *logos* or Latin *verbum* (a word; the Word) they used the word Word (e.g., John 1: 1, "In the beginning was the Word").

The word *logos* first appears in English language usage in the 1580s.

So, what are we to make of all this if we leave theology behind for a moment and focus on the origin and use of words to describe different experiences. If we are to believe, or at least presume, that words follow from experiences (i.e., "There must be a word for 'x'--if not, let's create one"; or, "Tell me, how you are feeling?"), the question is raised of how to describe or explain or interpret such an ineffable experiences as suggested by 'the Word'. How do we describe an experience of the logos or the Word? Do we tell a story? Do we preach a sermon?

Something happened to people early in the first century—something that was unique and unrepeatable for each individual. But the individual stories from these individual lives are long gone and we are left with the centuries of digesting and processing various translations and interpretations. We sing "Tell me the old old story" and we hear the church's story, not

---

284   "Even before John, then, there was a rich tradition, shared by the three principal civilizations of the eastern Mediterranean, that saw wisdom or reasoned understanding as the principle of creation: it was an Egyptian and a Hebrew, rather than a Greek, contribution *to personify this wisdom* [italics mine], as John does quite explicitly in his [Gospel]. ... Although this [i.e., the philosophical and linguistic differences between, e.g., Heraclitus and John] is a rather conceptualized, abstract way of looking at Christ as an agent in the world, we are now moving from abstraction to relations with persons" (Ostler, 2016, 73).

285   For example, Tertullian (160 – 220) translated *logos* as *sermo* (conversational discourse). The closer scholarly equivalent for *logos* at that time would have been to use *ratio* (rational explanation). Cyprian, Bishop of Carthage (210 – 258) also used *sermo*; his contemporary Novatian (200 – 258) used both *sermo* and *verbum* (meaning simply 'a word'). *Verbum* was used until the time of Augustine (354 – 430) who used both *sermo* and *verbum*.

In the late 4th century, Jerome used *verbum* when translating the Latin Vulgate Bible, the official version of the Bible for the next several centuries. Around 1520, Erasmus, when re-translating the Gospels into Latin, reverted to *sermo*: "He would have preferred *oratio* (speech) as a translation for *logos* but was stymied by its inconvenient feminine gender (Boyle, M.O. (September 1977). *Sermo*: Reopening the conversation on translating JN 1,1. *Vigiliae Christianae, 31* (3), 163 – 164)." Cited by Ostler (2016, 77).

any particular person's story. The old stories are long gone. Such common stories and doctrines are necessary for the life of a religious community. And, the ongoing process of continually reinterpreting the meaning of such old stories and the recounting of new stories continues.[286]

So, how might we summarize the immense complexity of Christian theology in one word? How about the Word?!

Worship

The word worship is related to many words which end in -ship, words such as apprenticeship, censorship, championship, citizenship, courtship, craftsmanship, dictatorship, discipleship, friendship, hardship, leadership, lordship, relationship, seamanship, workmanship, and so on.

The dictionary tells us that the suffix '-ship' means the state or condition of being something; or the position, status, or duties of something; or the skill or ability as someone or something.[287] However, '-ship' is not just the state or condition of something but is also the acts related to creating and shaping that state or condition. For example, citizenship is not just the condition or state of citizenship but the acts of a person who engages in citizenship. Or craftsmanship.

Or worship. The word worship comes from the contraction of worth + ship—that is, creating the state or condition of something having worth.

The suffix '-ship' comes from Middle English '-*schipe*' and Old English '-*sciepe*' (a state or condition of being). The related Old English word

---

286   "This was the popular, mythical side of the Greek spirit. ...sacred narratives such as Plato might adopt to justify claims that he could not back with reason. ... Greek myths were supposed to have a point. But besides seeing the point of a good story, Greeks were notorious for their relentless logic and devotion to Sophia (wisdom), following not the *mythos* but the *logos*" (Ostler, 2016, 72).

"It is a legacy of philosophy in Greek, and its intellectual style, to presume that highly abstract, and ultimately unverifiable, states of affairs can find a single, correct representation in the form of words. But the obligation to get that answer right, on pain of damnation, was also given a deeper bitterness by the sense of human, personal relations with God that derive from the Hebrew-Aramaic side of developing Christian background" (Ostler, 2016, 74).

287   The noun 'ship' describing large ocean-going vessels and the verb 'to ship' are unrelated to the suffix '-ship'.

scieppan means to create, to form, or to destine. These Old English words come from Proto-Germanic *skapaz* and *skap* (to create, to ordain, to appoint, to shape). The root of these words is PIE *(s)kep* (to cut, to scrape, to hack)—words which acquired in Germanic languages a specific sense of 'to create'.

The word worth has its roots in PIE *wert* and *wer* (to turn, to bind, to bend). From these PIE origins comes Proto-Germanic *werthaz*, a word which perhaps first meant 'to bend or to turn toward' and later came to mean 'worth' (that is, perhaps, 'worth' in the sense of 'bending or turning toward' something of importance or significance). From Proto-Germanic *werthaz* come related words such as Old Frisian *werth*, Old Norse *veror*, Dutch *waard*, Old High German *werd*, German *wert*, and Gothic *wairds*—all meaning worth or worthy.

From these sources comes Old English *weord* (significant, valuable; valued, appreciated, highly thought-of, deserving, meriting; honorable, noble, of high rank; suitable for, capable). By around 1200, *weord* had become the word worth and was used as an adjective to mean equivalent to, of the value of, valued at; having importance equal to; or equal in power to.

Old English *weord* also lead to the use of worth as a noun meaning value, price, the price paid; worth, worthiness, merit; and equivalent value amount, monetary value. From the early 13th century, the word worth was also used to mean excellence and nobility.

And so, at last, to the word worship.

The verb 'to worship', first seen around 1200, comes from the Old English noun *wordscip* (the condition of being worthy, dignity, glory, distinction, honor, renown) derived from combining *weord* (worth) and *–sciepe* or *–scipe* (to create). The original sense of the word worship is seen in the title *worshipful* (i.e., honourable); for example, as seen in the phrase, "Your Worship", used in respectful reference to the 'worth' or 'worthiness' of a law court judge or city mayor.[288]

---

288   Historically, "Your Worship" has been used in Commonwealth countries. In the United States, the equivalent term "Your Honor" is used.

Worship, as the sense of 'reverence paid to a supernatural or divine being', is first recorded around 1300. The noun worshipper comes from the late 14th century.

In its origins, we see that worship is not just a ritual act but is also an intentional creative act. In the 'bending toward' that which we believe to be of worth we create and 'give shape' to the expression of our respect and honour. We not only recognize the worth of something in worship but we create and give or add worth to the object of worship through our actions.

APPENDICES

Language Abbreviations / Dates

Ave	Avestan	3rd - 7th century CE (Sasanian Empire)
Grc	Ancient Greek	9th century BCE - 6th century CE
Heb	Hebrew	from 10th century BCE
Lat	Latin:	
	Old Latin	8th - 6th century BCE
	Classical Latin	1st century BCE onwards (scholarly use)
	Vulgar Latin	1st century BCE onwards (everyday use)
	Latin Latin	3rd - 9th century century CE
	Medieval Latin	9th - 14th century CE
	Renaissance Latin	14th - 16th century CE
	New Latin	16th century onwards
Non	Old Norse (ON)	8th - 14th centuries CE
PIE	Proto-Indo-European	Late Neolithic period, ~5,000 – 6,000 years ago
Gem	German:	
	Proto-Germanic	from 500 BCE
	Germanic	1st to 4th centuries CE
	Gothic	from 4th century CE
	Old High German	6th century
San	Sanskrit:	
	Vedic	2000 – 650 BCE
Classical	650 BCE - present	
Eng	English:	
	Old English (OE)/ Anglo-Saxon	mid-5th century - 12th centuries
	Middle English (ME)	12th - 15th centuries
	Early Modern English	15th – 17th centuries
	Modern English	from 1650

Centuries in which English words first seen

BEFORE 5ᵗʰ CENTURY

Adam
Eve

Christian

BEFORE 12ᵗʰ CENTURY

Amen
Bishop
Church
Deacon
Disciple
Easter
Epistle
Evil, as bad
Freedom
Glory
God
Heathen
Heaven
Helle (OE), as abode of the dead
Holy Ghost
Hymn
King

Kingdom
Life
Mass
Monk
Nun
Priest
Psalm
Satan
Shepherd
Sin
Shame
Soul
Will (noun, mental state)
Wise
Wisdom
Wit
Word

DURING 12th CENTURY

Ascension
Baptize
Blessing

Charity
Choir
Christianity

Demon
Death
Devil
Evangelist
Forgive, as a gift
Heresy
Justice
Mercy

Miracle
Paradise, Garden of Eden
Parson
Pastor
Passion, as Christ's suffering
Poverty, as destitute
Preacher
Virtue

DURING 13th CENTURY

Absolution
Blasphemy
Clergy
Conscience
Contemplation
Convert
Crucify, as verb
Crucifix
Despair
Discipline
Doubt
Faith
Forgive, as pardon
Free will
Fundament, as buttocks
Friar
Good
Gospel, re New Testament
Grace
Hope
Litany
Love
Meditation
Obedient

Paradise, any peaceful, perfect,
pleasant place
Penance
Prophet
Purgatory
Resurrection
Revelation
Sacrament
Salvation
Sermon
Spirit, as animating principle
Temptation, experience of
being tempted
Trinity
True
Virgin, figuratively chaste; *not* prior
sexual history
Worship
Witness
Will; i.e., free will

DURING 14th CENTURY

Alleluia

Angel

Annunciation

Awe

Bible

Blaspheme

Ceremony

Character

Chastity, as a virgin person

Christ

Christmas

Confession

Covenant

Cross, noun

Destiny

Diocese

Divine

Divinity

Doctrine

Eternity

Ethics

Eucharist

Evangelize, as verb

Exaltation

Font

Free, politically

Gentile

Guilt

Humble

Incarnation

Integrity, as purity

Justify

Lent

Lord

Messiah

Minister, to serve

Moral

Pagan

Parish

Passion, as strong emotion, desire

Pastor (noun)

Pilgrim

Pilgrimage

Praise

Pray

Prayer

Presence

Profane

Prophecy

Proverb

Reconciliation

Rector

Redemption

Religion

Repentance

Rite

Sacred

Saint

Sanctuary, immune from punishment

Saviour

Scripture

Secular, not religious; re types of clergy

Sect

Spirit, as divine mind, supernatural creature

Spirituality

Testament

Testimony

Truth

Tutor, as guardian

DURING 15th CENTURY

Beatitude

Belief

Chastity, as sexually pure

Fate, as predestination

Fundamental, as foundational

Gratitude

Hallelujah

Integrity, as wholeness

Intuition

Justification

Laity

Psalmist

Redeem, to buy back

Sanctify

Vocation

DURING 16th CENTURY

Afterlife

Altar

Apostle

Atheist

Atonement, to atone

Cathedral

Chorus

Conciliate

Creed

Ecumenical

Evangelical

Fate, as 'that which must be'

Guilty

Halo

Holy

Holy Spirit

Hymnal

Immortality

Jehovah

Liturgy

Meditate

Mission

Music

Passion, as sexual

Pulpit

Redeem, in theology

Responsible, as answerable

Righteous

Sanctification

Sanctuary, as refuge

Spirituality, quality of being spiritual

Temptation, as that which tempts

Truth, as in 'not false'

Tutor, as teaching

Virgin, literal sexual innocence

DURING 17th CENTURY

Apocalypse
Celibacy
Charism (early form of charisma)
Cult
Dogma
Evangelism
Fundamental, primary rules
Gospel, as any truth
Hell, as in KJV Bible
Hermeneutics
Hierarchy

Jesus, spelled as Jesus
Minister, high official
Missionary
Mystic
Numen
Passion, as strong enthusiasm
Pentecostal
Responsible, as accountable
Ritual
Self-righteous
Soul, as individual soul

DURING 18th CENTURY

Apologetics
Catechism
Evil, as 'evil' (a thing in itself, not
a descriptor)
Fate, as 'final event', that which
awaits at the end

Mysticism
Noumenon
Phenomenology
Responsibility
Secularization

DURING 19th CENTURY

Agnostic
Charisma, charismatic
Evangelical, protestant (a person)
Pagan, as pantheist

Parochial
Pastor (verb)
Secularist

DURING 20th CENTURY

Charismatic
Fundamental, as a
Protestant doctrine
Ministry, government department
Non-secular

Pentecostal,
Protestant denomination

Acknowledgements

For all those who love the origin of words, any words.
For all those who think that they've given up on religion.
For all those who think that they've given up on the secular.

For
Robert C Wild
Donald Grayston
Joseph W Mathews
William & Barbara Alerding

And for
Raymonde

Let me also express my gratitude and thanks
to all those who have contributed to the success of the
Online Etymological Dictionary.

Bibliography

Ayto, J. (1990). *Dictionary of word origins: The histories of more than 8,000 English language words*. New York: Arcade.

Barzun, J. (1986). *A word or two before you go: Brief essays on language*. Middletown, CT: Wesleyan.

Boas, H. C. (Dir.). Linguistics Research Centre, University of Texas at Austin. *Indo-European Lexicon: Pokorny Master PIE Etyma*. 8 Dec 2018: Retrieved from

http://www.utexas.edu/cola/centers/lrc/ielex/PokornyMaster-X.html
https://lrc.la.utexas.edu/lex

Blackburn, S. (2009). *Philosophy: The big questions*. London: Quercus.

Bonhoeffer, D. (1972). *Ethics*. New York: Macmillan.

Borg, M. (2014). *The heart of Christianity: Rediscovering a life of faith*. New York: HarperCollins.

Borg, M. (2018). *Days of awe and wonder*. New York: HarperCollins.

Brinton, L.J. & Arnovick, L.K. (2006). *The English language: A linguistic history*. Don Mills, ON: Oxford.

Brown, P. (2012). *Through the eye of a needle: Wealth, the fall of Rome, and the making of Christianity in the West, 350 – 550 AD*. Princeton, NJ: Princeton.

Brown, P. (2015). *The ransom of the soul: Afterlife and wealth in early Western Christianity*. Cambridge, MA: Harvard.

Bryson, B. (2001). *The mother tongue: English and how it got that way*. New York: HarperCollins Perennial.

Caputo, J. (2019). *On religion* (2nd Ed.). London: Routledge.

Chadwick, H. (1993). *The early church* (Rev. ed.). London: Penguin.

Claiborne, R. (1989). *The roots of English: A reader's handbook of word origins*. New York: Random House.

Critchley, S. (2014). *The faith of the faithless*. London: Verso.

Cunliffe, B. (2011). *Europe between the oceans: 9000 BC – AD 1000.* New Haven. Yale University Press.

Cunliffe, B. (2012). *Britain begins.* Oxford: Oxford University Press.

Ehrman, B. (2018). *The triumph of Christianity.* New York: Simon & Schuster.

Flavell, R. & Flavell, L. (1999). *The chronology of words and phrases: A thousand years in the history of English.* Leicester, UK: Silverdale.

Fredriksen, P. (1999). *Jesus of Nazareth, King of the Jews: A Jewish life and the emergence of Christianity.* New York: Vintage.

Fredriksen, P. (2012). *Sin: The early history of an idea.* Princeton, NJ: Princeton.

Gauchet, M. (1997). *The disenchantment of the world: A political history of religion.* (O. Burge, Trans.). Princeton: Princeton University Press.

Hillman, J. (1999). *The force of character and the lasting life.* New York: Ballantine.

Holy Bible: New International Version. (1984). Grand Rapids, MI: Zondervan.

Johnson. (10 Sept 16). Talking in tongues: Should religious language keep up with the times or stick closely to the original? *The Economist, 420* (9006), 72.

Kearney, R. (2002). *On stories.* London: Routledge.

Kearney, R. (2003). *Strangers, gods, and monsters.* London: Routledge.

Kearney, R. (2011). *Anatheism: Returning to God after God.* New York: Columbia University Press.

Kearney, R. & Zimmerman, J. (Eds.). (2016). *Reimagining the sacred.* New York: Columbia University Press.

Kennedy, J. (1996). *Word stems: A dictionary.* New York: Soho.

Kingsolver, B. (1999). *The poisonwood bible.* New York: HarperPerennial.

Liberman, A. (2009). *Word origins and how we know them: Etymology for everyone.* New York: Oxford.

Mallory, J.P. (1991). *In search of the Indo-Europeans: Language, archeology, and myth.* London: Thames and Hudson.

McCrum, R., Cran, W., & MacNeil, R. (1986). *The story of English.* New York: Viking.

Miriam-Webster Dictionary (10th ed.). (2000). (F.C. Mish, Ed.). Springfield, MA: Merriam-Webster.

Nussbaum, M. (2016). *Anger and forgiveness: Resentment, generosity, and justice*. New York: Oxford University Press.

Online Etymology Dictionary. (D. Harper, Ed.). Retrieved from http://www.etymonline.com/

Ostler, N. (2006). *Empires of the word: A language history of the world*. New York: Harper Perennial.

Ostler, N. (2016). *Passwords to paradise: How languages have re-invented world religions*. New York: Bloomsbury.

Pagels, E. (1995). *The origin of Satan*. New York: Random House.

Picard, M. (2013). *The bedside book of philosophy: From Plato to Paradoxes: Thinking through the ages*. Hove, UK: Quid.

Pujol, O. (2019). The ancient roots of Indo-European languages. *National Geographic: History, 4* (6), 12 - 21.

Robinson, M. (2019). *What are we doing here?* Toronto: McClelland & Stewart.

Rollins, P. (2015). *The divine magician: The disappearance of religion and the discovery of faith*. New York: Howard Books.

Stark, R. (1997). *The rise of Christianity*. New York: HarperCollins.

Stevenson, V. (1999). *The world of words: An illustrated history of Western languages*. New York: Sterling.

Taylor, C. (2007). *The secular age*. Cambridge, MA: Harvard University Press.

The Concise Oxford Dictionary of English Etymology. (1993). (T.F. Hoad, Ed.). Oxford: Oxford University Press.

The Oxford Dictionary of Word Histories. (2002). (G. Chantrell, Ed.). Oxford: Oxford University Press.

The Stanford Encyclopedia of Philosophy. (2019). The Metaphysics Research Lab: Center for the Study of Language and Information (CSLI), Stanford University.

Thomas, L. (1990). *Et cetera, et cetera: Notes of a word watcher*. Boston: Little Brown.

Tillich, P. (1966). The significance of the history of religions for the systematic theologian. In J.C. Brauer (Ed.), *The future of religions*. Retrieved from http://www.adwaitha-hermitage.net/tillich/Concrete-Spirit.pdf

Tillich, P. (1987). *The essential Tillich: An anthology of the writings of Paul Tillich.* (F. F. Church, Ed.). Chicago: University of Chicago Press.

Tillich, P. (2005). *The new being*. Lincoln, NE: University of Nebraska Press.

Visser, M. (2002). *Beyond fate*. Toronto: Anansi.

Wynn, T. & Coolidge, F.L. (2013). *How to think like a Neandertal*. New York: Oxford.

Index